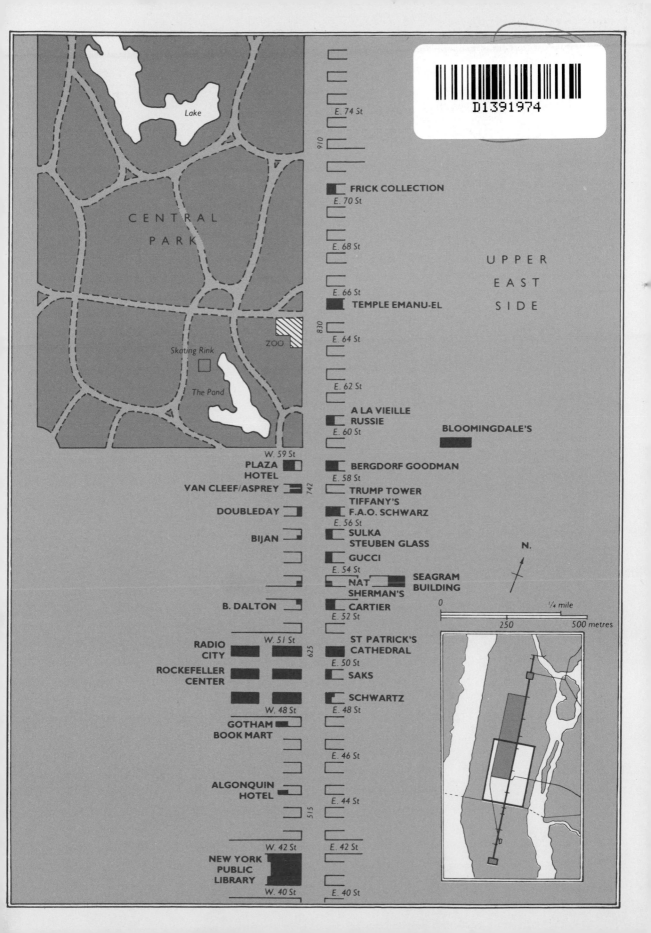

A WALK UP
FIFTH AVENUE

A WALK UP FIFTH AVENUE

Bernard Levin

JONATHAN CAPE
THIRTY-TWO BEDFORD SQUARE
LONDON

In Memoriam
Tom Walsh

First published 1989
© Bernard Levin 1989
Jonathan Cape Ltd, 32 Bedford Square, London WC1B 3SG

A CIP catalogue record for this book
is available from the British Library

ISBN 0–224–02619–4

Printed in Great Britain by
Butler & Tanner, Frome and London

Illustrations

Acknowledgments

I have, I hope, acknowledged in the text the authors and publishers of all the books I have quoted, but two stand out as being particularly helpful in the depths of their insight into New York: Saul Miller's *New York City Street Smarts* and Jerome Charyn's *Metropolis*. New York being what it is, a complete list of all the people who willingly gave their time and advice would be as long as the book; I thank them all, for from all of them I learned about their city and its most famous street. Some, however, went so far out of their way to help that they must be named. Charlie DeLeo, *genius loci* of the Statue of Liberty, took care of me and my vertigo when I went to the very top of his beloved Lady; Malcolm Forbes gave lavishly of his time, and to every request replied, 'No problem'; Jim Dwyer, who knows more about what goes on beneath the streets of Manhattan than most New Yorkers know about what happens above, shared his knowledge most generously; Vartan Gregorian, then President of the New York Public Library, lit up the interview room with his knowledge, understanding, enthusiasm and energy; the officers and men of the 369th Regiment made the Bronx ring with their hospitality; Marylou Whitney, learning what I was doing in New York, instantly invited me to her party; Bijan Pakzad gave me the run of his amazing emporium for an entire day; the members of the New York Diamond Club did everything short of giving me a sackful of diamonds; Jerry Levene taught me to shoot; Rabbi Ronald Sobel spoke many words of charity and wisdom; Steven and Kappy Mott (two of the happiest people I ever saw) fed me from their lavish farm nineteen floors up; Mother Hale, amid the bitterness of Harlem, had no bitter word to say; and New York's Finest showed me what they had to put up with in fighting crime, and why they were inexorably losing the fight.

At home, Oula Jones once again deployed her incomparable skill in indexing; I am not quite sure how anyone brings zest to such a profession, but she does. Brian Inglis, the gimlet-eyed, read the proofs with his usual care. My secretary, Catherine Tye, kept the aspidistra flying while I was away – her patience and dedication stretch far beyond the office work, and make her an ever-present help in trouble – and Margaret Grant retyped the entire book with remarkable speed and accuracy.

The members of the team who made the television programmes were once again almost exactly the same as those who had worked on the previous two travel-series I have done. Rarely have I known such a band of friends, and never have I worked with such meticulously skilled professionals. To Bernard Clark (Producer), Laurie Choate (Director), Graham Edgar (Cameraman/Director), who also took the still photographs, Steve Egleton (Sound Recordist), Nathalie Ferrier (Assistant Producer) and Mark Milsome (Assistant Cameraman), I offer my warmest thanks for the friendship and work alike.

CITIES CHANGE; more curiously, even if they don't change, opinions of them do. It is the attitude itself that undergoes transmutation. In *New York Observed*,★ there are three vignettes of the city, written in 1916, 1929 and 1949 respectively. The first is by Joyce Kilmer, and has a beautiful period charm; but it is the lost innocence of the city, looked at today, that turns it into poetry.

The dwellers in a great European city would give their proudest avenue of great shops and rich clubs some dignified and significant title, like the Rue de la Paix or the Friedrichstrasse. The Asiatics would give it a name more definitely descriptive and laudatory, like 'The Street of the Thousand and One Mirrors of Delight'. The New Yorkers, laconic and Olympian, designate it by a simple numeral. They call it Fifth Avenue.

It comes partly from the national reticence, this prosaic name of a poetic thoroughfare ... Also it is a phase of our democracy. We will not seem to exalt one avenue over another ... Fifth Avenue sounds to the uninitiated no more wealthy and aristocratic than Fourth Avenue ...

To give a street of wonders an austere name, to build palaces and fill them with offices and shops – these are the acts by which Americans are known. And especially does the New Yorker delight in the whimsical, the inconsistent, the unexpected. He is like a child who likes to dig in the sand with a silver spoon and to eat porridge with a toy shovel ...

★ Abrams

Well, the Rue de la Paix is not what it was, and the Friedrichstrasse is no more; she could, of course, claim to be right about not exalting one avenue over another: I have *never* heard anyone in New York call Sixth Avenue The Avenue of the Americas, though that is surely because it is such a ridiculous name, not because of the levelling tendencies of Americans. (Nobody insists that Amsterdam and Columbus Avenues should be numbered.) But who would now think that reticence is a national trait of Americans, or believe that New Yorkers delight in the whimsical, the inconsistent, the unexpected, or that the New Yorker is like any kind of child, let alone the kind who likes to dig in the sand with a silver spoon and to eat porridge with a toy shovel? Indeed, who now thinks that a New Yorker would eat porridge at all, with any implement, or even know what porridge is?

Theodore Dreiser's view of Fifth Avenue was rather less lavender-scented. Kilmer was writing on the eve of America's entry into the European war; Dreiser, thirteen years later, on the eve of the Great Crash. Even so, can this be the same city, the city of reticence, of prosaic outlook, the city of which 'It may be objected that the sponsors of Fifth Avenue did not foresee its destined splendour'?

Nowhere is there anything like it. My City. Not London. Not Paris. Not Moscow. Not any city I have ever seen. So strong. So immense. So elate.

Its lilt! Its power to hurry the blood in one's veins, to make one sing, to weep, to make one hate or sigh and die . . . Winey, electric! What beauty! What impressiveness! . . .

. . . a callous, money-seeking and unsentimental city, as one looks here and there. But lyric, too. And spendthrift. Frittering, idle, wasteful – saving nothing, hoarding nothing, unless maybe, unmarketable dreams . . . to this hour I cannot step out of my door save with a thrill responsive to it all – its grandeur, mystery, glory – yea, Babylonian eternity . . .

. . . Ho! one may cry aloud for aid and not be heard; ask for words only and harvest silence only, where yet all is blare. Or be harried by too much contact, and fail of peace; be driven, harried, buried by attention. God!

. . . here it runs, like a great river; beats and thunders like a tumultuous sea; or yawns or groans or shrieks or howls in sheer ennui.

. . . We are here together, seeking much, straining much. You, I. We are yearning to do so much here in my city – be so much – have some one group or phase or audience, or mayhap one other somewhere in all this, to recognize just us – just you – me. And not always finding that one. My fateful city!

Look at that passage: 'spendthrift ... wasteful – saving nothing, hoarding nothing, unless maybe, unmarketable dreams ...' Soon it would be Black Friday and 'Buddy, can you spare a dime'; Dreiser, gloomy enough at the best of times (he must have been drinking when he wrote that dithyramb) would become much gloomier; but it is interesting to hear the note of frenzy amid 'Babylonian eternity' (the point about Babylon being that it had fallen many centuries before), singling out not only the beauty but the impressiveness and defining both in terms of the beats and thunders of a tumultuous sea and a chorus of yawns, groans, shrieks and howls, yet where a man may ask only for words and harvest nothing but silence.

Move on another twenty years. Governor Roosevelt of New York has been elected President four times since Dreiser wrote, and is four years dead; the Depression has come and gone, and so has the Second World War. The arch and whimsical E. B. White, strict grammarian of the *New Yorker*, takes up the story:

> The city is like poetry: it compresses all life, all races and breeds, into a small island and adds music and the accompaniment of internal engines ... The genteel mysteries housed in the Riverside Church are only a few blocks from the voodoo charms of Harlem. The merchant princes, riding to Wall Street in their limousines down the East River Drive, pass within a few hundred yards of the gypsy kings ...
>
> Manhattan has been compelled to expand skyward because of the absence of any other direction in which to grow. This ... is to the nation what the white church spire is to the village – the visible symbol of aspiration and faith, the white plume saying that the way is up. The summer traveler swings in over Hell Gate Bridge and from the window of his sleeping car as it glides above the pigeon lofts and back yards of Queens looks southwest to where the morning light first strikes the steel peaks of midtown, and he sees its upward thrust unmistakable: the great walls and towers rising, the smoke rising ... this vigorous spear that presses heaven hard.

Foiled again; three in a row. Imagine voodoo charms in crack-strewn Harlem today; indeed, imagine a world so long gone that 'voodoo' and 'charms' can be put together in a phrase. The Towers of Trebizond, too, are not what they were; it was unfortunate for White that he was writing on the eve (how many eves New York's unfolding story has had!) of the worst era in Manhattan's construction history, an era in which the Seagram Building could be hailed as a masterpiece and win every architectural award. All the same, and forgetting the anachronisms like the summer traveller in his sleeping car, we can hear the last, expiring breath of a still patrician city, with streets that could be walked at night and where nearly half the men wore hats, and television was the latest toy.

The truth about New York today is as elusive as ever; but that is the truth about New York. Whatever Fifth Avenue might have been called in Europe or the Orient, a walk up it from end to end demonstrates the city's perpetual *restlessness*, its implacable determination never to keep still long enough to be defined. This is true socially, artistically, intellectually; but it is at its most noticeable in the city's architecture. Somebody must know exactly how many prominent buildings on New York's most prominent thoroughfares were put up only after the Second World War and have been torn down and replaced; somebody must know how many such replacement buildings have themselves been torn down and replaced, and how many sites have been subjected to the same process *three* times, all in the past forty-odd years. It is not the least of New York's ironies that the city with the buildings that are the most difficult to erect and to demolish has more erecting and demolishing than the shacks of Mexico City's shanty-towns. One day, the Landmarks Commission will don impenetrable disguise, wait till night, and by the light of the moon will designate every building in Manhattan an irreplaceable treasure, not to be touched by the profane hands of the wrecking crews. Then, and only then, will New York be written about in a way that makes it possible for the writing to last longer than what it describes. All cities deteriorate; that is the Iron Law of cities. Jane Jacobs has argued in a series of books that cities *do not have to* deteriorate, but I think she has practically given up denying that in fact they all do. If all cities deteriorate, do all their principal arteries also and inevitably do so? Probably; look at London's Oxford Street, which is a disgrace to a wealthy capital city, and would be something of a disgrace in Beirut or Kinshasa. Look, more closely, at Bond Street; the signs of decay are not so obtrusive, but they are there. (Do not look, for if you do an uncontrollable shudder will come upon you, at Edinburgh's Prince's Street, once one of the noblest thoroughfares in all Europe.)

Why? It is a circular argument which maintains that cities deteriorate because the inhabitants lose their pride in them, for why do they do so? They throw down more litter (in London, the incidence of littering has increased to exactly the same extent as the number of prominent litter-baskets, a fact that will give you the creeps if you think about it long enough), but again, why? The planning authorities relax their severe codes, so Colonel Sanders and Mr McDonald flourish, to the further decline of the streets they conquer, but such decisions themselves must have a cause, a reason: what is it?

Fifth Avenue, like most of its principal partners (certainly Sixth, Seventh, Madison, Lexington and the wandering Broadway) is much more difficult to judge in this context. The great streets of New York are unique in one respect: they have always encompassed a very wide variety of qualities; they are the least homogeneous of major thoroughfares. Perhaps that is because of their length; when a street can be anything up to a dozen miles long, it is unlikely to keep the quality all along its length. But although a rough map of Fifth Avenue's different natures could be compiled (Washington Square to 30th, say, for innocence, up to the beginning of the Park for the fiercest thrust of retail commerce, the great apartment blocks up to the end of the Park for wealth, the rest for Harlem), it remains true that the mix is by no means sharply delineated. Take the rue Faubourg St Honoré, or Bond Street even now, and compare them to that great stretch of fine stores on Fifth Avenue. From, say, F.A.O. Schwarz, Tiffany's and Steuben Glass at the top of one side and Bergdorf Goodman and Van Cleef on the other, down to, perhaps, Saks on the East side and Mikimoto on the West (a span of ten blocks), the shops can hold their own with their European sisters. But there is one crucial difference: in London and Paris their Fifth Avenues are all of the same high quality. In the real one in New York, the most elegant places rub shoulders with shops selling gewgaws, cut-price electronic equipment, marked-down photographic materials, T-shirts and the like. It is, no doubt, a tribute to America's devotion to both democracy and commerce; if you've got the money for the rent (I sometimes wonder where it comes from, considering what real estate on Fifth Avenue costs), then no other store should have the power to do more than look down its nose at the brash downmarket newcomer.

So it is difficult to see whether Fifth Avenue has declined. But it has. I have long since lost count of the years over which I have seen, on every visit, that same 'Closing Down – Everything Must Go' sign, but it is a symbol of gentle and not catastrophic decline; if it were not so, surely the Fifth Avenue Association would have told the store to put up or shut up. (I suppose I mean put up or shut down.) The buildings are grimier, too, which no doubt can be blamed on exhaust pollution, but they are less often cleaned, which can't. The pot-holes, of course, have been there since mastodons and brontosauri roamed the primeval forest of Manhattan, but it is not just nostalgia that convinces me that they are bigger, deeper and more rarely fixed. (Saul Miller, in his book *Street Smarts*,* claims that New York has solved the pot-hole problem by passing a law making it impossible

---

* Holt Reinhart Winston

for anyone to sue the city for damage incurred through hitting a pot-hole. I can well believe it, though I *can't* believe his other claim, to the effect that city-wide, in winter, *thirty thousand pot-holes a week* are filled. To be fair to Mr Miller, I don't think he believes it, either.) Quite certainly the standard of driving down Fifth Avenue has fallen desperately low, while the level of anger behind the wheel has risen dangerously high.

On my earliest visits to New York, it was possible – it was not even eccentric – to *saunter* up Fifth; no-one would try it today. To saunter it is necessary to have a sufficiency of both time and space, both of these now rare and getting more so; the likelihood of having your pocket picked has grown vastly (sauntering includes window-gazing), and God knows manners have deteriorated. And they may have deteriorated even further than it seems; the buses, even the newest ones, carry signs saying No Littering, No Smoking, No Radio Playing, which is all most commendable; but there is another clause which says No Spitting. Now I remember that London buses and street-cars before World War II had such an injunction against spitting, but it has long since vanished; I don't believe it survived the war. Yet spitting is as nasty a habit as ever it was; what has happened in Britain is that people have unanimously educated themselves to regard spitting as wholly unacceptable at any social level. The result is that the sign has disappeared because there is no need for it. But it seems that it *is* needed in New York, and indeed in Fifth Avenue itself. As for the cart-vendors, they used to be among the Avenue's most engaging sights and pleasantest dispensers of very fast food. Today, the carts are standardised, the quality of the produce poor, and the stench of rancid fat coming from the hot-dog carts unbearable. (Concomitantly, the police hassle the vendors more, though not, alas, on grounds of quality.)

Of course, the further down the Avenue you go, the worse it becomes. There is no good restaurant on Fifth at all any more (whatever happened to Longchamps?), and although McDonald's have refrained from coming up further than 34th Street (sited conveniently across the street from the Empire State Building so that the visitors, when they have finished, can refresh themselves), Fifth is a culinary desert below as well as above.

Of course, the Fifth Avenue Association does what it can, but not only is it constantly trying in vain to put salt on the tail of the street's decline, it is actually accelerating it. True, the Association tries to keep out the rip-off shops, projecting signs, and other immediately obvious eyesores that would lower the tone. But in the same breath, the Association *boasts* that it is supervising the erection of a thirty-floor office building between the Empire State and the Public Library, as if two of the most glorious buildings in the entire City, let alone Fifth Avenue, needed to be set off by a demonstration of really *good* architecture.

It is possible to deplore what might be called the internationalisation of Fifth Avenue, where names such as Gucci, Asprey, Sulka, Van Cleef and Arpels, Aquascutum sprout along the street as they sprout along the most fashionable streets of the most fashionable cities; but at least such names are a guarantee of quality. The one-off names can announce pride and perfection – I think of A la Vieille Russie on the corner of East 59th, or that weird place Sac Frères in Bond Street; but they can also be fly-by-nights, and lower the tone. And I suppose that tone, if the word is used rightly, is the test. Slowly and subtly, Fifth Avenue's tone has changed, not for the better. The entirely residential stretch opposite the Park, say from the Pierre Hotel to the Nineties, which takes in the Museum Mile, has always set the tone, rather than the glittering shopping stretch, and it is still very largely what it always was: elegant, handsome, grave, clean, attended, quiet. But more and more, that length of the Avenue begins to seem like another street altogether, divorced from its lower limbs and secretly despising them. (Presumably, its upper limbs, beyond the Park, always have been despised.) To walk, on the eastern side, from 62nd to 95th is still a pleasure, a soothing balm for the spirit, even if you don't like the Guggenheim. (And if you don't, you need only to retrace your steps a dozen streets and cross the road; surely you like the Met?) But more and more, that soothing balm is needed to counteract the slowly advancing – infinitely slowly advancing, yet never actually stopping – deterioration of the thirty or forty blocks below the Park. The Iron Law of cities cannot be denied; they do deteriorate. Even Fifth Avenue.

★   ★   ★

In the introduction to the most comprehensive guide to the architecture of New York City, the one compiled by the American Institute of Architects, the editors identify nine chronologically successive historical styles of building, starting naturally with Colonial and finishing with Modern. Of the seven in between, *five* have, as an appendage to the category, the word 'Revival'; thus, Greek Revival, Gothic Revival, Renaissance-Baroque Revival, Roman Revival and Romanesque Revival.

When New Yorkers visit London for the first time, and venture on the Underground or subway, their first surprise (the second is that they don't get mugged, stabbed or offered cocaine at reasonable rates) is at the very great depth of the stations and the tunnels, compared to what they are used to at home. On making enquiry of a knowledgeable Londoner as to why this should be so, they are told that London stands on clay, whereas New York stands on rock, so London must dig far deeper.

In those two areas of limited mutual comprehension, there lies much to contemplate. The New Yorker concludes that the London Tube is unsafe, since the roof will inevitably cave in on him with a horrid squelching sound, and the Londoner begins to panic at the thought that all the buildings he sees around him in New York, though they have the appearance of having been built at any time since the fourth century B.C., have in fact been put up since he went to bed the previous night.

The New Yorker's predicament cannot be my concern here; but I am myself a Londoner visiting New York. Its architectural achievements are not confined to any one area, and certainly not one Avenue, though there are a good number of interesting buildings on it: I followed my street from bottom to top many times, and one of these marches was devoted entirely to the architecture of it, as you shall hear. But just as no-one, to whatever part of the city his visit on business or pleasure may confine him, would imagine that what he saw about him defined the character of Manhattan's buildings, so Fifth Avenue cannot be taken as representative of anything but itself, if that. Midtown Manhattan offers a cityscape that is unique, literally unique; there is nothing quite like it, and very few things even nearly like it, anywhere in the world. There are parts of Chicago and Los Angeles and a few other American cities that are superficially reminiscent of it, but keener inspection reveals that many tall buildings do not make a Manhattan. One obvious difference is in the width of the roads where the tall buildings stand; the Manhattan ones are much narrower than in such pseudo-replicas as Dallas or Kansas City, and this in itself makes the whole feel and nature of the city different. No doubt the nature of Manhattan is governed by the size of it; those twenty-five square miles do not hold the world's record for resident population density, but I doubt if there is any city of comparable size in the western world which can compete for the number of people who could be counted in it at noon on a busy working-day in the tourist season. (To start with, it is estimated that $3\frac{1}{2}$ million people come into Manhattan every day to work there.)

Manhattan, then, had to grow upwards because it could not grow outwards. And it packed its streets so closely for the same reason. But the history, though fascinating, and the historical explanations of the city, have nothing to do with what the visitor actually *sees*, not only on his first visit but again and again as he returns for more.

When I first visited New York, very long ago, I took advice from knowledgeable British friends who had been there many times and American ones who lived there or spent much time there. I filled a stout notebook with details of what I should wear, where I should stay, what notable signs I should seek out and what people I should call, which plays I should see and which areas I should avoid after dark, how the subway works and where the buses run, what tip a taxi-driver will expect and what he will say if he doesn't get it. Thus equipped, and feeling like an expert already, I arrived, to realise that nobody, whether indigenous or inquiline, had told me that it was beautiful, let alone that it was – as I instantly felt and have most passionately believed ever since – one of the most beautiful cities in all the world, indeed one of the most beautiful man-made sights that man has ever made.

That, I allow, is coming it a bit strong. But those who dissent, I have found, make the mistake of adding up the parts to make the sum. You cannot treat Manhattan like Central London, where you can say: here are the Houses of Parliament, and there Trafalgar Square with Nelson on his column, and here is the splendid vista down the Mall, and there is the noble dome of St Paul's, and here the still handsome sweep of Regent Street, and we are sorry about Tottenham Court Road. London was not planned like the grid of Manhattan, but that is not the clue; London *is* the sum of its parts, and the fine things to be seen in it do, combined, make it memorable and attractive. But New York must be, can only be, taken in a single gulp, and from the Battery to Harlem, wherever you are, that gulp takes in the same elixir.

For New York, understood aright, is magical. The first sight of those vistas, with the giants marching down the canyons and gullies, *literally* takes the breath away; you gasp for air, so stunned are the senses at a sight so mysterious, so mighty, so proud and so tall. Of course, if you look at single buildings, you will be frequently disappointed in their quality, and rightly so, for Manhattan has its share, a substantial share, of duds. But the magic of Manhattan is not that the vistas outweigh the dudness; it is that the duds themselves are transformed when regarded not as individual *objets d'architecture* but as fragments of a whole. It took several years of travelling to New York before I could cure myself of the habit of walking along any midtown Avenue or even Street with my head thrown right back and staring at the sky.

Of course, the image of New York is of a hard town, even a brutal one, and where crime is concerned that is obviously true; it is also true that New York is tough in business and tough on those who fall through the net; those are aspects that no-one can deny, and fewer people than ever ignore.

But there is another, quite different, soft side to New York; though the citizens will deny it with their last breath, it is a *sentimental* place. Look at the entertainment it flocks to: musicals built a mile high on hokum, so only they have happy endings; terrible plays like *I'm Not Rappaport* (I wouldn't be surprised to learn that it is still running); movies like *Love Story* and *On Golden Pond*. Look at its pets: dogs outnumber cats (it's three to one the other way in London), because dogs are themselves incurably sentimental, while cats will give their whole hearts to nobody. Look at its alms-giving, not all founded in guilt. Look at its Christmas; Charles Dickens could step straight into New York and recognise it as his own. (It was New York which first thought of 'painting' Christmas trees in left-on light bulbs on its skyscrapers.)

Under its rough hide, New York is a softie; it has the romantic view of itself that O. Henry popularised. Again and again, he paints the city as a place of almost oriental magic, a place where wonderful, unexpected things happen, where adventure beckons on every corner, where a prosaic, mundane scene can turn in an instant into the basis of love at first sight, where a magic carpet is parked at every kerb.

And this means not only that New York tolerates the World Trade Center and the Trump Tower; it means that the secret which New York is at such pains to hide is that it feels the same way about its architecture that I do, though I come from a truly hard city, and one that is getting meaner all the time.

New York permits itself to be seen as sentimental over a few special buildings; the Flatiron and the Chrysler, for instance. But many a business-man, after a hard-bargaining business lunch accompanied by no more than six jumbo-sized martinis, would love to walk away as I do, head back, eyes popping and to hell with the collisions.

Take the word 'skyscraper' itself; surely it is a word that only a city which believes in magic would take to its heart. A Mr Moser, in 1883, was the first to use the word to mean a tall building, but the etymology is unimportant (quite apart from the fact that Chicago probably beat New York to the building of the first one). But what a word, and for what a thing! One day when it was raining I went up to the top of the Empire State Building on this walk of mine. There was not much to be seen but cloud, but *the clouds were below me*; that was the point. Here and there the spires of these great secular churches poked through the clouds, and I realised that, from the top of those, people could see my ladder to heaven, as I could see theirs. That is a familiar sight from an aeroplane, of course, where it is mysterious and wonderful enough; but to experience it in the middle of a great city is indeed to scrape the sky, and the sight of those questing topless towers of Ilium, planted like trees in the clouds that swirled around below their summits, was to understand again why O. Henry (New York knows, which London does not, that *The Gifts of the Magi* has a *happy* ending, not a sad) called it Baghdad-on-the-Subway. One day, staring at the sky, I shall be knocked over by Harun-Al-Rashid.

But my dangerous way of seeing New York is in fact the only way it can be seen at all. Lovers of Manhattan have to reconcile themselves to the strange and appalling fact that the city has, and can have, no vistas. The 'setback' rule, by which the higher a building goes, the more it has to be recessed from the street, constitutes only the slightest palliative; the truth is that the only views in midtown Manhattan are the foreshortened ones up and down the Avenues and East and West along the streets; what you cannot do in New York is get back far enough to grasp the overall shape and nature of the buildings right across the street. And that extraordinary fact has, of course, its origins in the grid system. The villain of the story, though like so many men who have caused great harm, he was wholly innocent in intention, was John Randel. Reporting to the city, which had set up a commission to draw up a street-plan for the fast growing metropolis, Randel, I trust in fittingly sepulchral tones, said:

> A city must be composed principally of the habitations of men, and straight-sided and right-angled houses are the most cheap to build and the most convenient to live in.

But only, alas, if the men never want to venture out from their straight-sided and right-angled habitations, and, more to the point, if they never want to see sunshine. (Has anyone worked out the area, in square feet, of sidewalks and roads in Manhattan which are *never* touched by the sun?) The regular depth of the grid poses many more problems than that, but its fundamental flaw has nothing to do with the practical effects. The grid, for all its simplicity and convenience (the Manhattan traffic would have been hell whatever shape the city was built in, as soon as there were enough vehicles to pose the problem), is an attempt to make rational that which cannot of its nature be rational – the way human beings live. There are many planned cities in the world: Washington DC, New Delhi, Paris, Brasilia. But the first is planned (in the grid sense) only in its central, administrative quarter; across the river you are into the trees, and it is no distance to the other three sides and freedom. Much the same can be said of Delhi, and beyond the walls the city sprawls like any other Indian city.

Paris has some wonderful vistas from the central node of the Etoile, but they do not give a feeling of rigidity, presumably because although they look as if they were built to a single plan, in fact they grew over two hundred years. (And it is only on the map that the boulevard Périphérique looks like the walls of an ancient city.) Only Brasilia tried to do what Manhattan did, and those who built it had learned the lesson of Manhattan; there are no rigid lines, let alone grid-patterns (there are no traffic-lights either, for that matter). Yet even Brasilia could not impose its architectural will, however fluid its plans, and was bewildered to discover that, in James Elroy Flecker's words, 'Men are unwise, and curiously planned'.

There remains Manhattan and its grid, with Fifth Avenue pushing up it like an armoured column racing ahead of the main army and counting on the infantry to do the mopping up. It is true that most of Manhattan's business is housed amid the lines of the grid; still, that leaves plenty of living to be done in it. No-one, as far as I know, has done a psychological study of its effect; it certainly hasn't made New Yorkers tidy, or even conformist, though I cannot believe it hasn't made them bored. It is ironic that although Manhattan is, of all the world's city centres, the most given to pulling down buildings and erecting new ones (all books on Manhattan's architecture are out of date in a few years – imagine that being true of London, let alone Oxford! – and the American Institute of Architects' guidebook has a section labelled 'Necrology' for those buildings of interest which have been pulled down while the book was being compiled), the one thing that restlessness cannot touch is the criss-cross pattern out of which they are plucking the buildings doomed to die, and into which they are inserting the ones destined to be born. It is not surprising that many New Yorkers, and even more of New York's visitors, find after a time in the grid that they must flee to the haven of irregularity in southern Manhattan, where the streets sometimes wander at odd angles, and in any case have names. (Mind you, a Londoner, or any Indian, would find even the Villages intolerably restricting quite soon.) Like all Englishmen, I intone the familiar rubric: I love New York, but I wouldn't want to live there. Gradually, over the years, I have begun to surprise myself by feeling that I could, after all, live there, *but only far downtown*.

But those 'Revivals', now. Britain had a 'Gothic Revival' in the nineteenth century, though it is difficult to see why, considering the quantity of real Gothic that remained. The revival gave us the Houses of Parliament (but it wouldn't have done if some thoughtful fellow hadn't accidentally burned the previous building to the ground), perhaps the greatest masterpiece of architecture put up in England since Vanbrugh's day, and surely not surpassed yet, nor like to be. The 'Gothic Revival' had an astonishingly long life; as late as the 1950s, those submitting plans for a new Coventry Cathedral were formally enjoined, in the conditions they had to meet, that mock-gothic would not be acceptable. But New York holds a different kind of record; the present Gothic St Patrick's, finished in 1888, replaced the original St Patrick's, built in 1815 and sited downtown, which was destroyed by fire in 1868. It was restored, *but in Gothic*, so that for a time, until the downtown one was stripped of its original status, there were two Gothic St Patricks in New York.

New York prides itself on its modernity; not for this city are the carefully-tended colonial areas of Boston, the *vieux carré* of New Orleans, the preservation in Philadelphia of every stick and stone that the Founding Fathers might have hit while aiming at the spittoon. New York, indeed, came late to 'Landmark' legislation. Yet the yearning for something old, which has to be translated as something which *looks* old, will not be denied. New Yorkers jeer at the bizarre juxtapositions of styles in the houses of Los Angeles, where an Egyptian temple rubs shoulders with a Polynesian long-hut, and a Wild West stockade with an Oriental palace, but New York is in no position to jeer. Walking up Fifth Avenue with the AIA handbook symbols in mind, I counted fifteen buildings from the 'Renaissance/Baroque', six from the 'Gothic', two from the 'Roman' and one each from the 'Georgian' and 'Greek'. Yet there are no Renaissance Men in New York, today, except in a strictly metaphorical sense, nor have the Goths been seen in these parts for some time, and that goes also for the ancient Romans and Greeks; finally, Britain has not had a George on the throne since 1952, and *he* wasn't the George who gave his name to the style. After all this, it is reassuring to learn that the New York 'landmark law' can protect any building more than thirty years old, and the number which have been 'listed' is now approaching 20,000. (Entire districts, such as Greenwich Village, have been served with landmark orders.)

Still the building goes on, preceded by the demolition. At any given time, between fifty and a hundred buildings are going up in Manhattan, and since Manhattan is not exactly in the middle of Kansas, and nobody is going to be allowed to erect a thirty-floor Hilton in the middle of Central Park, something each time has had to be removed before being replaced. But the incessant building, in so tight-packed an area as Manhattan, poses special problems. First, how do you get a building down before putting one up on the site? In places where the buildings are less close, they can be blown up; modern developments in the science of demolition have been remarkable in the way many small packets of explosive, strategically placed, can bring down a building and keep the debris almost entirely inside the ground plan. But however fine the tuning, you cannot do that in Manhattan, and the removal of a forty-floor building with a steel frame, which was, after all, built to stand up, is an appallingly arduous task. Remember that even when all forty floors are shrouded in scaffolding (and, in New York, netting also) there is practically no room to swing the traditional metal ball that cracks a building, and demolishing it by hand and pick would take so much time that another Revival would have come, and possibly gone, before the job was done.

Yet New York buildings come down at astonishing speed; almost from week to week, where there was a towering presence there is now a cleared site, and foundations going in. That, however, is nothing compared to the speed at which Manhattan buildings go *up*. The building-rate is speeded, of course, by the fact that so many tall buildings are uniform from top to bottom – the upended box theme; but even allowing for that, the progress is, certainly by European standards, exceptionally fast.

Sometimes, New York buildings *fall* down, with massive loss of life. And on one occasion, as the head of the Department of buildings told me, there was a different kind of scare. Only a few days earlier, he was told that there had been a dynamite explosion up-town, on a construction site. He rushed to the place, to find that a compressed-air hose, used to provide energy for the drills, had burst, sending debris and people flying across the street. Terrorist explosions in the modern world hold only prosaic terrors; but do you remember the Great Alligator Scare? It began with a belief (quite unfounded) that the smart set were giving each other baby alligators as pets, and soon it was believed that no New York apartment was without one. The next step was that the smart set, tiring of the beasts and feeling it was too much trouble for them to dispose of their unwanted friends to a zoo or an aquarium, the owners were confidently said to be getting rid of them by flushing them down the lavatory. So far, so good, but the legend was only working up to its climax. Down in the darkness, the wet and the sewage, the little creatures began to grow, and in no time at all, beneath the streets of the city, huge, savage alligators were roaming, fighting *and breeding*. Before long, it was 'known' that a growing number of underground workers were missing, then that street manhole-covers had been seen to fly out of their settings, and were followed by dreadful snouts, equipped with rows of huge and hideous teeth.

★   ★   ★

Washington Square, where Fifth Avenue officially begins, is New York's village green. It has no duckpond, and the villagers don't play cricket, though they certainly play everything else; it has, however, as every village green must have, its official eccentrics, one of whom is on show now, a man with a cat – a cat, not a dog – on a leash, and not just a dog-leash but a real dog-harness, obviously strong enough for a Doberman (*absit omen*), though the ginger puss thus restrained is remarkably well-behaved, as well as perfectly groomed, and hardly as big as a Jack Russell. It is plainly as little concerned as its owner is, or for that matter the bystanders, as the curious duo wend their way through the crowd.

As befits a village green on a sunny Sunday, the crowd is thick, good-humoured and wanting to be entertained. There is no lack of entertainment; jugglers, comedians, conjurors and fire-eaters abound, urged on by the children with grandstand views from their fathers' shoulders, while vendors wind in and out, doing a vast trade in ice-cream and soft drinks. And some of the entertainers are of the finest quality. Three unicyclists, for instance, cleared a space and began a startling routine; not content with the most elaborate arabesques, their unibikes obeying them like the most obedient skate-boards, they paused a moment for an assistant to light a set of torches, and set off again as soon as they were all burning. The brands were about a yard long, and for about half of their length they were covered in matted fabric, steeped in spirit; they blazed merrily – no mere glowing, but real flames – and the three exceptionally intrepid performers proceeded to spin about the square, in a series of intricate but almost formal patterns, as they juggled with their torches – three for each of the team – as imperturbably as they would toss and spin Indian clubs. But they hadn't finished; as soon as they had collected an appropriate ration of gasps and applause, they changed their act.

Hitherto, they had been content to juggle their torches in a series of solos, though that had been startling enough, particularly when they began to do the Indian-club juggler's trick of throwing it up, and catching it, behind their backs. (But the Indian-club juggler does not, after all, set fire to his clubs, nor does he usually display his dexterity while riding a unicycle.) Now, however, the dauntless three, while increasing the speed of their weaving progress, began to throw the blazing torches to one another, sometimes curving them over the heads of the crowd like the flaming arrows of Red Indian movies.

Gradually, the flames died down, and the three musketeers dismounted, to a huge roar of approbation – and, perhaps more appropriately, a collection. They passed among the crowd, encouraging munificence with the old – indeed traditional – busker's trick: one of the collectors would suddenly shout to his colleagues on the other side of the square 'Hey – a ten-dollar bill!' They deserved it, but they were not finished, for their encore was to be more spectacular yet. One of them produced a skipping-rope, and began to circle the arena; violating every one of Newton's Laws of Motion, he proceeded to jump the bike off the ground with the use only of his knees, and skipped the rope beneath it. Faster and faster he sped round, the rope making a permanent circle to the eye, as it went over his head, under his wheel, over his head. Then, when the applause was at its greatest, he tossed the rope away, snatched from the hand of one of his colleagues a sword – visibly and undoubtedly a real sword, not a trick one – and, never slackening his pace round the square, he swallowed the thing. Carefully, slowly, it disappeared down his gullet, and the crowd actually, but not surprisingly, fell silent at the sight of a man unicycling round and round with the hilt of a sword sticking out of his mouth and the rest of it inside him.

I couldn't get near him for the cheering throng that surrounded him when he finally dismounted and held out a hat; I wanted to tell him, if he didn't know it, the story of the small boy at the circus, who insists that his father must take him round backstage, so that he can meet his new hero, the sword-swallower. The genial artiste welcomes the tongue-tied and saucer-eyed child, who finally recovers his power of speech and asks 'Please, mister, how do you become a sword-swallower?' His hero shrugs: 'You swallow a sword,' he says. 'If you live, you're a sword-swallower.'

But still there was more to come: the Famous Washington Square Small Boy Trick was about to be performed. It was preceded, I may say, by the entrance into the square of a mounted policeman, who was not, happily, about to arrest anybody, least of all the bike-skipping, torch-throwing, sword-swallowing entertainer, but merely wished to add to the enter-tainment by parading his particularly gentle and well-behaved horse round the square, for the delight and instruction of the children. It worked, too; after an initial hesitation, many a tiny hand reached up to stroke the horse's nose or pat its side, while the cop beamed upon us all. Then, as if on cue, he moved to the side: it was time for the Small Boy Trick.

The entertainers called for a volunteer among the children; no hesitation here – they hurled themselves forward. The winner, bursting with pride, was a tiny black fellow, perhaps five or six years old. 'We are going', he was told, 'to make a glass of Coke disappear.' The child was given a glass, and a can of Coke was opened and poured into it. He was told to lift the glass up, holding it very carefully with both hands, and put it on his head, still clutching it and taking care it remained upright. The star performer did as he was told. Then the patter began: the magic was very difficult to operate, he must concentrate very strongly and fiercely if it was to work, he mustn't for a moment relax his grip on the glass, if he forgets for even a moment, it won't work. Junior was practically exploding with the intensity of his concentration – he had long since stopped breathing – and then, as the mumbo-jumbo reached a climax, one of the conspirators tiptoed up behind him with a straw, and carefully drank the whole glass, while the crowd, self-sworn to silence, watched enraptured. 'Now,' they said, 'lift the glass down – be careful, hold it tight – in front of you.' Junior did as he was told, and very wonderful was the look of utter stupefaction on his face as the glass that he knew was full, and that he had never for a moment let out of his hands, was plainly empty, with only a little froth to show that the Coke had ever been there.

'Don't worry,' he was told, 'we're going to magic it back.' Again, the patter, again the instructions, again the iron grip of the glass, empty this time, by the two little hands on the little head; again the mumbo-jumbo, and again the conspirator's silent approach, now with a full can of Coke, to be poured silently and carefully into the glass. And again the unbelieving amazement, as the glass, lowered inch by inch, turned out to be full again.

It was a happy crowd, as befits a village green, and it was clear that it was a people's festival, and a local people's one, at that. There were out-of-towners and upper-enders, and tourists and me; but mostly the crowd consisted of those who live down this end of the Avenue, and beyond it. Though the excitement of the acrobats had gone, there were still the buskers; the guitar-playing was hardly Segovia, but notably better than, say, the performers in the London Underground, for these can really play and really sing, and as a background to the crowd and its pleasure it could hardly be bettered. And another thing: the place was a lot cleaner and tidier than back home; these people care about their village green, for all that it has no duckpond, and is not green at all.

An elderly man tugged at my sleeve. 'Did you know', he said, with no preamble, 'that this place used to be a cemetery?' I said I didn't. 'Yup,' he said, 'a cemetery for paupers – what they call a potter's field. You know why it's called a potter's field?' Now that is one of the countless items of haphazard knowledge that my head is uselessly crammed with, and I said I did. He looked at me very suspiciously; he was clearly used to asking the question and no less used to his triumph when the answer was no. Before he would question me further, I told him. He was a sport; instead of looking crestfallen, his eyes lit up, delighted to find a fellow-serendipitist in

Washington Square. 'But did you know', he went on, 'that they're still down there' – he stamped on the ground – 'because the cemetery was just filled in and covered over?' That, I did not know, but I was enjoying as much as he was the bits and pieces of knowledge which we had, so I countered with that pleasant little Venetian courtyard, raised above the ground, which is not just a cemetery covered over but a plague cemetery, and no visitor can traverse it without a shudder if he knows the story.

So we chatted, my fellow-magpie and I, tossing riddles back and forth, till he said, 'Come with me'. He took me through the massive and handsome arch – somewhat reminiscent of the Arc de Triomphe but rather more of the Marble Arch – and told me that it had been erected to mark the centenary of Washington's inauguration as the first President of the United States. But he couldn't tell me on what occasion Washington had said the memorable words that adorn the arch: 'Let us raise a standard to which the wise and the honest can repair. The event is in the hand of God'. We shook hands and parted. (What the guidebooks don't tell you, incidentally, about the Arch is who designed it – or rather, they tell you who designed it but hope that you can't remember why the name is so familiar. The architects were McKim, Mead and White, a very successful firm, and it was the White – Stanford White – who was responsible for the Arch's design. But his name will go down in history for a much more spectacular reason: he was the victim of the most notable murder but one to have taken place in a theatre. White's former mistress, Evelyn Nesbit, married Harry Thaw, who suspected her, probably rightly, of two-timing him with White. While she was on the stage, Thaw entered the theatre and shot White dead.)

★   ★   ★

And so my journey began, with a remarkable realisation. As I looked up Fifth Avenue from Washington Square, the Empire State Building naturally loomed over everything. But the sight of it made clear that the Avenue runs, as they all do, apart from Broadway, absolutely straight from end to end. The ground dips and rises but never deviates to the left or right; I was, after all, looking up some thirty blocks, though that is nothing compared to the view *down* the Avenue from where it ends at 141st Street, when the dead-reckoning makes the Empire State Building visible, exactly where it should be, more than a hundred blocks away.

Here, where Fifth Avenue starts, is the last place on the whole massive thoroughfare which could be in London: Washington Mews, which originally *was* a mews, is a tiny and delightful cul-de-sac, fiercely neat and ordered, spotlessly clean, with creeper festooning almost every house. Not only is it the only spot in Manhattan that might be found elsewhere in the world, it is the last restful sight from here to 105th Street, where Central Park ends in that magical formal garden. Whatever else Fifth Avenue is, it is not restful.

I celebrated the start of my march with a drink in Number One Fifth Avenue (the capitals are theirs, as well they might be). It still has traces of the *art-deco* of the jazz age, though the nostalgia is very faint; still, to be Number One Fifth Avenue is a considerable achievement in itself. Less remarkable, where achievements are concerned, is the outdoor art show. For these are the 'Sunday painters', and the four syllables make the heart sink under their weight.

I have long given up inspecting the hopeful amateurs (to say nothing of the hopeful but unsuccessful professionals) who exhibit their creations on the railings of Hyde Park and the Bayswater Road. When it started – first, I think, on public holidays, and only later as a regular occurrence every Sunday – there were, amid the dross, a few pictures by young almost-artists which showed the true stigmata: passion and single-mindedness. You could imagine them living in the traditional garret, not noticing the cold, not dreaming of fame and riches, not worried about where the rent money is coming from next week, just painting, because they must paint or burst.

Even that does not guarantee that the painter is an artist; but anything less makes it very sure that he isn't. After a time, the handful with promise disappeared; their instinct told them that they must pursue a different path to success. Their instinct was right, for the rows of paintings were soon broken by oases of mass-produced 'souvenirs' for the tourists, and then the pictures themselves began to be mass-produced – shoddy reproductions of well-known pictures and lifeless drawings of the London sights the souvenir-strewn tourists had come to see.

The Fifth Avenue outdoor show has so far not sunk that low. And yet the Washington Square School (to think that the Salmagundi Club, the home of real artists for more than a century, is just round the corner!) cannot be distinguished by the naked eye from the Hyde Park Group.

There is a distinction to be made. Sunday painters are of two kinds, and only one of the two depresses me. The kind that doesn't comprises the genuine amateurs, painting solely for their pleasure, with no ambition beyond their own enjoyment of what they are doing. They do not depress me, because they do not depress themselves, and merely feel better when they have finished. And so they should, considering their subject matter.

There are the same luscious blondes in fields, a very long way after

Renoir. There are the same idyllic scenes on pools and leaves and flowers which are not really by Monet. There are the same bright cut-out colours in abstract shapes all too easily distinguishable from Matisse. There is even technical facility – sometimes at a surprisingly high level – to eke out the windswept beauties who didn't quite sit for the pre-Raphaelites, the Indian brave on his horse, the guitar-player, the boxing match, Paris in the snow, the baby on the rug, the picnic, the colourful perspective view down the Avenue.

But there is also, ascending over the whole concourse like a sinister cloud, the belief among the other category of exhibitors that if only the world will open its eyes, their work would be on its triumphant way to eternal fame and honour. Ah, the monographs on their work three centuries hence; the university courses in their brush-technique; the biographies; above all, the walls of every great gallery in the world, alive and quivering with their masterpieces.

But the world will not open its eyes, except to wipe away a tear of sympathy. The truth is that the rarest commodity in the world is not gold or diamonds or uranium or even happiness. It is genius, which cannot be created. It can be encouraged (though not *dis*couraged – another one in the eye for the Manichee), it can be polished, it can even be guided, but it cannot be brought into existence by any action or belief or desire. ('I can call spirits from the vasty deep.' 'Why, so can I, and so can any man, but will they come when you do call for them?') No-one knows where genius comes from, no-one knows why a finger points at a baby in its cradle – *this* baby, *this* cradle – or who says, when the finger points, 'You are Beethoven', 'You are Dickens', 'You are Rembrandt, and you will live for ever'. Stravinsky got it right, though the yearning hopefuls at the bottom of Fifth Avenue will never believe it: 'Nothing is certain about masterpieces,' he said, 'least of all whether there will be any.'

★   ★   ★

First, however, I had to get there, which could be said of most of the people who made up the extraordinary stew (surely a closer description than the more familiar 'melting-pot') that the United States became when she opened her gates to the huddled masses of countless lands, yearning to be free. There are, of course, many studies of the successive tides of immigration into America; none that I know properly expresses the astounding nature of the vision that made it possible. Throughout history there have been huge migrations, vast population shifts, flights from conditions too terrible to be borne, mass expulsions; but the great American experiment had no precedent and has had no successor, and among the many remarkable aspects of that deed is history's failure to make due acknowledgment to its quality.

Acknowledgment made, a man would have to have a singular lack of imagination if he was descended from immigrants anywhere and not interested in knowing more about how it happened. And I have more than the usual interest, for an odd reason. The number of nationalities I might have had is alarmingly large. Ignoring the likelihood that my forebears came from the Middle East in the first place as too remote to count, the most obvious possibility is that I might have been Russian, since that is where my maternal grandparents came from. Next, I could have been Lithuanian, for so indeed was my father. When the great wave of Jewish emigration from Tsarist anti-semitism began, towards the end of the nine-teenth century, the refugees all made for Stettin, then a German city; it was the port of embarkation to all the countries willing to accept them. But many, seeing no point in going further, stayed where they were and took German nationality; the lucky ones were old enough to be dead by the time the Final Solution was under way. My mother's parents, declining the opportunity to become German themselves, boarded, together with my grandmother's brother, the first boat that held out the promise of taking them; it was bound for the United States, thus offering me a fourth choice of nationality. But my grandmother became ill, and could not sail, so she and my grandfather left the boat and remained in Stettin until she was fit to travel again; meanwhile Great-uncle Rudi left on the America-bound boat and made his life there, as an orchestral violinist, in Chicago.

By the time my grandmother had recovered, the next boat was going to London, and to London they went, to live there till their deaths much more than sixty years later; they were never naturalised. Score five. My mother was born in Britain, and I was, and am, a native British citizen. But there was still one more nationality that I might have acquired: South African. My parents parted when I was three years old, in the depths of the Depression, and my father went to South Africa, where it was well known that the streets of Johannesburg were paved with gold, to build up a successful business and then send for the family to enjoy the fruits of it. But neither the building nor the sending – nor, *a fortiori*, the fruits – ever materialised.

So I inspected the Statue of Liberty with a better reason than most. They are free with their statistics there, starting with the ominous news, displayed on a board just outside the entrance, which read, 'Two hours from this point to the top'. The extraordinary time for the climb, however, is governed not so much by the height to be attained as by the number of visitors wishing to attain it. The giant plinth has a lift in it, which cuts down the labour of the journey, but today it was out of order, and special attention was directed to the illuminated sign inside the entrance hall which warns those in ill health, and particularly with any kind of heart trouble, not to attempt to scale ('Because it's there') the mountain.

I went up from the ground floor to the observation deck in the tiniest lift I have ever seen; it was hardly bigger than a coffin, and held only two people, both of them uncomfortably. The lift had been put in a year or two before, when the Statue (which was in an advanced and dangerous state of disrepair) had been closed for many months for renovations; it was said that the lift had been added so that Mrs Reagan could go to the top for the ceremony of re-dedication. There are two spiral staircases, one inside the other, and so there should be, since neither of them is wide enough for more than one person, and passing would therefore be impossible, so there is one staircase for going up, and another for coming down. (But what happens when someone with heart trouble scorns the illuminated warning and in consequence expires at the top – or, worse, half-way up? More disturbing still, what happens if someone has a heart-attack and does *not* immediately succumb; how do they get a doctor up? In the Nancy Reagan Elevator, perhaps, but that has no intermediate stops, so it leaves untouched the problem of how the doctor, having arrived at the top, can get down past the crowd coming up, as far as the patient. Ah, he can take the down staircase, when all he has to do is to tell those descending in front of him to hurry along. But that won't do, because unless he is himself on the staircase, be it up or down, on which the tragic event is unfolding, he cannot get to the dying man – I am now assuming that he *is* dying – because it is impossible to get from either of the staircases to the other. Meanwhile, what of the sufferer; whichever staircase *he* is on, the crowd wants to get past him, but they can only do so by climbing over him. Moreover, there is no public address system on the staircases, so neither the ascending nor descending visitors would have any means of knowing that anything untoward had happened, and the people on the staircase that was blocked would become angry, claustrophobic, alarmed, or all three, unless the message with the sad truth was passed from mouth to mouth, up or down as required, though that, of course, is exactly how the game of 'Chinese whispers' is played, with a line of people whispering a message along it from one end, to see how garbled it will be by the time it gets to the other, as in the old chestnut 'Send reinforcements, the regiment is going to

1   *Starting: the village green*

2

3

advance' – 'Send three-and-fourpence, the regiment is going to a dance'. On the whole, the illuminated message about the dangers might well be made more prominent still, and have the customers' attention drawn to it even more forcefully.)

The most notable and startling thing about the Statue of Liberty is that it is *flimsy*. Once you are inside it you can see the shell very clearly and closely, and instead of the massive thickness of iron, reinforced by (if not entirely lined with) bricks, stone or marble, which the visitor might expect from the huge size of the statue itself, the fabric can be seen to be so thin that a finger could apparently be poked through it. It couldn't; nonetheless, the copper 'skin' is only 2·5 millimetres thick, and probably a good deal less, because that was the original thickness of the copper sheets, and they were hammered thinner before being installed. Also it shakes.

It does worse than shake. But before I got to the worse, I met Charlie DeLeo, the Keeper of the Flame. Charlie – he proclaims it himself, so I am not embarrassing him by repeating a whispered confidence – is in love with 'the Lady', as he calls her. He really is the Keeper of the Flame, because one of his duties as general maintenance man is to replace the light bulbs in the torch itself; but for him, the title sums up his attitude to his job and to the mythical goddess whom he serves, for he is no less dedicated to his mistress than were the Vestal Virgins whose task was to keep a sacred flame alight in the temple of their faith.

Charlie DeLeo has been the Lady's protector for sixteen years. He knows every square inch of her, inside and out, quite literally. He came originally as a visitor, fell in love with her, applied for a job and got it. Rather touchingly, he calls himself the Quasimodo of the Statue of Liberty, but he is certainly its expert; while the reconstruction was going on, he was there every minute of the day, helping to solve problems that only he fully understood. His philosophy of his job is based on one simple precept: 'I want to give something back to the Lady.' A devout Christian, he glossed it thus: 'Too many people in the world are just taking and not giving, so I want to increase the giving.' And then he said, 'When I'm right up at the top of the crown, in the tip of the flame, I feel close to God, and I always pray. I come up here and I pray for all the people who are suffering – in all religions, it doesn't make any difference to me.' He even likens the light of the torch to Christ, the Light of the World.

And another thing: when the Lady was built (she was unveiled in 1886) there was no such thing as a security problem, nor indeed was there until only a few years ago. Blowing up the Statue of Liberty would be something of a coup for any one of the hundreds of terrorist groups in which our

2 Is it a bird? Is it a plane?   3 No, it's vertigo

world abounds, but Charlie is a match for them, too: 'I know every nook and cranny, everywhere you could hide something, everywhere you could leave things, and if I see anything suspicious, a parcel or anything, I call Security right away.'*

Rashly, I asked him if I, too, could go right up to the top, right to the flame. That was my first mistake, because the only way up to it was by an absolutely vertical metal ladder. Charlie did not know the word vertigo, but he understood the nature of it, and was extremely solicitous at getting me up and (which is always worse for the vertiginous) down.

I stepped out on to the narrow platform that runs right round the flame, and instantly discovered the full horror of the Lady's construction. If the whole structure shakes, this topmost part *sways*. There was a flimsy railing, and there was Charlie's steadying hand on my arm, but all I could think of was the Hitchcock film in which the villain falls off the Statue of Liberty, and does so in a singularly nasty manner. He has been chased up the Statue by the detective, and they wrestle at the top; the villain pitches out over the rail, and the detective catches him by the cuff of his sleeve, clutching his nefarious prize, who is dangling over the abyss, until reinforcements arrive to haul the miscreant back over the rail and take him down. And then Hitchcock cuts, in close-up, to the shoulder of the villain's jacket, and, one by one, the stitches that join sleeve to body begin to go. The detective's grip on the bottom of the sleeve is still firm, but at the top it is coming away. Wider and wider grows the split, until the last threads snap, and the villain hurtles down towards the sea, with the detective still clutching an empty and detached sleeve.

Charlie got me down the ladder safely. A remarkable man.

I walked down the rest; from the observation platform to the plinth elevator there are 168 steps, which is exactly twice the number I have to climb from my street door to the door of my flat. They say that the entire climb, from ground to crown, is the equivalent of 22 storeys, but that includes the plinth, which is 142 feet high, the Lady herself being 151 feet. It suddenly occurred to me that Great-uncle Rudi would have seen the Lady in all her youthful glory, with the copper still unoxidised, when he arrived off New York; he sailed for America in 1888, only two years after the Statue was finished. Even now, when New York is familiar to me, and the Lady fixed as a symbol in the mind's eye of countless millions who have never seen her in reality, even now the trip across the water, with the incomparable sight of that skyline, makes me catch my breath. What Great-

---

* But (see the doctor's dilemma) how is Security to get to it if it is half-way up?

uncle Rudi must have thought can hardly be guessed at; he must have felt that he had arrived in the Promised Land. I suppose he had.

No-one can leave the Lady without a basket of facts, least of all me. She was built by Auguste Bartholdi, who was also responsible for the Lion of Belfort, a huge sandstone figure let into the hill below the town, to commemorate Belfort's heroic feat of standing the German siege through-out the Franco-Prussian War. For the very complicated engineering, he turned to Gustave Eiffel; visitors to the Lady who know Paris will recognise the criss-cross struts inside the Statue's shell as similar to the bracings of the Eiffel Tower. Bartholdi was obsessed by the monumental statues of ancient Egypt; one of his inspirations for the Statue was the Colossus of Rhodes, which also bestrode a sea harbour.

Her upraised arm is 42 feet long; she weighs 225 tons; she is lit by 107 1000-watt bulbs, all tended by Charlie DeLeo; and each of her eyes is $2\frac{1}{2}$ feet wide. And another thing, perhaps the most haunting fact among the countless facts that make up the Lady and her legend; her face is that of Bartholdi's mother. Did ever son more nobly salute the womb that bore him? (Yes; but only one.)

After the Statue of Liberty, Ellis Island. The words mean little today, and I imagine that even most Americans hardly know of its existence. But the grandparents of millions of them would have known, and for many the knowledge would lead to a shudder. A mile off the lower end of Manhattan, Ellis Island was, until its closure in 1954, the filter and sieve through which all immigrants passed into the New World – or were turned back within sight of it. The total number of immigrants who ran the Ellis Island gauntlet was around 12 million; Great-uncle Rudi was one of them.

When Ellis Island ceased to act as port-in-the-storm for the huddled masses yearning to be free, it was abandoned, and the Great Hall (its correct name was the Registry) through which those millions shuffled, bewildered, with their meagre possessions in bags and bundles, was left to rot. When I got there, reconstruction and renovation were in full swing; there are to be conference-rooms, sporting facilities and restaurants, but the centrepiece of the new Ellis Island is to be a Museum of Immigration. It wasn't difficult, despite the ruin and the bustle, to conjure up the scene at the end of the nineteenth century and beginning of the twentieth (Ellis Island's heyday). The huge, arched ceiling is to have its beautiful tiling restored; every time a workman dropped a plank or banged a rivet into a metal beam, the echo rolled along it, and brought the dead to life.

Few societies, at any time in history, have ungrudgingly welcomed immigrants from other lands, particularly lands where the customs and the language were very different from those of the indigenous. The United States, not much more than a century old, was no exception; the unique generosity of which I speak was not universal, and as the wave grew higher, indignant citizens turned to with mops to push it back. An Immigration Restriction League sprang up, appalled by these uncouth mongrel breeds, with the patriotic societies and the labour unions (as always and everywhere in fear for their jobs), prominent in its membership; in reply, a Liberal Immigration League came into being, among *its* ranks there were the steamship companies and manufacturers short of hands, also looking after their own interests. The rules about restrictions and exclusions sound as though no further tightening of the valve could be thought necessary, or indeed possible:

> ... idiots, insane persons, paupers or persons likely to become a public charge, persons suffering from a loathsome or dangerous contagious disease, persons who have been convicted of a felony or other infamous crime or misdemeanour involving moral turpitude, polygamists, and also any person whose ticket or passage is paid for with the money of another or who is assisted by others to come, anarchists or persons who believe in or advocate the overthrow by force or violence of the Government of the United States or of all government or of all forms of law, or the assassination of public officials, prostitutes and persons who procure or attempt to bring in prostitutes or women for the purpose of prostitution, those who have been, within one year of the date of the application for admission to the United States, deported ...

In addition, immigrants could be refused entry if they were suffering from epilepsy, tuberculosis, leprosy, trachoma, ringworm, parasitic disease or amoebic dysentery, hernia, deformity, heart disease, arthritis or varicose veins.

And yet, despite these catalogues, it is salutary and astonishing to learn that the principle on which the immigration laws was based was that if an immigrant did not fall within any of the legal or medical prohibitions he or she would invariably be allowed in; the idea of restricting immigration *as such* came much later. (Even literacy was not a requirement.)

The immigrants came from everywhere, and from all trades and social classes, with every language and custom, every belief and practice. But the group which came in the greatest numbers was that of the Jews. It is ironic that one of the world's oldest and most deeply-embedded legends is that of the Wandering Jew, as though such a figure is unique, whereas the truth is that for two millennia the Jews have been wanderers over the face of the earth. Sometimes they have wandered for knowledge; sometimes for trade and gain; but mostly they have wandered in search of a land which would let them live in peace and freedom. To this day, there are still countries in which Jews live in fear or under restriction, countries which will neither let their Jews leave nor let them alone, countries with laws which apply to Jews but to no other citizens, countries where the persecution of Jews is tolerated by the rulers and countries where it is encouraged by them. No wonder that as the long lines of immigrants shuffled through the Great Hall towards their destiny (Ellis was always overcrowded, and in the peak year, 1907, an average of 3300 immigrants *a day* landed there), they wondered whether, as they had been led to believe, this was at last the country they had been seeking throughout the centuries, the country that would take them in and let them stay for ever, to live and work and pray like any other citizen.

From the beginning of the new century, there was reassurance for them in the Great Hall itself; Jewish societies had established themselves in America, and their representatives were on Ellis Island to help those stunned by culture-shock, and – more practically – to help them find jobs, relatives and synagogues.

The First World War stopped all that. The Russian Revolution was seen as a threat to the United States, and the wave of ur-McCarthyite political repression, under the leadership of ur-McCarthy, Mitchell Palmer, flooded over the immigration movement as well. Quota laws, for so long demanded by the indignant citizens and the patriotic societies, were introduced, and the great infusion was over. Today, the immigration laws of America are much less restrictive than they were at their worst in the 1920s, but they will never again be as free as they were in that truly golden age when the dazed arrivals looked up at the echoing ceiling in the Great Hall, wondering whether this was a dream or a nightmare or reality, and wondered all the more intently when a member of one of the Jewish help societies tapped them on the arm and offered them a kosher meal.

The story of the Great American Flood, the flood that poured out of the east to travel and settle in the west, is one of the most heartening of mankind's achievements. The wanderers travelled over unimaginable distances with unimaginable difficulties; they arrived penniless, ignorant, illiterate, with nothing material, carrying a different culture, puzzling attitudes, strange feelings, new relationships and a very old religion; they did not have even the language of their hosts; a whole generation had to pass before they could believe that the persecutions and the pogroms were over for ever in this extraordinary land; and, having survived, they set themselves to thrive, and did.

This mighty statue, and the derelict island not far from it, symbolise, and whatever happens to immigration policies the world over will continue to symbolise, that longing for freedom which is embedded in the heart of every human being, and which will not be silenced or stifled or rooted out, but will on the contrary continue to grow and to clamour for fulfilment, until it is satisfied in a land in which it can flourish. For tens of millions of such human beings that land has been the United States of America, and their first inkling of it was the sight of that Lady of Hope, whose correct title is 'Liberty Enlightening the World'. Truly, 'I was a stranger; and ye took me in'.

★   ★   ★

I met one of them early on. The garment trade in New York has had a long and colourful history, starting with the immigrants who filled the sweat-shops, going on with the melodiously-titled Ladies Garment Workers Union, and now one of the greatest industries of the developed world; the mass production of simple, but excellent clothes – excellent not least in design – has been one of the most important social developments of modern times, especially because from clothes the whole gamut of manufacture was run in the provision of well-made, well-designed, increasingly inexpensive goods – furniture, linens, luggage, pots and pans, crockery and cutlery, travel, carpets, radios and televisions, cars, tape-recorders and cassette-players, food (perhaps second only to clothing in the size of the explosion), heating, lighting, houses, newspapers and magazines, tools, bicycles, and almost everything else that formerly was either the province of the wealthy, or shoddy rubbish.

And here I was at the epicentre of the earthquake. It is a dress-making establishment, though strictly it doesn't *make* dresses, it only cuts them – the making is done upstairs. But the application of mass production to dresses is demonstrated here in the most spectacular fashion. The factory floor extends for 150 *yards*, and down it run gigantic tables 30–40 yards long, on which weird machines run up and down, peeling off from a huge, continuous roll of cloth what becomes a pile of layers of fabric, in a standard width, anything up to a foot thick. When the desired height of the pile is reached, the machine which dispenses the cloth retires, and the cutting-machines take over; they cut the pattern right through the heap which, depending obviously on the nature of the cloth, can be up to 250 layers thick. Now do the arithmetic: if the cloth rolled out is 40 yards long and 3 yards wide and 250 layers thick, and assuming that the cutting-patterns (which are laid on the cloth) have been fitted so as to get as many dress shapes on to the cutting area as geometry will allow, how many dresses come off that table?

Pass; but it is a lot. In fact, it is 200,000 dresses a week, as the boss, Joe Vitriano, told me, and they all go upstairs to be stitched, where the same vast expanse (Joe said his floor is one-and-a-half football fields long) is waiting. Now 200,000 dresses a week from what is only one of thousands of dress-making factories testifies to the stupendous demand for good, attractive clothing at comfortable prices that the modern world exercises. Who first spotted the fact that the poor, though they could not buy expensive things, exist in such numbers that it was worth making cheap things for them? And then who took it a step further, and argued that the poor would buy more such things if they were made attractive? His name, like the inventor of fire, the wheel and husbandry, is forever lost; but at least we know who matched the new mass manufacturers with a new mass form of retailing – Marks & Spencer. Has anyone ever seen anything badly designed or badly made in Marks?

Then I went upstairs. Down below they cut the cloth; above, they sew the garments. Harvey was as genial as Joe, and as forthcoming, but he had a revelation in store for me. The factory was humming with the noise of a couple of hundred sewing-machines; the women sat in rows and, well-practised, finished a blouse or a skirt in a few minutes. If this was a sweat-shop, it was an uncommonly pleasant, airy and bright one, and the downtrodden wage-slaves looked no less uncommonly uptrodden. They were all Hispanic, mostly middle-aged, all well-dressed. I asked Harvey how many such factories he had, scattered about the city, and he told me seventeen. And were they all staffed entirely by Hispanics, like this one? No, in fact this is the only one. And the others? All Chinese. *All* Chinese? Yes.

I asked the obvious question, and the answer illuminated the world. Because, he said, 'the Jews and the Italians are now doctors and lawyers'. The history of the nineteenth and twentieth centuries lay bare before me, a history charted by the fate of the successive waves of immigrants into the United States and other industrialised countries. Every such wave inevitably gravitates to the worst-paid, most-exploited jobs; it is largely the reluctance of the indigenous to take such jobs that leads to the immigration. But generation by generation, the newcomers fight their way out of the trap into the mainstream of society. More; because they have indeed to *fight* their way upwards, they have honed their skills, organised their intelligence, toughened their ambition, with the result that they not only get out of the trap, but find themselves far up the ladder of success. That story has been most dramatically acted out by the Jews; but a less spectacular version of the drama has been played by other immigrant groups.

So I asked Joe what is going to happen when the Chinese are doctors and lawyers, and he said, 'It has started already'.

It has indeed, as Daisy Tsui had just demonstrated. *New York* magazine ran a feature on 'The 20 most important people in New York in 1988'. The net was cast ingeniously wide, including not only the Mayor and Felix Rohatyn, but a young drug-pusher specialising in getting schoolchildren hooked on crack (importance need not be related to virtue) – and Daisy Tsui.

She is eighteen years old, and has just been accepted for Harvard, where she will study biochemistry. Her father left China for the United States at about the time she was born; he worked in a Chinese restaurant for seven years, to save enough to bring his wife and daughter to America. She arrived knowing no word of English; her parents can still speak nothing but Chinese. After elementary school, she went on to Stuyvesant High, considered the best in the city. She ended there in the top five in a class of 709. She was not lonely, incidentally; the school has a rigid system of admission on examination results only, and 9200 children applied in 1987 for one of the 750 places available; the school is now 40 per cent Amerasian, though the national population figure is 1.5. (She won't be lonely at Harvard, either, where 14 per cent of the current intake are of her origin.)

Are the Chinese cleverer than occidentals? The experts say no, as does common sense; *no* ethnic group is in general cleverer than any other, a fact which has long been fiercely debated, most fiercely in the case of the Jews. But the story of immigrant Jews – immigrant not only to the United States – is the most striking *confirmation*, not refutation, of the truth that Jews in general are no more brainy than other people in general. The Jews were the first to realise that they would get no help from those who had taken them in, other than the taking itself; from Ellis Island on, they were on their own. This strengthened their determination – their *need* – to be successful, and two further strands helped to weave the rope on which they pulled themselves up. The first was the help that the Jews gave each other in their days of struggle, and the second was the deeply ingrained Jewish belief in learning. That threefold advantage, born of necessity, carried the Jews to success (and to resentment of their success, though that is another story), and an almost identical pattern of motivation has inspired others who inevitably started at the bottom to get to the top. And now, it seems, the Chinese are climbing the ladder, and becoming doctors and lawyers; it seemed time for me to ask Joe what was going to happen when *they* were all doctors and lawyers. And he said, 'I don't know. There aren't any more groups to come.'

It was an amazing statement, yet it obviously corresponds to reality. He went on to say that I could see the process happening right here if I knew where to look. In this factory the Spanish employees are unionised and they work a thirty-five-hour week. But in the other factories the Chinese are not unionised, and they work seventy hours a week. 'Think about it.'

I did think about it, but Joe had to leave before I could offer him the fruits of my thinking. He handed me over to a very remarkable man, Sol. Sol was a Jew of Polish origin; he had been in a Nazi concentration camp, survived it, and gone to the United States at the end of the war. When he landed, he could not speak a word of English, but he built up his own garment business, and prospered greatly. He sold the business not long ago, but retirement was irksome, so he joined Harvey.

He took the argument about post-industrial society much further. He pointed out that the very things this firm was making were being made in Asia for a third of the cost but in the same quality. 'Listen,' he said; 'the stores in America can buy our goods for ten dollars and sell them at twenty dollars. But they can buy the same quality items from Asia for *three* dollars and still sell them at twenty dollars. So why should they pay us the other seven?'

He went further still. He insisted that manufacturing industry is going to die all over the western world, because the east, the raw, developing east, is going to be able to undercut anything the west can make by an enormous margin, tariffs or no tariffs. I offered him the example – a good many years ago, moreover – of the British motor-cycle industry, which dominated the world for so long, but has now disappeared entirely, with not a single British firm making motor-bikes in Britain and the industry taken over by the Japanese. 'Oh, you wait,' he said; 'the Japanese are falling into the same trap – the Taiwanese and the South Koreans and the Thais are going to do the same thing to the Japanese that the Japanese are doing to the west. You'll see.'

But this wise and far-seeing man had not finished with his philosophy. 'We're not going to starve', he said. 'Sure, manufacturing industry will die out in the United States in the next ten to fifteen years, but the service industries will grow correspondingly. But that isn't enough.' 'How do you mean, isn't enough?' I asked him. 'Look', he said, holding out his hands and turning them first palms up, then down. 'Men have to make things with their hands,' he said; 'they've always had to. That's why we have hands. But what kind of a world is it going to be when all you've got is one man saying I'll flip your hamburger and you'll flip my hamburger?'

I asked him if he knew Primo Levi's book, *The Wrench*. He didn't. I told him he would enjoy it; I forbore to say that he would recognise himself in it. For Levi's book is a marvellous, uncompromising hymn to *homo faber* from *homo sapiens*, an argument from the deepest and oldest impulses in mankind. The hero of *The Wrench* is a construction engineer, constantly called in when difficult building needs a special approach; but the heart and savour of the book lies in his lust for work, for using metal and wood and brick and concrete and machinery, forcing them all to give up their secrets and bend to his will. Perhaps building dams and derricks is far from making mass-produced skirts, but as Sol talked the distance shrank, and any kind of work that consisted of *making* was as good as any other.

'But I have no complaints about this country', he said. 'I came here with nothing, I built up my own success.' I told him of the feeling that always possesses me when I come to America, and particularly New York, the feeling that America has never lost the belief that by hard work and determination *anything* may be achieved, whereas in Europe it has almost died out. 'That's true,' he said; 'I only hope my children don't ever forget it.' His son, he said, is a plastic surgeon, his daughter a lawyer. He repeated, 'I came here with nothing, I have no complaints about this country'; and as he thought about his children, he smiled, for the first time.

I left thinking not so much of Joe and Sol, as that remarkable phrase of Joe's: 'there aren't any more groups to come'. It obviously wasn't meant literally; for one thing, if the Soviet authorities allow genuinely unrestricted Jewish emigration there could be a new Exodus for half a million people. What is Emma Lazarus going to say when such a Diaspora lands, bringing nothing with them but a determination to succeed at once, rather than waiting for two or three generations as their ancestors did?

The history of immigrants has been thoroughly explored; studies of the effect of *emigration* on the lands thus abandoned have been largely confined to such narrow fields as that of the harm Nazi Germany did to herself by driving so many German-Jewish scientists abroad and, more recently, the decline in the quality of Soviet orchestras denuded of so many Russian-Jewish players. But I know of no study – perhaps it is considered too delicate a subject – of the quality – the genetic quality – of nations stripped of their best; for surely it follows that those who nerve themselves to face the hazards and hardships of emigration must be mostly the people with greater hardiness, character, strength of will, enterprise and intelligence. I have often wondered whether the wretched stagnation of Ireland is due to the fact that, generation after generation, their best and boldest have left their native country, never to return.

More facts. Even before the First World War, four-fifths of the population of New York City were first or second generation immigrants. At this moment, almost 30 per cent of the city's population were not born in the United States. That Harvard intake which included Daisy Tsui may not be all it seems; some of the Ivy League colleges have been accused of instituting a *numerus clausus* in the case of the Chinese applicants, so that their astonishing success rate may be actually understated. (A pit of irony yawns at our feet; the battles over quotas that kept Jews out of the best American Universities finished decades ago. If the barriers, rusty now, yet perhaps still serviceable, are being hauled out and re-erected before the Chinese, it would seem that a vital lesson still needs to be learned: have not the Jews of America contributed gigantically to its life, culture, prosperity, power and international standing? And who shall say that the Chinese, left to themselves and their qualities, will not do the same?)

More facts. The flower and vegetable retail trade in New York is now run almost entirely by Koreans. There are a million Italians in New York City. Of all the people in the world who leave the country they were born in and settle in another, two-thirds fetch up in the United States. There are no Amerindian geographical enclaves in New York, but in Astoria, in the borough of Queens, there are 70,000 Greeks, which is more than any city other than Athens and Sydney. Between 1820 and 1920, well over 30 million immigrants had been admitted to the United States. More than 30 languages are spoken in New York. Nobody knows, even roughly, how many illegal immigrants there are. Despite the gradual but apparently inexorable decline in the number of Jews in New York, there are *still* more Goldbergs than Smiths in the phone book, but in Britain there are *already* more Patels than Smiths in the Bradford phone book. In the implications of those two pairs of juxtapositions lie the history, and perhaps the future, of the world.

★   ★   ★

At this point, I played hookey. Though it was off my line of march, I couldn't resist an invitation to visit the Federal Reserve Bank of New York, particularly as I had been promised, by the hospitable authorities of the Bank, some remarkable sights. Nor did they exaggerate.

I began with the department in which banknotes which have outlived their time – too torn or dirty to be put back into circulation – are disposed of. First, the packets are unwrapped and introduced to a computer which counts them, having been instructed as to which denomination it is to count, and how many notes of that denomination. When the computer reports that that job is done, it is dismissed with thanks, and the next process begins. The stacks of currency, 10,000 notes in each, are picked up and delivered to a projection on the machine; from this, they are automatically fed into a sorter. The sorter spits on its hands and gets to work.

Each note passes over a series of sensors: one detects the denomination, the next checks for authenticity (by seeking coded metallic matter in the note), the next determines whether the note is torn, and the last learns how dirty it is, which is measured by the quantity of light it reflects – the dirtier the less. Notes which fail the cleanliness or integrity test go straight into a hopper where the work of destruction begins.

The hosepipe which sucked in the notes that had been sentenced to death ran through the wall at the end of the machine; I learned that on their way upstairs they had been shredded horizontally into strips an eighth of an inch wide (which means fifty strips), and for good measure the denominations are mixed when the shredding is finished. Then, after the dust had been extracted (because if it wasn't the operators would choke to death quite quickly), the shredded money fell into two huge hoppers; two metal plates swung out from the walls and pushed the debris down; as more fodder fell, the plates crushed it into a more and more compact form, until eventually the entire hopper was one solid cube, and a cut-out stopped any more shredded wheat falling. Then the door at the end of the oven swung open, unseen hands slapped a sheet of cardboard on each side of the cube of compressed dollars, further invisible wizards bound the whole thing in wire, and a truck took it away.

Each bale weighs 450 lbs, and 16 such bales leave the premises, well and truly shredded, each day, with a face value – when it had a face – of more than $20,000,000. Assume a five-day week, and a few public holidays; 875 tons a year, 5 *billion* dollars disposed of. Where now are your millionaires who light their cigars with ten-dollar bills? Where are those who charge their extravagant friends with throwing money away? Where are the pessimists who refuse to join get-rich-quick schemes because it would be like tearing up dollar bills? If this be extravagance, it is extravagance on a scale that makes beggars simultaneously of Croesus, Timon, and the Medicis.

But when the bales of murdered money have left the premises, where do they go? What does one *do* with $3\frac{1}{2}$ tons of shredded dollars a day? What wide variety of ingenious uses have ingenious users put it to?

The answer is full of irony: *there is no use for it at all*. Until 1981, the notes were burned, reduced to a very fine ash – they say as fine as talcum powder – which could be disposed of, albeit with some difficulty. But since then, environmental concern has dictated that no more such burning may take place; whence the bales, and whence, also, the increasingly desperate search for a saleable use for them. A handful of the stuff is made into novelties like mock golf balls, another handful is taken by charities who like to put shredded notes in jars and sell them; but a fortune awaits the man who can think of a use for the stuff, a use which someone would pay for. (Having learned of the Fed's tragedy, I enquired as to what, then, does become of the stuff? I was told that it was dumped as infilling when new buildings are being put up. And nobody doing the building could be prevailed upon to pay for it.)

The compressed shreds looked like some kind of unappetising breakfast cereal; there was a splendid grizzled old hand operating the hoppers and the compressing, who had been there since long before the system changed over from burning to baling, and he was touchingly fond of his machines. It occurred to me that, over the years, he had had through his hands far more money – far more by thousands of times – than all the greatest millionaires of history put together. I was about to tell him so, when I was struck by the thought that he might not be altogether pleased.

And then I descended into the bowels of the earth, to see the gold. Gold is neither the rarest nor the most valuable of metals; whether it is the most beautiful is a matter of individual taste. Yet no other metal – no other natural substance, not even diamonds – has even a fraction of the mystery, the awe, the reverence, the greed, the longing, the satisfaction, the trust that gold inspires, and always has inspired. In every land and in every epoch, if the stuff could be found and dug up, or got from a more fruitful nearby soil by barter or force, it has been sought after, fought after, thought after, bought after, and none but the greatest saints and most severe ascetics have been immune from its lure. As currency or as ornament, hidden beneath the floorboards or lying in bank vaults, this yellow thing is a magnet with the unique property of attracting human beings, who have only to scent it far off on the wind, or to catch a glimpse of it winking in the sun, to be helpless in its thrall.

In Wagner's *Das Rheingold* it takes its place as the only substance more valuable than love, and at the same time the substance most likely to lead to murder (ultimately, it leads to the end of the world); with this giant metaphor he measures the unassuageable longing for power that consumes mankind, and depicts that longing with such consummate art that a blind man who knew nothing of music could hear the gold shimmering in the orchestra.

In Peter Shaffer's *The Royal Hunt of the Sun* the metaphor is made even more explicit, and the great roll-call of the sources of the Inca's gold, now needed in his greatest extremity, echoes the Muster of the Ships in Homer:

> Atahuallpa speaks! Atahuallpa needs! Atahuallpa commands! Bring him gold. From the palaces. From the temples. From all buildings in the great places. From walls of pleasure and roofs of omen. From floors of feasting and ceilings of death. Bring him the gold of Quito and Pachamacac! Bring him the gold of Cuzco and Coricancha! Bring him the gold of Vilcanota! Bring him the gold of Colae! Of Aymaraes and Arequipa! Bring him the gold of the Chimu! Put up a mountain of gold and free your Sun from his prison of clouds!

At the Federal Reserve Bank in New York, they brought me to the gold. As the statistics rained about me, and threatened drowning, I think I heard that there is more gold in this building than in the whole of Fort Knox; I certainly heard that the gold in the more famous cave is all American; the rest of the world's treasure is here.

No-one, from the President of the United States to the President of the World Bank, is allowed into the innermost recesses of the cave where lies the petrified substance of the sun unless he is accompanied by three guards, no two from the same department. The Virgil at my elbow as we descended into the Seventh Circle pointed to a section of blank wall: 'Let me show you', he said, and went to a huge wheel. As he turned it, a crack appeared in the wall, and two doors swung silently open. They were fully three feet thick, and as they parted, the pins, six inches in diameter, slid out of their housing, looking like monstrous fangs; these lock into position across the two halves of the door as it swings shut.

It swung open; and there was the gold. The bank offers guided tours, but these do not penetrate into the Holy of Holies (how naturally the phrase came to mind!); thrice guarded, I was led to the real thing.

The real thing is very real indeed, but it is the sense of sound, not of sight, that is affected first. For the vaults are silent; so silent that it is a positive, an almost tangible, feeling. The guards moved as if they did not touch the floor; not a jacket rustled, not a key jangled; my Virgil was struck as dumb as they. I had to break the spell, and did so with the obvious question: what is the value of all the gold here? He told me that it was 14 million dollars, but immediately added that that was the wholly artificial standard price – gold bought outside, on the market, would cost ten times as much.

Wagner came back to me; this was Fafner's cave, where the dragon lay asleep, his hoard around him, while the hero approached, sword ready, for the final battle. The walls were divided into caves of various sizes, presumably depending on the quantity stored by this or that country. Each cave had a number, but no name; only those whose business it was to know could say 'This is Belgium's gold, and this is Ecuador's'. (There are some eighty hoards altogether.) The slabs of gold were arranged, for the most part, like the bricks in a wall. Moving round the room, I suddenly came upon a cave that could only have belonged to Aladdin himself, or at the very least Harun-al-Rashid. A vast wall of gold faced me, thirty feet across and twenty high; how far back it went I could not see. Whose it was, I could not guess; presumably South Africa does not store her gold here? Surreptitiously, I hoped it was Britain's.

I followed my cicerone into another sanctum. 'This', he said, 'is where the gold is weighed.' In the centre of the room there stood a huge set of scales, eight feet high, each pan a massive platform. I assumed that this was only for very rough computation, for those who wanted to know no more exactly than half-a dozen ingots one way or the other. Not a bit; not even a little bit. 'Watch', he said, pointing to the pendulum on the central post of the scales, which was enclosed in glass; he took out a crisp new dollar bill and tossed it on to one of the scales. As I watched incredulously, I saw the pointer shift; it stopped at three-hundredths of an ounce, which, it seems, is the weight of a dollar bill. I goggled at my guide, and again, laconically, he said, 'Watch'. He took out another dollar bill, and showed it to me: 'This one's dirty,' he said; 'watch'. He threw it on to the other scale; almost imperceptibly, the pointer swung. It stopped at four-hundredths of an ounce; there was a hundredth of an ounce of dirt on the bill, and the machine had measured it. 'That's nothing,' he said, and waved his hand over the scale; the pointer moved. It could measure the weight of a handful of air.

I raised my camera to take a picture of this magical machine, but my guardian angel touched my arm; I sensed, rather than heard, the three guards moving towards me. 'Sorry,' he said, 'nobody takes pictures down here.' I could well believe it.

We went back into the golden room. I wandered round the walls again, thinking about this extraordinary substance, for which so many have died and so many been slain. I turned away, and saw a trolley stacked with ingots, and a guard sitting on the end reading a newspaper. I suddenly felt nothing; there were perhaps two or three hundreds slabs on the truck, but the thrill had faded. I realised what had happened; for more than half an hour I had been steeped in gold, heaps and hills and mountains of it, and I was gorged with the feast. Can one, then, have too much gold? The world has certainly never thought so; did the custodians, down in this subterranean treasure-chamber, become blasé? I looked over the shoulder of the guard who was reading the paper, inches from a couple of tons of gold; he was engrossed in the sports section. Virgil bade me pick up a slab about the size of a book, and I thought, as I failed to move it, let alone pick it up, that this must be the Bank's regular joke – nailing an ingot to the floor. Not a bit of it; I had forgotten, if I ever knew, that gold is *heavy*.

Virgil accompanied me to the upper air, and I went away in a thoughtful mood. I was thinking of a short story by Lord Dunsany that I had read decades before, and had not thought about since. It told of an island in the middle of a lake, somewhere in the remotest depths of Latin America. The seeker after treasure would make his way to the edge of the lake; there was no boat of any kind, and if he wanted to reach the island he would have to swim to it. But any traveller who had got this far *did* want to get to the island; that was why he had made the journey, because the island was piled high with chunks of solid gold, guarded by mysterious priests, who presided over a strange ritual. When the swimmer scrambled up on the island shore, after a very taxing swim – it was a large lake, and the island was exactly in the middle – he was told that he was free to take as much gold as he wanted, without payment or ceremony. The priests told him that he would be given a box, and when he had filled it with as much gold as he wished to take, it would be shut and locked, then bound, with further locks, on his back. He was then free to return to the lake shore, and the gold was his from the moment he landed.

The traveller who is telling the story describes his wonder, and how he began to stuff the box full of gold. Then, gradually, he begins to think. Those priests, they looked impassive, utterly so. The box, it was of metal; heavy. The gold was heavier still; the swim had been strenuous without any burden on his back. He looked again at the priests, with their faces of unconcern, and looked again at the far shore. Then he threw all the gold back on to the pile, tossed the box after it, and dived into the lake. He got back to the shore almost spent, and gazed back at the island, and at the priests, still sitting calmly and unmoving.

*   *   *

4 *The immigrants' route*   5 *The immigrants' landfall*   6 *With onions? And ketchup?*
7 *The song of the shirt*   8 *Malcolm Forbes reads a bedtime story*

4

5

7

8

Four blocks up; a hundred-and-thirty-seven to go. And the first pause is at 12th Street, where the memories of the dollars and the gold are most apposite.

Malcolm Forbes entered the room, briskly; a man of slightly below average height, looking far younger than his sixty-nine years, asking 'Where do you want me?' The chair from behind his desk was fetched and placed, and he sat down. 'Thank you,' I said. 'No problem,' said he. Mind you, in position, he was a good ten feet nearer the splendid Rubens at the end of the room.

Some rich men do not enjoy their riches; a fearful limitation. Malcolm Forbes is not one of them. Downstairs in the Forbes building there is a delightful museum, beautifully arranged, and open to the public without charge. It contains his collections: huge armies of toy soldiers (he mentioned demurely that he had another 140,000 not on show), an ocean of toy boats from every era of American shipping, walls full of historic documents, and a separate gallery filled with the most luscious Fabergé *objets d'art*. His hot-air balloons, many of which are made not in the familiar shape but in the form of gigantic castles, elephants, whales and motor cars, cannot be accommodated in Fifth Avenue, so he keeps them at his château in Normandy, and they form the only balloon museum in the world.

Yachtsman, fox-hunter, tennis-player and, most notoriously, motor-cyclist (I watched him roar off down Fifth Avenue when we parted), Malcolm Forbes undoubtedly enjoys his wealth. Indeed, he said so very plainly when I asked him why he didn't retire, saying that he could live in luxury and enjoyment for the rest of his life. 'But I do live in luxury and enjoyment right now,' he said '*and* I enjoy working.' Then he sat up sharply and added, 'Retirement kills more people than work ever did, you know.'

An eloquent man, something I had not been prepared for. Also a frank one; he laid out his attitudes to poverty and wealth in a manner that could easily be caricatured.

In this country you don't basically have a sense of class; a sense of us versus them. There are ideological arguments, usually by intellectuals who've had all the benefits of an education, decrying the arrogance of a self-made businessman. In this country you go through phases, but it's very seldom 'down with the rich, do away with the rich'; it's 'how do I get a piece of the pie, how do I get more than I've got?' So you don't get that kind of resentment. Oh, you do when somebody acts like because they've got money they're entitled to be at the head of the queue. But that's an individually created resentment, and it's deserved. But overall I don't think you get the kind of traditional feeling of

9 The topless towers of Ilium

'they've always had it and they don't care if we get any.' I think that in the streets of Harlem they don't regard Fifth Avenue with hatred; they want to know when some elements of it are going to reach into Harlem.

That speech would once have been widely regarded in Britain as nothing but an excuse by a very rich man for not caring about the poor. But it is, as even a slight acquaintance with the United States reveals, perfectly true. It is very convenient for Malcolm Forbes, of course, but that doesn't alter the extraordinary fact that it corresponds to American reality. It also, though not to the same extent, corresponds to the reality in Japan, West Germany and Italy, and in many other countries.

But the most remarkable phenomenon of recent years is that the contrary attitude, which for so long seemed inextricably embedded in Britain's social relations, is now fading, being replaced by the American approach of 'How do I get a piece of the pie?' instead of 'How can I stop the boss getting another piece of the pie?' Americans are quite unable to understand me when I tell them that not so long ago British workers in their millions were quite content never to buy a bigger or better Ford if by thus denying themselves they could prevent the boss from buying a bigger or better Mercedes. It is not difficult to see how this attitude arose, or at least how it was perpetuated: the ethos of British trades unions, combined with the appallingly low quality of their leaders, led to an ugly and mean-spirited combination of resentment, indifference and pessimism.

Now, however, such feeling is diminishing rapidly. And it is precisely when – indeed, *because* – so heartening a change in attitudes is taking place that voices can be heard in reproach. Materialism is decried by those with an ample store of materials; consumerism is denounced by those who have spent their lives consuming and have every intention of continuing to do so; greed is anathematised by fair round bellies with good capon lined.

Those who once patronised the poor have become indignant because the poor have begun to get richer; worse, the poor have begun to emulate their betters, taking holidays elsewhere than in Benidorm, eating in restaurants they once did not aspire to, even travelling first class on trains. We should remind ourselves that revolutions are not always noisy, nor accompanied by bloodshed; there are the silent, peaceful ones, too, and it is one such that is changing British society for the better. *A bas les aristos!*

Forbes is a candid man, too. He did not shrink from making clear his belief that colour has much to do with economic situations; he even suggested that Britain was no longer the most tolerant country in the world, and that that was because of immigration. Nor was he put out (though he

paused awhile before answering) when he described his Fabergé masterpieces as illustrating the extravagance of the Tsarist court, and I asked
him if they did not now illustrate the extravagance of the Forbes court.

Very few men of enormous wealth who have built it up themselves,
either from nothing or from adding to and extending an inherited business,
have been free of ruthlessness; how could they be? Multi-million pound
deals and bids and mergers are, in a sense, fights, and fights with enormous
purses for the winners. Let us leave out of consideration those tycoons who
have broken the law, and take only the legitimate ones. They cannot afford
sentiment or even kindness towards their opponents in the opposite corner;
the bulls and bears of finance are baited with sharp-toothed dogs, because
the beasts are needed for dinner. But there is another distinction: what is
the quality of their enjoyment of the battle? If today's tycoons are, in their
way, as ruthless as the 'robber barons', many of them clearly have a zest
and relish for dancing on the financial high wire that the originals did not.

It can have nothing to do with the amount of money victory in the new
battle brings in; we are talking, after all, about men who already have
countless millions. Nor is it that the struggle becomes all-important, a goal
in itself. The truth is that they are enjoying themselves, not just with the
money they make, but in the making of it. Rupert Murdoch and Robert
Maxwell are not at all similar figures; but they both have a whale of a time
planning their next coup, carrying it out, fighting off the opposition, staying
one crucial length ahead of the field. These plainly share the happiness that
Forbes enjoys. To gamble millions just for fun may be thought, by more
sober citizens (and particularly un-millioned ones), to be inexcusably child-
ish. It occurred to me only after I had left Malcolm Forbes that it may not
be wholly coincidence that he collects, and in immense numbers, toy
soldiers.

I returned to his wish to keep working, and he rose handsomely to the
bait:

To me the day is a joy to get up to, for the things I do. You see, it's not work
except in a technical sense, if you love what you're doing. It's not the balloons,
it's not the motor cycles; if I could do only one thing it would be at my desk
writing and running this business. The other things are completely good fun,
but they're not working. The working is the most fun, and I'll keep it up until
physically I'm not able to. We often joke, my children, about how accountants
and tax people say you should give away your business to your children; well,
I've given them equity, but I've often told them I'm not going to give them

fifty-one per cent because probably the first thing they'd do would be to fire me.

Mind you, he is not entirely free of the more traditional weaknesses of the super-rich; he collects honorary degrees the way other people collect stamps. He is a Doctor of Law twenty times, a Doctor of Letters four times and of Humane Letters fourteen times, of Business Administration four times, of Journalism thrice, of Commercial Studies twice, and of Humanities, Fine Arts and Literature once each. He also has an honorary degree in something called International Entrepreneurship from something called the Armand Hammer United World College of the American West, though that last one sounds as though you can get it through the post, or even in a shop selling T-shirts and tin trays bearing the legend 'Everything I like is illegal, immoral or fattening'. (One section of the wall of his office is hung with the robes and hoods of all these doctorates, and a magnificent rainbow spectacle they make, though some of them look quite remarkably implausible.) He is also, by the way, a Commander of the Order of Ouissa-Alaoyite, an Associate Commander Brother of the Most Venerable Order of the Hospital of St John of Jerusalem, a Knight Grand Cross of the Most Noble Order of the Crown of Thailand and a Paramount Chief of the Nimba Tribe.

Before leaving, I had one more visit to the Fabergé gallery; it was full of children, very small ones, making an amazing din, and taking, as far as I could see, no notice at all of the treasures gleaming under the lights of their glass cases. Fabergé wouldn't have minded, I suppose. Nor, come to think of it, would Malcolm Forbes.

★　　★　　★

At the other end of midtown is a very different kind of billionaire. Donald Trump clearly enjoys his billions as much as Forbes does, but in a very different way. Down at 12th Street there is a man of great sophistication; up at 57th there is a genuine naïf. Their respective attitudes to themselves, their money and the world are fascinating to compare and contrast.

When I call Trump a naïf (I have, incidentally, never had the pleasure of meeting him), I am mindful of his success; though there was money in the family, this is no playboy, rolling his father's dice. Trump's successes, which are numerous and colossal, were made by him, through his almost infallible instinct for a deal that will ensure that the high cards fall in front of his place, not his rival's. (Though his book, *The Art of the Deal*, is so gushing, so innocent and so useless as a textbook for budding billionaires that it *must* have been written entirely by himself. He presumably made enquiries to learn whether Shakespeare would be interested in ghosting it, and moved on when his calls were not returned.)

Trump, by all accounts, including his own, is really interested in nothing but his business and the spoils of it (he bought Khashoggi's yacht), though he is not above thinking seriously about nuclear proliferation. Put it this way: on Forbes' desk there was a pile of new books, including the Ellmann biography of Wilde. Whether they were there for reading or for ostentation I have no means of knowing, but I would not be surprised if it were the former; no, I *would* be surprised if it were the latter. What does Trump read? Again, I don't know, but my capacity for surprise would instinctively be the other way round. Besides, Trump is a teetotaller, without medical or religious reason; beware a man who doesn't know what the First Miracle was about. (Beware even more, though for different reasons, a man who counted the late Roy Cohn as a friend as well as a lawyer; even the turbulent rivers of twentieth century American law and politics can rarely have spawned a more vile scoundrel.)

The enthusiasm of Trump is obviously genuine; he not only enjoys his life, his wealth and his achievements, but his zest for the battle is plainly undiminished – indeed, it plainly grows greater. It is clear that he is not wounded by the portraits of him as a bullfrog and vulgarian (though the vulgarity of his buildings – most notably the atrium of the Trump Tower – cannot have been rivalled since the casinos of Las Vegas were built). His hornswoggling is breathtaking; he induced – if indeed a stronger word would not be more appropriate – the city of New York to grant him property-tax exemptions worth hundreds of millions of dollars, and he bought his huge resort at Mar-a-Lago, in Florida, by unabashed blackmail: he told the owners that if they wouldn't sell he would put up, between them and the sea, a huge and hideous building – and a building that Donald Trump himself would characterise as hideous would have been hideous indeed.

Donald Trump is not invited to the parties where old money rules. What is so fascinating about him is that he obviously doesn't mind, indeed, he probably despises those who give the parties as much as they laugh at him. His brashness, his absurd vanity, his childlike glee in his success, his transparency – all these are the signs of a man who cannot be put down by sneers, whose enjoyment of the riches he has gained by his own intelligence and understanding is whole-hearted and unabashed. There he stands, the American Dream come true, saying you, too, could become a billionaire –

I did. And if you fail to emulate me, don't show your envy – it will only make you look foolish, and won't worry me at all.

Is there an Achilles heel to this extraordinary man? Perhaps there is; once, in an interview, he dropped his guard. 'I wonder', he said, 'how many people would stay around if I didn't have my money. Maybe not many would.' That was what Timon of Athens discovered the hard way, and Timon was neither the first nor the last. I doubt, though, that Trump spends much time on such pessimistic and misanthropic feelings. It is not that he dislikes being cynical about his friends, nor that he ever doubts his money-making mission, nor that, surrounded by billions of dollar bills, he feels lonely. He puts such thoughts from him because – oh, most emphatically and undoubtedly because – he cannot envisage a time when he won't have his money, for that would mean that he had failed. And who ever thought, even for a moment, that Donald Trump might fail? Certainly not Donald Trump.

★   ★   ★

Just off the Avenue at 16th Street is a place with the stirring name of Revolution Books, and also, in case foreigners should hesitate, Revolution Livres and Revolution Livros. Mind you, on the next corner there is the Book Review Restaurant, and when I first saw it I thought it must be a place where all the literary giants gathered to talk about books and the arts, while humble hangers-on like me could sit at their feet and admire their shafts of insight, their quips and gambols that were wont to have the table on a roar. I also convinced myself that the fare would be simple but delicious, oysters on the half-shell, Nurnberger Röstbratchen, real Sachertorte and of course infinite quantities of the finest coffee. Thus inspired, I went in, and found myself in what might have been the original Greasy Spoon Café, with not a sign of Saul Bellow, let alone the oysters. No amount of examination or enquiry reveals how it got so inappropriate a name.

Barnes & Noble are more easily identified; the policy of discounting books is widespread in New York, indeed in America, since there is no Net Book Agreement to stop it. But Barnes & Noble take it much further than any other bookstore, slashing the prices of books before they even get into the store, and the rapid multiplication in the number of their stores demonstrates that it is good business; they have a slogan remarkable even in so self-confident a town: 'If you paid the full price for it, you didn't get it at Barnes & Noble'.

The truth is demonstrated at their Fifth Avenue store at 18th Street; there are two stores, in fact, facing each other across the Avenue, the one on the western side being a repository of textbooks and study materials, a vast, three-floor market for those who want to learn, discover or confirm. But on the eastern side is the general discount store, even bigger than its brother, and so stacked with prices-off bargains that they have had to adopt the supermarket system and provide trolleys for the customers to wheel about the aisles.

The chain bookstores in New York – B. Dalton and Doubleday as well as B&N – all have at least one branch on Fifth Avenue, and most of them are open late – Doubleday till midnight, a most civilised hour for a bookshop to close. They are also security-conscious to an uncomfortable degree; at some, the browser, on leaving, must go through a scanner, at others security men peer into bags. Well, shoplifting is very big business everywhere in the advanced world; that, I suppose, is how you know that it is advanced. (There is an old story of a party of shipwrecked travellers who fetch up on an unknown shore, and go in fear of savages, until they come upon a clearing in which there is a gibbet with a body hanging from it, whereat their spirits lift, because they know they are in a civilised land.) When, incidentally, did shops change their ancient rubric, 'Shoplifters will be prosecuted', to '*Thieves* will be prosecuted'? Blunter, I suppose, and spades must be called spades; and surely a shoplifter is a thief. But the world gets harsher in more ways than one.

All newspaper men love cities in which they can get tomorrow's papers tonight. In London, it used to be impossible, and as far as most of the dailies are concerned, it still is, though the Sundays can be bought at a dozen or more spots in the centre of the city, from 10 p.m. or so on Saturday night. In New York, all the papers (but 'all' in New York would be a gorgeous joke to a Londoner or even a Parisian) are available in the early evening, and on Saturdays from mid-afternoon.

The reason for their early appearance is obvious: the size of the three New York Sundays is such that most of their countless sections have to be printed far in advance, and might as well be sold when ready. (The earliest editions available come without the first news section.)

It is Saturday evening, and I am staggering home with the Sunday *New York Times*. (One Sunday just before Christmas 1988 it turned the scale at 11 lbs 2 oz.) I make myself comfortable on the bed and face at once one of New York's most extraordinary phenomena. For surely the *New York Times* is a very strange phenomenon indeed.

The strangest aspect is literally obvious: its layout and design suggest that the editor and management don't want anybody to read it. Page after page of editorial matter is composed of hideous slabs and blocks of grey, none bearing any relation to its neighbours. There is no attempt to emphasise or even define the significance of a story, no use of contrast in headlining, no sense of a page that has been composed, put together, made of ingredients which support and reinforce each other. The use of photographs is lamentably haphazard; they seem to have been dropped from a great height and printed where they fell. Cropping is not so much badly done as apparently unknown; the typefaces used in the news-pages' headlines suggest that a bygone editor once took pity on the niece of one of his friends because the girl wasn't quite good enough to get into art school and invited her to design a series of headline alphabets for the paper, which are being used to this day – often in, I may say, anything up to *eight* faces on one page.

If the paper has no layout men, it *a fortiori* has no sub-editors. I am a particularly prolix writer, and have frequently been the despair of the editor on every paper I have worked for; but if I wrote at the kind of length the news items in the *New York Times* run to, and to so little purpose, I would surely be certified or fired or both. On and on, for column after column, runs a story about the poor quality of the garbage collection in Queens or the new thief-proof design of parking meters; there is no idea of how a story should be shaped, cut or presented, no attempt to catch the reader's attention early (a practice at which the *Wall Street Journal* is exceptionally good, and which is not at all difficult to learn). The notion that a headline should not tell too much of the story beneath it has plainly never entered anybody's head; again and again a triple-decker makes reading the item unnecessary. As for the headlines themselves, they can be savoured at their gorgeous worst on the page devoted to engagements and weddings; I append a few which are genuine ones, not parodies by me: 'Dentist affianced to Miss Copeland', 'Susan L Breshears Exchanges Vows With Birch Bayh 3rd, a Fellow Lawyer' and 'Sybil Peyer has Nuptials'. Mind you, the Sports section can do quite well with 'Hamill Assails Skating Trend', and so can the Arts pages with 'New Museums Harmonize with Art'.

But once a reader starts collecting NYT headlines, there is nowhere to stop. 'Finding High Rate of Threatening Radon Levels, US Urges Tests of Houses'; '2 Women Succeed as Producers, But Easy Street Is Down the Road'; 'Opera in Which Solos Are Pre-Eminent'; 'Schools Responding to Beeper, Tool of Today's Drug Dealer, by Banning It'; 'Beetle, Fire's Precursor, Riddles Western Pine'; all these stretched right across the page, some of them double-decked. 'Human Immune Defenses Are Transplanted in Mice' was very modestly displayed down-page, but the paper's honour was saved by the photograph which accompanied it; it was of a white mouse, entirely indistinguishable from any other white mouse. Still, nothing could challenge – until the next time, I suppose – the one that stretched clear across the page, reading 'Safety of Grapefruit Called Into Question'.

Its scrupulousness (every day there is a section called 'Corrections', where the most minute errors, many of no consequence at all, are put right) is genuine, its integrity unquestionable, its coverage of the United States unrivalled, its investigations thorough to the last detail, some of its correspondents the world's best (and bravest), and if the gargantuan size of its Sunday edition is daunting, the reader has no difficulty in throwing away the sections that are unwanted before turning to the ones that are more appealing. Yet it always looks hideous, and there is almost no story printed in it that would not be greatly improved by being reduced to half its length.

The explanation is obvious; it has no competition. The fact that a city as big, powerful, sophisticated and rich as New York cannot now provide a second 'quality' daily (it used to have eight) is as extraordinary as it is shocking. The economics of newspapers constitute a mystery far more profound than the question of what song the sirens sang, or what porridge had John Keats; I take it, though, that the lack of a second serious newspaper serving the New York area *is* a matter of money. Yet I cannot believe that the American entrepreneurial spirit, which is real enough, balks at the problems the launch of such a paper would entail. If no-one will bell the cat, the *New York Times* will remain one of the world's most thorough and most honourable newspapers, but it will also remain one of the world's most unreadable – and, I suspect, the most unread.

*   *   *

At 13th Street, there is an odd contrast: on the eastern side there is the Lone Star Café, which for some reason has a monster prehistoric reptile on its roof, a *Tyrannosaurus rex*, glaring down at the passers-by as though he means to eat them all. Right across the road, however, is the Parsons School of Design, and *its* distinction comes from the fact that it is one of the few institutions housed in buildings which live up to their intentions. (Is there a more hideous blot on London's environment than the monstrous junk-pile of a building which houses the Department of the Environment?) The Parsons School of Design has been most handsomely designed. It is tall and very thin, only three windows wide, and it goes up fourteen floors, ending with some handsome crenellations at the top in a very attractive white mixture of brick and stone.

But the sight of it awakens again an echo which I have been hearing for a long time now. It is nudging my subconscious more powerfully than ever, and surely it must soon burst into real life and declare itself. For the moment, I go on uptown, little knowing that every step I take is bringing my realisation to the surface. There are two buildings, for instance, respectively on the western corner of 14th Street (which houses the Research Institute of America), eleven storeys high with an overhanging stone eave, and on the eastern corner of 15th, similar to the Parsons School though a little wider; both most gracefully proportioned. On the eastern side of 16th there is another, in red stone, beautifully decorated, yet another of these wonderfully proportioned unrecognised masterpieces, exuding an infinitely ancient harmony. There is another on the corner of 19th, its façade built round noble pillars, with an extension on the roof looking like a series of dormer windows. Beside it, on the opposite corner, is yet another, the handsomest yet, as tall and elegant as a fashion model, done in white stone.

But here I must temporarily abandon my hunt for the elusive echo to contemplate something more mundane, something that has long passed into the American language, and even earlier into American folklore: the wooden Indian.

In this case, some forty wooden Indians. On the corner of 22nd there is a cigar store. That is a phrase which in itself is redolent of American history, for of course it sells cigarettes and tobacco and pipes and many things that have nothing to do with smoking at all; it reminds us that cigarettes are relative upstarts in the smoking world, whereas the cigar was known and smoked long before anyone thought of rolling the tobacco in paper, and the pipe, at any rate the clay pipe, was familiar for centuries before that. But where there was a cigar store, there was always a cigar store wooden Indian.

Poker players are enjoined to give nothing away by their facial expressions; they must play like a wooden Indian. Politicians who must not give political advantage to their opponents by indiscreet statements remember to be as silent as a wooden Indian. There is a song about 'The pessimistic character with the crab-apple face'; clearly, he has no more juice or spirit in him than a wooden Indian.

Why the wooden Indian became associated with the cigar store I do not know, though social historians may. But any investigation should start here, where the window is so crammed with them that the wares the shop actually sells are hardly visible, where on both sides of the door (which faces the corner directly) there is an honour guard of them, where inside the shop they stand opposite the counter in impressive muster, and where finally the overflow is accommodated in the store-room, a long, narrow hall made narrower by the silent witnesses.

They are for sale, too; they start around $200 and go all the way up to $1500. How do you value a wooden Indian? Somehow those blank but piercing stares put me off anything as mundane as an explanation. With the wooden eyes following me, I move on.

Just off the Avenue at 22nd, there is a building called the Sidney Hillman Health Centre. I guess that not one New Yorker in a thousand now knows the name; it wouldn't surprise me to find that most of the staff don't know who he was. But he was a great man. Hillman was one of the group of labour-leaders in the twenties and thirties who organised and led trades unions for the lowest-paid workers; his great colleague was David Dubinsky, who was the head of the Ladies Garment Workers Union. Hillman and Dubinsky, and Sidney Hook (who is still alive and flourishing) were among the heroes of my youth; I used to hear about them and their work and achievement from Harold Laski's lectures. But their work touched upon one of the most puzzling mysteries of American politics. These men were socialists, though of an unwaveringly democratic stripe; they were often smeared as communists, though they knew, and made clear, that the communists were the greatest enemies social-democrats could have. There were other figures in and around the movement: Upton Sinclair, for instance, also falsely tagged as a communist, but too wild to buckle down to the slow, patient work of politics, and Norman Thomas, the perennial Socialist candidate for the Presidency, and earlier on, Eugene Debs, and John Dos Passos, though he moved far to the right in his later years.

These men had talent and political understanding, and in the Depression they also had a huge opportunity. Yet they were never able to establish a significant position for democratic socialism in the spectrum of politics, and nobody since them has even seriously attempted to do so. Why would not the seed germinate? It cannot be because of the rigidity of the two-party pattern; Britain's was far more rigid, yet the Labour Party cut its way into the system in an astonishingly short space of time. Nor can it be explained in terms of the politics of the parties, where left and right, in party terms, are almost meaningless. And none of the other arguments – Marxism was suspect as an alien creed (though they weren't Marxists), the unions were far less willing to move into politics than their British counterparts, collectivism could never make headway against the race-memory of the pioneers – seem sufficiently convincing to explain the failure. The long reign of Roosevelt, who had been swept into office in 1932 precisely because so many people saw in him the rescuer of the downtrodden, must have hampered any serious movement towards social-democracy, but, after all, by 1932 Britain had had two Labour governments.

The mystery remains. What is certain is that the dream of Hillman and Dubinsky and their kind will now never come true. If socialism, however democratic, has never established itself in the United States, the worldwide retreat from socialism that has been going on for a decade or so will ensure that the ground will remain hard, and indeed grow stonier still. Sidney Hillman is rightly commemorated in the downtown health centre, but those who dreamed of a greater memorial in the shape of a socialist United States must sleep on.

★   ★   ★

In the life of every Avenue in Manhattan there comes a moment when Broadway, lurching diagonally up the grid, cuts across it. In the case of Fifth this happens at 23rd Street. On the eastern side of Fifth there is a tiny park, Madison Square, where the original Madison Square Gardens stood; but it is no use my closing my eyes to conjure up the historic occasions it has seen, from world championship prize-fights to crucial political rallies. I know no city in the world so adept at rolling up its past behind it like a carpet; there must be fewer ghosts in this place than anywhere else on earth. It is a strange thought – at least it is to a Londoner – that if a time-traveller from no further back than the nineteenth century walked right up Fifth Avenue, he would recognise only one building in the whole street: St Patrick's Cathedral.

Away with such intimations of mortality, for it is right here, where Broadway and Fifth meet, that there stands a building which not even New York would dare to pull down, and if the idea were ever to be mooted the citizens would surely rise *en masse*, link arms around it, and cry in all the thirty languages of the city, 'They shall not pass!' The Flatiron is rightly one of the best-loved buildings in all the city; it gets its name from the fact that a cross-section of it would indeed be in the shape of an iron, and the reason for its curious form (Richard Shepard, in his book *Broadway*★, says that 'When seen head-on from the north end, it looks like nothing so much as the prow of a giant ocean liner cleaving the traffic-flecked streams on either side as it sails uptown') is nothing but geometry. Draw two parallel lines, vertically, on a piece of paper. Then draw two more across them, at an angle of forty-five degrees. The space between the upper of the two

---

★ Harry Abrams

cutting lines and the upper limb of the two vertical ones on the same side is indeed shaped like a flatiron, and that is how it had to be.

The Flatiron is elaborately carved; its limestone has weathered well. I have never been inside it, though living or working in the prow of the ship must be a strange experience, since the walls are always threatening to close in and crush the occupant. The House of Mr Tripp's Coachman, in Amsterdam, comes to mind. One day Mr Tripp, a wealthy burgher, overheard his coachman sighing to a friend 'I would be a happy man if I had a house no wider than Mr Tripp's front door', whereupon, Mr Tripp set to and had a house built for his coachman that was indeed exactly the width of his own front door, and there it stands to this day. (Mr Tripp's, however, has long since disappeared; there may be a moral in this.)

From here I can see a rather childish-looking clock high up on the Metropolitan Life Insurance building, one of the very few public clocks Manhattan can boast. (That being so, it is a pity that the clock is insisting that the time is three minutes past twelve when it is in fact twenty past one.) And here, too, is a funeral monument, the obelisk surmounting the tomb of General Worth, a hero of the war with Mexico; it is said that he is the only famous man actually buried beneath a New York street. (And how famous, today, is he?) Leaving the General, and turning again to Madison Square, a curious episode of New York history rises to the surface; when France gave the Statue of Liberty to the United States, she omitted to throw in a plinth, so the recipient nation had to raise the money for one of their own. One of the fund-raising schemes was the exhibition, in Madison Square, of the arm and the torch of the Statue.

But I must press on, leaving Broadway behind, though not before discovering from Richard Shepard's book that the first illuminated sign to glitter over Broadway stood high on a building which stood where the Flatiron now lords it, and it said 'Buy Homes on Long Island Swept by Ocean Breezes'. The message would be terser today.

And then, between 26th and 27th Street, comes 225 Fifth Avenue. After the first floor, which is in white stone, it becomes red brick, with pretty stone and metal balconies, a strikingly handsome outside fire-escape, fine friezes running right round the building just beneath the eaves. And at last I realise what I am being reminded of; the reminder is almost embarrassing in its implausibility, yet I am not, cannot be, mistaken. I am in Venice, on the Grand Canal.

Scale down those ten-, twelve-, fifteen-storey buildings, New York's downtown version of the skyscraper. They would fit, without any need of further alteration, into the stretch just below the Rialto Bridge, where those square, white (now, of course, discoloured) palaces stand. The one – I can never remember its name – which houses the police headquarters, to say nothing of the Vendramin-Calergi, would not be ashamed of the Fifth Avenue palaces as neighbours, rather would welcome them. Presumably (though why should I presume it?) none of the New York architects of the Venetian stretch had the comparison in mind, but it is there, and very striking it is.

At the corner of 27th Street, there is a shop called Julie Pomerantz. That is neither here nor there, but it opens a well of memory for me. During the Second World War, my family connections in America included a family called Pomerantz. Friends of Great-uncle Rudi? Relations of Great-aunt Min? I can no longer remember. But what I remember very well is that the Family Pomerantz had a son, and they named him Joseph Stalin Pomerantz.

You have to be of my generation to understand that apparently lunatic decision. When the Western Allies were fighting Nazi Germany, the Soviet people were our brothers-in-arms, and there was a huge cult of admiration of Stalin, as the leader of our gallant Russian comrades. Few of Stalin's admirers knew – or, more exactly, were willing to face – the truth about his murderous tyranny, though well before the war the knowledge was available; in any case, wartime conditions meant that criticism of our heroic allies was severely frowned upon – indeed, in Britain it could come under the rule against 'spreading alarm or despondency', which was a criminal offence.

In the United States there was rather more scepticism about Stalin, but not enough to overcome the believing, and besides, it was true that the Soviet armies were battling the Germans, so, in accordance with the old maxim, 'My enemies' enemies are my friends, my friends' enemies are my enemies' Stalin was enrolled in the ranks of those who were fighting to make the world safe for democracy, and all the Family Pomerantz did was to take the enthusiasm somewhat further.

Joseph Stalin Pomerantz must now be in his late forties, always supposing that he didn't hang himself long ago, or die in the electric chair for the murder of his parents. (No doubt, the American practice of the forename and middle initial provides enough camouflage for all practical purposes; 'Joseph S. Pomerantz' does not itself provoke suspicion, though from time to time he presumably has to fill in forms with his full name.) Why do parents do these things to their children? Well, whatever the reason, I send friendly greetings to Joseph S. Pomerantz of New York City, and assure him that his secret is safe with me.

Another pause. At 29th Street stands the Marble Collegiate Church; 'America's home-town church' it calls itself. Founded in 1628, it says, chartered by William III in 1696 (eight years after the Glorious Revolution which finally decided that Britain would be a Protestant country). Very well; but here is another notice which tells the passer-by, and for that matter the intending worshipper, that it is open only on Sundays. Hm; is trade so slack that the place is open for business only one day a week? (It is not so on the corner of 53rd and Fifth, where there is a most welcoming establishment.)

But all this is by the way; what stopped me was a plaque on the wall which revealed that the Minister from 1932 to 1984 (which must itself be some kind of record) was Norman Vincent Peale.

That was once a name to conjure with, and only a few days earlier the name had popped up in the newspapers. Assuming that he must have been dead for many years, I thought the references must be to a son, or even grandson, but no, it was the old boy himself, and the reason for his appearance in print was that he was celebrating his ninetieth birthday. Well-preserved, well-deserved; but thereby hangs a tale. The text of the plaque runs like this:

> From the pulpit of this venerable church, this man, with matchless eloquence and person-to-person persuasiveness, sent forth a message that has circled the globe: he taught that positive thinking when applied to the power of the Christian message could not only overcome all difficulties but also bring about triumphant lives. Let all who worship here, then, be open to Dr Peale's momentous message.

Nothing wrong with that, though a strict stylist would say that the threefold repetition of 'message' mars the flow of the prose. But Peale, in his day (the 1940s), had a huge *réclame* and a vast following. He was the first clergyman to get a countrywide audience (before television, remember) by preaching absolutely straightforward orthodox Christianity. Before him there had been Father Divine and Aimee Semple Macpherson and the violently anti-semitic Father Coughlin and many much madder and more crooked than those, but Peale eschewed both the barnstorming form and the dubious substance, and led his flock into the paths of righteousness.

Only, and this is the point, it was a fairly nauseating kind of righteousness. His most famous book, though he wrote many, was *The Power of Positive Thinking*, and the title alone provides a clue; it could have been a manual of success in business, marriage or sport. Peale, glad-handing his followers in his sermons and books, provided pre-cooked health-food religion for those whose stomachs were too feeble to digest the hard gristle of the real thing; think positive, and all your troubles will fly away, because daffodils are beautiful and Jesus wants you for a sunbeam. Peale wasn't a fanatic or a charlatan, let alone corrupt like the televangelists with their vast fortunes (though the proceeds from the sales of his books must have been enormous), and I don't suppose he did any harm at all. But even if there had been ubiquitous television in his heyday he could hardly have been more widely-known; I cannot remember which was the musical that contained the lines:

> Norman Vincent Peale
> Tells us how to feel,
> Big deal!

I doubt if St Francis would have had much time for him, except in the sense that St Francis had time for everybody. Well, he's ninety, and here is his church, and it's open only on Sundays. Happy Birthday.

So I took myself to the little church around the corner, or, more exactly, to 'The Little Church Around the Corner', for by that name it is known and loved. I had assumed that the name was given to it in derision, to contrast it with the neo-Gothic splendour of the Marble Collegiate Church, but the true story is much better. The Little Church Around the Corner (its real name, which nobody uses, is the Church of the Transfiguration) has a considerable history. Its first Minister, the Reverend George Houghton, was a remarkable man; he brought the Oxford Movement to the United States, was the first to set up a breadline for the unemployed, and sheltered runaway slaves.

Well, in 1870 George Holland, an actor, died, and the friend in charge of the obsequies, Joseph Jefferson, wanted the funeral to be held in the Marble Collegiate Church. But in those days, actors were regarded not only as raffish folk but as irredeemable sinners one and all, and the pastor of the fashionable Marble Collegiate was scandalised at the very suggestion. With, presumably, a sniff of disdain, he said to Holland's friend that he believed that the departed actor might be accommodated at 'the little church around the corner'. 'Then God bless the little church around the corner', said Jefferson, and stomped off to make the arrangements. To be fair to Peale, I am sure that if he had been rector of the Marble Collegiate in 1870 he would have accepted Holland.

Anyway, the name stuck, and ever since has been used in pride and affection. So it should; it is a tiny, simple, unornate Episcopal chapel, its

10 But how do they clean the windows?   11 Easy: the human fly

12

intimacy felt at once, its modest charm obvious without being intrusive. And what is more, it is open every day of the week.

To be even more fair to Peale, or anyway his church, I have to say that I finally found it open, and explored it. It is indeed impressive, with a splendid vaulted roof and a handsome, ornate organ, which has one property I cannot remember ever seeing before. The organ pipes are split between the two ends of the church; presumably each 'set' fairly divided, lest all the treble should be at the back and all the bass at the front. It reminded me of that most imaginative stroke of the builders of the Royal Festival Hall organ; churches and concert-halls have long given organ-designers an opportunity to shape the placing of the pipes in elegant patterns, but they were, presumably by tradition, always symmetrical. The RFH organ, however, abandons symmetricality; the pipes are clustered in groups apparently at random, and the informal effect is most pleasing.

It is probable that the Empire State Building and the Taj Mahal are the two best-known man-made edifices in the world, and in all the history of the world. When I say 'best-known', I mean no more than 'known to exist'; millions who pass that test could pass no other – they haven't visited either, could not draw even the roughest recognisable sketch, even would not recognise them without further clue in a photograph. Yet countless millions know that there is an edifice called the Taj Mahal, and another called the Empire State Building. Why? Why have those structures – which in appearance, site, character and function could not be more different – worked their way into the human consciousness as no other buildings, old or new, dramatic or sedate, history-soaked or uneventful, have? St Paul's and St Peter's, Windsor Castle and the Tower of London, the Golden Gate Bridge and Sydney Opera House, the Berlin Wall and the Parthenon – all have to cede the first two places to these, if the only test is the knowledge of their existence.

The Taj Mahal is a long way from Fifth Avenue; let us concentrate on the best-known *modern* edifice. The Empire State Building, to look at – and immediately we face the first problem, which is that it is practically impossible to look at it. The configuration of Manhattan's canyons is such that there is no vantage point at street level, other than almost exactly dead opposite, from which its soaring size and shape can be seen – not seen *well*, but seen at all. And even looking at it from directly across Fifth Avenue gives no idea of how it fits into its surroundings, what its proportions are, what kind of an architectural statement it is making. It is a solemn thought that a visitor only one block away in any direction would not know that it was there.

12 That which cannot buy happiness

'New York's skyline' means three wholly different things. Originally, it meant New York as seen from the water – indeed, the concept was formed by the view from the ship as it came in to dock, in the days when visitors arrived by sea. There, before them, was the New York skyline, the great fist of skyscrapers, looking, because of the difficulty of seeing the perspective, as though they were all clustered together on the waterfront. But there is another meaning to the phrase: the truth about the New York skyline is that in most of Manhattan there is no sky to be seen, if you think in terms of sky as canopy and back-drop, against which the urban scene stands out in a series of vistas like ranks of soldiers – irregular soldiers – on parade, one behind the other. In Manhattan, no such sight is to be seen. Look up, and the sky is either unrolled over you like a bandage stretched laterally along the street you are on, or is a floating mass entirely untethered by the buildings it hovers above. There is, and can be, nothing like the vistas of other cities, in which you can look to your left or right and see a series of buildings stretching further and further into the distance. Go to the foot of Brooklyn Bridge, and look back at Manhattan. Then go to the foot of Westminster Bridge and look back at central London. They might be two entirely different civilisations. As far as town planning goes, I suppose they are.

Very well, if I can't see the Empire State Building, and thus begin to solve the mystery of its worldwide familiarity, I shall go up it, and see what I can see of New York from the top. And there, of course, was the third meaning of the New York skyline; the glorious view from the sky itself. Mind you, just as the canals of Venice cannot be seen from the top of the Campanile (every visitor remarks on this phenomenon, not knowing that every one of his predecessors has done the same), it is impossible to deduce the grid system from what can be seen far above it. (Far indeed; a European city-dweller has to come to terms with the fact of a building that is a quarter of a mile high.)

No-one is permitted to go to the top of the Empire State Building without being bathed in the usual (usual for New York, that is) flood of statistics. Ten million bricks, 1,000 miles of elevator cable and 7 miles of elevator shafts; the weight (how do you weigh the Empire State Building?) is 365,000 tons; it has 2 million visitors a year, 3400 workmen built it (14 were killed in accidents), the ventilation system passes a million cubic feet of air a minute through it; the record for running up the stairs (1860 of them) is twenty minutes; construction riveters' pay was 1.92\frac{1}{2}$ an hour.

And it holds one more record. The estimated cost of building it was $44,000,000, and that was what the developers raised; the sum included clearing the site, which included the old Waldorf-Astoria Hotel, which made 16,000 truckloads of rubble. But the cost was in fact $25,000,000; the Empire State Building must have been the last great building ever put up for very substantially *less* than the originally estimated cost.

'How high', said the head of the developers' group to the architect, 'how high can you make it so that it won't fall down?' This was going to be, and for many years was, the tallest building in the world, but until the very moment that it was opened, the builders were nervously looking over their shoulders at the Chrysler Building, which was racing the Empire State into the sky; there were even fears on the Empire State that the cunning Chrysler team had concealed a vast spire inside their building's shell, to be fitted at the last moment and enable the Chrysler to claim the blue riband for height.

Perhaps it was that just claim – 'The tallest building in the world'– which so caught the imagination of the world that the imagination has never struggled free, despite the fact that it has several times been surpassed in height, not least by a spectacularly unworthy rival – the cowardly twin towers of the World Trade Center. All the histories of the Empire State's construction record the incredulity of the world, which would not believe that such a building could stand, if only because it was sure to be hit by lightning sooner or later, when it would inevitably crumble and collapse to the ground. (It has been struck by lightning thousands of times since it was built; that is what lightning conductors are for.)

And the date of its construction – it was opened on 1 May 1931, in the heart of the Depression (it was the slump in prices that had enabled the building to be 'brought in' at so much less than the estimate) – must also have contributed to its fame. In a world of poverty and unemployment, stagnation and drabness, with breadlines everywhere, this great finger pointing to the sky must have seeped into the world's mind and fostered hope there. And just as it challenged despair, it also outfaced the dull, grey world of economic failure; the Empire State Building, even today, is bright and colourful, a true beacon blazing excitement to the heavens and, more important, to the street below, and the passers-by. (Which reminds me; there is still another impediment to seeing it, and this one the strangest of all. If you walk down, or up, Fifth Avenue on the eastern side – that is, the side where the Empire State stands – you can easily walk right past it without noticing it. There is nothing to make you look up at that point, nothing to draw your eyes to the heavens.)

It was time to go inside and look around. They keep their building in immaculate order, I must say. The famous Art Deco motifs run through the whole building; the entrance hall is full of the Building's colours, silver and bronze – they are on the handrails on the staircases and on the trim round the lights, and of course the great mural which is the first thing a visitor sees if he comes in through the Fifth Avenue entrance. While I watched, a janitor came out with a long-handled velvet mop and lovingly went over the mural and the marble floor beneath it.

I called on Jack Brod, who has been here longer than any other tenant; he is in the diamond and precious metal business, and has his office on the sixty-sixth floor (the Building is non-residential). He is seventy-nine years old, and a landmark in himself, and he is looking forward to his next birthday because the place in Colorado where he goes for his annual ski-ing holiday allows free use of the ski-lifts and other facilities to people over eighty. He had moved into the Building fifty-seven years before, while it was still under construction. Had he had this particular office all that time? No, when he first came, he was on the twentieth floor, and the sixty-sixth floor hadn't been built. And he remembers well the day the plane hit the building.

The war was over, though only just; Jack Brod was still in the Air Force, and had left the building to return to his base. On the way, he remembered something that he had to discuss with his secretary, and called the office. When he got through, she was screaming hysterically, and he could hear uproar in the background; when he asked her what was happening she screamed 'They'rc bombing the building! They're bombing the building!' 'Who's bombing the building?' 'The Japs, the Japs, the building's on fire!'

'I thought', said Brod with considerable understatement, 'that she might have gone mad.' Then he heard a radio news bulletin. The power of human unreason is limitless; the war with Japan had ended, but so extraordinary, so inexplicable, was what had happened, that that fact was swept away, and a Japanese bombing-raid called in to explain. He added some fascinating details that I had never heard before. First, only two people were killed; that was because it was a Saturday, so a lot of businesses weren't operating. Second, one of the plane's engines broke off and went straight through an office window and straight out at the other side, then fell on to the flat roof of a building below; no-one was hurt. And he confirmed what I have always thought of as the most macabre fact of the entire macabre incident; the plane cut one of the elevator cables, and a girl operator fell, in her elevator car, sixty floors to the basement, and suffered only minor injuries. What did she think about? Presumably, she had no idea what had happened, and simply concluded that the cable had snapped. And what did she *do*? Did she keep jumping, on the apparently logical, but in fact erroneous, belief that if she was in the air when the car hit the floor she would be less likely to be killed? And what did she think when it did hit the floor and she was *not* killed? (I was reminded of an accident with no such happy ending; a few years ago, a Japanese airliner, shortly after taking off from Tokyo, broke up in mid-air. One of the wings came off, and what remained spiralled down like the sycamore pods children play with, throwing them into the air to watch them going round and round as they fall. But there were no people in our sycamore pods.)

As we talked, Mr Brod unbuttoned his jacket, and I raised an eyebrow when I saw a gun stuck casually in his belt. We talked about security, and once more I reflected on that most extraordinary fact about our world, that security as we know it today, ubiquitous and a standard feature of our lives, is less than twenty-five years old. It began with aircraft hijacking, which is in itself a remarkable thought, because hijacking has been possible, for money or politics, ever since regular scheduled civil flights began (which was in the 1930s), and there have been bandits and robbers and fanatics since Heidelberg Man was a boy. Yet nobody did in fact hijack an aeroplane – let alone put bombs in one, timed to go off during the flight – until the 1960s. And now no office building of any size or significance is without security men and devices, and no-one anywhere boards a plane without being scanned or searched or questioned or all three. (Brod told me that he was so used to the gun, which he had worn for all the fifty-seven years he had been in the Empire State Building, that several times, while going to board a plane, he had forgotten he had it, and calmly walked through the scanner with it stuck in his belt, and when the scanner beeped, and the guard motioned him forward for a manual search, he had realised that in a few seconds the guard was going to find it, and he had to indicate its presence rather rapidly.)

At that point, most appropriately, I heard the shrilling of a police siren, and I was about to ignore it when I realised we were on the sixty-sixth floor, and concluded that *I* had gone mad, because of course it was quite impossible to hear anything that far down. But when I mentioned my hallucination, Jack Brod said no, it's very mysterious, but the higher up the building you are, the clearer you can hear the street sounds. And on one occasion he was very glad of the phenomenon, because it was the only time his office had been robbed; four men burst in, held up the staff and began to stuff jewellery into bags, when a police siren, hundreds of feet below, sounded so loudly that the gang thought that the cops must be in the building and coming through the door, so they got out quick – they took about a quarter of a million, but if they hadn't heard those sirens, he said, 'they would have cleaned us out'. And had he ever had to use the gun? Yes, once.

A man bought a fifty-five thousand dollar necklace and paid with a certified cheque. But before he left, we checked with the bank, and found that it was a dud. So he was just leaving the office, and I ran out after him, he was waiting for the elevator. I fired two shots into the air, to warn him, and then he turned round and I saw he had a gun himself, and it began to look a little like High Noon. Anyway, I fired again – I didn't want to kill him or injure him seriously, I just wanted to stop him leaving with the necklace, so I fired low and hit him in the foot. But he still got away, and went to a hospital, limping, I guess, and he was arrested there. And I've never had to use the gun since.

I asked him if the Empire State was a happy building, and he said yes it was. First, it's famous all over the world; when he advertises on radio, nobody needs to write the address down. And there is a fellow-feeling in the place; he threw a cocktail party, a year ago, on the top, to raise money for the Boy Scouts, and they made $25,000 just from the people with offices in the building.

And I love the building, it's part of me. I just signed my seventh lease, it takes me up to October 1st, 2000. It's like home to me – most of the time I'm awake I spend in this building. I have made no plans to retire.

And were people disappointed when it ceased to be the tallest building in the world? Well, he said, it bothered the owners of the building a little because the World Trade Center was built with public money. 'But it didn't bother me.'

Then he began to reminisce. In his own business he has seen an entire social revolution, which has meant that buying objects of gold and silver is not confined to the rich; whereas once the purchase of something in precious metal virtually defined enormous wealth, now middle-class, middle-income people think nothing of buying a golden bracelet. But the price of gold itself is the most striking example of the change: 'I've seen gold go', he said, 'from twenty dollars an ounce to nine hundred and fifty. I think it goes back to King Midas; it's in people's minds that gold is everything. It doesn't erode, it doesn't rust, it's sanctified. It's been treasured for three thousand years, and everywhere.' I thought of the Federal Reserve Bank, and my Virgil bidding me pick up a chunk of it.

Then I met Terry. There are very few sights in the world of which it can be quite literally said that no-one, however eloquent and with whatever descriptive powers, can convey their essence to another person, so that *only* 'the sensible and true avouch of mine own eyes' will suffice. These most rare visions are generally the great wonders of the world; but a few of the incommunicables are less mighty, more domestic. Such a wonder is Terry, or, to be exact, what Terry does for a living.

Terry is a tall, good-looking young man, in a smart, close-fitting (it had better be, considering what follows) uniform. We met in one of the Empire State's offices. We talked a little; he was a cheerful, as well as a pleasant, man. Then it was time for him to demonstrate what he had come to do. He went over to the sash window to open it, but it was stuck fast; he took a can, sprayed some fluid round the edges, left it for a moment or two, then tackled it again. This time the lower half easily slid up to its full distance. I was about to make a note to ask him what was in the can of magic unglue, when he jumped out of the window; perhaps I should have said earlier that we were on the seventy-eighth floor, and Terry is the man – one of two – who cleans the windows. And he *did* jump out of the window.

Is it a bird? Is it a plane? Is it Superman? No, it is Terry, at his daily labours. On the Empire State Building there are no window-sills; I imagine skyscraper architecture dispenses with them for reasons of safety. And in the days of the Empire State's building, 'cradles' were unknown. How, then, do Terry and his mate clean the outside of the windows? Well, Terry was there to give me a demonstration of how it is done.

Round his waist is a stout canvas belt, reinforced with leather; from it are suspended various pouches for the tools of his trade. On each side of his waist, the belt has a buckle, in a leather seating. To this buckle there is attached a strip of webbing; at its other end there is fixed a sliding metal bolt. (The whole thing is rather like an airline seat belt.) Now watch carefully.

On either side of the window there is a tiny metal plug, screwed into the stonework, in shape rather like a mushroom, projecting about three-quarters of an inch. Terry leaped up on to the interior window-ledge, turned to face into the room, then, in a gesture like that of the limbo-dancer going under a bar of fire, went out of the window backwards. As he did so, he stretched out his left hand, holding the bolt in which his strap ended. With practised ease, he slid it over the little metal button in the wall, gave it a tug, then cupped his hand over the lower edge of the raised window; now the only part of his body inside the room was his left hand – no, the fingers of his left hand. Another graceful movement, and he had the bolt over the matching plug on the other side. A heave, and he had his feet braced against the wall at the bottom of the window; *then he swung himself back into the arc formed by the straps which were now attached to his belt at one end and to the wall-plugs at the other end, pushed himself out with his feet, and began to wash the window.*

I do not believe that I have ever come closer to being violently sick. Even sticking my head – and *only* my head – out of the window to talk to him made me dizzy and clammy with vertigo; Terry continued to smile. I asked him why he wasn't afraid. He laughed, audibly and quite genuinely. I asked him if a head for heights was inborn, and he said no, it can be learned. 'Not by me', I murmured, and asked him how long he had been doing the job. 'About five years.' And how long would he stay at what is certainly a young man's work? He shrugged. (Reader, have *you* ever seen a man shrug while hanging from nothing seventy-eight floors above Fifth Avenue? I have.)

Is it true, or a legend, that looking down is the worst of being high up? 'No, it's true.' 'So I suppose you take care never to look down?' 'Oh, no, I look down all the time' – and he pushed himself out a little further and twisted his body so that he could get a better view of most of Manhattan spread out seventy-eight floors beneath him.

I learned from Terry that there were 6500 windows in the Empire State Building, that the two intrepid stuntmen (comrades-in-arms of the Blondini Brothers, scaffolders to the nobility and gentry, in Frank Dickens's *Bristow* strip-cartoon) take four months to do them all, whereupon they start again, Forth Bridge fashion; that he starts at the top and works down, that the upper windows are easier to clean than the lower ones because they don't get the street dirt, that he has never met a pigeon while doing the upper floors, that in winter he knocks off work when the temperature falls below 30 degrees, that the first window he ever cleaned in this fashion was on the fifteenth floor and he did feel a little shaky at first, and that he has never dropped anything. Oh, and that he has never had a dream in which he fell.

I have done my best to bring Terry and his work to my readers. But I assure them that I have failed. The nonchalance of Terry, and the blood-freezing things he does, cannot be conveyed to those who have not seen him vault lightly out into space, a thousand feet above the hard pavement of Fifth Avenue, without a parachute. In particular, no-one who hasn't seen it can imagine, with no matter how fecund an imagination, the sight of Terry leaving all manual contact with the building and swinging himself back into his harness as though it was an armchair, balancing himself as he does so with his feet against the rim at the bottom of the window.

He came back into the room; only 6499 to go. I shook his hand; mine was trembling. He picked up his bucket and his tools, slid the ends of the harness into their seatings, bade me good morning, and went on his way next door to make it 6498.

I never caught sight of King Kong. But I had a different kind of glimpse, of the difference between New York and London, that I suspect will remain with me for the rest of my life. When I emerged, the sunny day I had left outside had vanished, and rain was teeming down. There were no taxis to be had, of course (it was rush hour as well), and the nearest bus-stop was a Niagara away; I would be drowned getting to it. At that moment, a man materialised – it is the only possible word – apparently out of the pavement, with a huge sack and a cry of 'Umbrellas, umbrellas, three dollars an umbrella'. Now a three-dollar umbrella is most unlikely to have an ivory handle and gold trimmings, but with any luck it ought to keep the rain off, and three dollars was not exactly a king's ransom. I joined the crowd jostling for his wares (we were all sheltering under the Empire State's awning), and handed over my three dollars. He gave me a flimsy but perfectly serviceable umbrella, and before I stepped out with it over my head, I watched the crowd a little longer; the money and umbrellas were changing hands at such a rate that he had altogether stopped shouting his wares and their extremely modest price. Well, I thought, there is a true entrepreneur; he spots a need, he supplies what is necessary to fill it. What is more, he is plainly a *wise* entrepreneur; instead of concluding that the people under the awning must be so desperate for umbrellas that they will pay any sum asked, he lowers the price dramatically; that way, there will be no arguments, no bad feeling, and a great rush to buy.

Dry beneath my umbrella, I walked to the bus-stop, thinking hard. For what I had just witnessed had conjured up most vividly an episode I had read about at home, only a few weeks before. Exactly the same thing had happened; a sudden downpour showing no sign of stopping; a crowd sheltering beneath an awning (Selfridge's awning, actually), a man seeing an opportunity to make some brisk trade arrives with a suitcase of cheap umbrellas. And then the two identical scenes diverge sharply; the English entrepreneur was arrested and charged with obstructing the pavement.

I made the comparison in my head, but the Lord heard it, and rewarded me for my generosity to my host city. Even as I squelched along, a cab drew up beside me, and the passenger made to get out. A dozen figures on the sidewalk sprang forward, but before anyone else could get to it, I had hold of the door-handle like a commissionaire, and all I had to do was climb in as the providential passenger climbed out. As the rain streamed down, and the cab crawled, horn blaring, through the traffic, it was time to think about the cabs here, and cabs there.

New Yorkers visiting London are apt to complain, even if only after they get home, about our plumbing, our currency, our Sundays, our habit of forgetting people's names, our airports, our customs officers (look who's talking), our habit of driving on the wrong side of the road, the complexity of our titles of nobility, our hotel rates, our pop-singers, our accents, the temperature at which our homes are kept, our toilet-paper, our habit of calling private schools public schools, our drink laws, our television, our system of clothes-sizing, our unintelligible sports, our political system, our laziness, our national boasting, the length of our history, our patronising attitudes, our race relations, the lesser members of our Royal Family, our popular newspapers, our other newspapers, the lack of punctuality and cleanliness of our trains, our unwillingness to be shown photographs of their family, our swear-words, our statuary, the strictness of our firearms legislation, our food (look who's talking), our lawyers (look who's talking), our lack of enthusiasm for ice in drinks, our night-clubs, our furniture, our lavatorial comedians, our class system, our women's appearance, our religion, our dislike of Americans, our dislike of the Irish, our dislike of all other foreigners, our telephones, our confidence tricksters, our amazing disregard for the problems of the disabled, the words of our National Anthem, our beds, our soap, our homosexuals, our National Health Service, our cigarettes, our automobiles, our shop assistants, our electric sockets, our prostitutes, the lack of regularity in our street-system, our public holidays, our zoos, our habit of queueing, our hairdressers, our children and our weather. But they *never* complain about our taxicabs.

The reason is, of course, the quality of New York's, which can provide a British visitor not only with a subject to add to *his* list of complaints about the United States, but a source of wonder and conversation for years afterwards.

Let us begin, though it may not be the worst, with the ignorance of New York cab-drivers – their ignorance, that is, of New York. The grid system, of course, means that the Manhattan hack does not need to memorise a list of street-names and where they are to be found. But an Englishman will expect that if he tells a driver to go to a particular famous hotel, theatre, store, museum, office-building or restaurant, he will be taken there. His shock when he discovers that the driver does not know, without further instruction, where to find, say, the Plaza Hotel, F.A.O. Schwarz, the Brasserie, Lincoln Center or Washington Square, is considerable. (I once told a company of friends at dinner that that very day I had encountered a cab-driver who didn't know where the Empire State Building was, only to have my sensation put in its place by a fellow-guest who said she had recently found one who didn't know where Grand Central Station was.)

There are other shocks in store for the New York visitor who hails a cab. One of them – which is actually getting worse, year by year – is the very high probability that the driver does not speak English and exhibits no wish to learn how to. A New York friend told me that this problem is caused by the constantly growing number of illegal immigrants; the literacy tests for naturalisation still exist, but the 'wetbacks' and others with no authorisation to be in the country will naturally have no incentive to learn the language, since they cannot present themselves for citizenship without risking deportation. It seems a plausible explanation, but does not touch the more urgent mystery: why do they all have to become taxi-drivers?

For that matter, why don't they keep their cabs even moderately clean? Why don't the licensing authorities at least see that the cab is fit to drive? (I once rode in a cab which had clearly been hit broadside on, and damaged so extensively that the passenger door wouldn't close. The rust at the point of impact was such that the cab must have been on the road in that condition for weeks, if not months.)

Oh for The Knowledge, and regular inspection, and at least a rudimentary grasp of the language! For those, I would exchange all hope of solving the final mystery of the New York cab-driver: why is he so bad-tempered? Clare Boothe Luce said 'The rudest human beings in the world are New York City cab-drivers,' and they are still single-mindedly devoted to the cause of never losing the title. Driving in Manhattan's rush hours would be enough to try anyone's patience, indeed *is* enough, as the symphony of horns, for hours on end, testifies. But don't they ever get used to it? And that's no excuse anyway, for they are just as curmudgeonly when sailing down Fifth Avenue on a sunny Sunday morning with no other traffic to speak of. Of course, the New York taxi-driver who is constantly auditioning for the part of a New York taxi-driver in a film about New York is the greatest menace of all; their terrible jokes, their assumed Bronx accent, the stump of a cigar, which is their regular prop, their comments on the Mayor, the President, the Ayatollah, other drivers and the weather – these will make the passenger long for a hack who drives through the pot-holes for kicks, and has only as much English as will enable him to spend the journey snarling. And not only snarling; I have never found the courage to suggest that my cab-driver might usefully go home and take a bath after he has dropped me off, and very rarely asked him to turn the radio off. (I would have had the law on my side in the latter instance; there is no authoritative ruling, as yet, on the former.)

But New Yorkers love the London taxi, and well they might. Mind you, when the Londoners ride the New York buses, the boot is on the other foot. Here they come, my compatriots, not to burn the White House again, but to be almost equally tiresome. I was on a Fifth Avenue bus; it stopped, and a young, obviously English, couple got on, and asked the driver for two tickets to the Empire State Building. The weary look that New York bus-drivers adopt when they are particularly struck by the manifest injustice of the universe crossed his face, and he said, 'It's two dollars'. One of them produced a ten-dollar bill and waited for the tickets and the change; Jehu's weary look deepened. 'Coins,' he said, gesturing at the machine which takes the money, 'or tokens'. (The machine, incidentally, bears lucid and clearly-printed instructions, including the news that the driver does not give change, and indeed has no access to the money in the machine. The couple searched respectively their pockets and handbag to see if they had any two-dollar coins, which was unlikely, because there is no such thing as a two-dollar coin. Jehu's appearance was now that of one who is expecting to be hanged any minute for a crime he has not committed; the whole exchange had taken place in the stairwell of the bus, and the door was still open. I fished in my own pockets for the tokens I knew to be there, but before I could come to their aid – *largesse oblige*, after all – they turned, bewildered and crestfallen, and got off. Jehu pressed the button that shut the doors, with more than ordinary force, and the bus proceeded on its way downtown.

I reflected on the remarkable fact that people would come 3000 miles to a country they do not know, without obtaining the most elementary information, to be found in any guidebook, on how things are done. True, it is the New Yorkers who are the very worst travellers in the world when it comes to the conviction that everything everywhere will be done the way it is done back home; they tend, when they discover that it ain't necessarily so, to be not only bewildered, but genuinely angry, presumably at the impertinent claim of the natives to do things their own way. But there are certain kinds of English tourist who do not simply go on the British equivalent of the assumption that the whole world is permanently on New York time, but who are too lacking in imagination to do anything about their lack of understanding of the customs of the country. It is true, of course, that New York buses are wonderfully uninformative; they display nothing like the itinerary of the route on a London bus, and only a few of the bus-stop posts give any information about the route; there is no equivalent of the very detailed list of the stops and even timetables that London bus-stops always carry, though there are bus-route maps you can buy, as there are subway-maps. As for the timetables, a schedule for a Manhattan bus-route would invariably be a work of fiction, and any expectation that the driver could keep to it would do nothing but deepen the lines of suffering on his face.

There are, of course, other means of transport in Fifth Avenue. One day, travelling down the Avenue in rush hour, I saw a man on roller-skates. I had seen others, but those all looked sporty, light-hearted and consciously eccentric in the pleasantest way; this one looked exactly like a respectable businessman. He was dressed in a dark, conservative suit and carried a real businessman's briefcase; and yet he was skating down Fifth Avenue with immense skill, and with an air that suggested that he did it every day and did not consider it surprising. As he came alongside my taxi, I wound down the window and introduced myself, asking him whether he was doing it for a bet or a diet; in reply, he fished out his wallet, took his business card out and handed it to me, then waved and whizzed on (considerably faster, I may say, than my taxi or the rest of the wheeled traffic). From it I discovered that his name was Eric Nalven, that he was indeed a businessman, specifically a banker, and that he had his office in the Tishman Building, the one cursed with the number of the Beast – 666. Intrigued, I got in touch.

He explained that he lived uptown, that to come by car to Fifth Avenue was madness, that at rush hour skating was much faster than a cab or a bus (there he was demonstrably right, for a three-toed sloth is faster than Fifth Avenue in rush hour), and that it was good exercise.

He had been doing it for some years now, and naturally knew every wrinkle. He surprised me by saying that the cab-drivers were the most implacable of his enemies: 'They hate your guts,' he said, 'they'll cut you up – anything for a fare.' Bus-drivers were much better – 'They're big, they know they're powerful,' and car-drivers have a tendency to giggle. What was his biggest problem? 'Pot-holes – you have to watch out for them.' And isn't he constantly wondering if he's going to be knocked down? 'Well, put it this way – if you're gonna get hit by a car you want it to be a Jaguar.' And had he ever been hit? 'Yeah, twice – both times from turning my head to look at a red-head on the sidewalk.'

Next day, he gave me a demonstration; as I drove down the Avenue, he followed behind, and at once I realised what his greatest problem must be, far worse than any pot-hole or bad-tempered cab-driver; it was that roller-skates have no brakes. He is moving, after all, at about twelve miles an hour; what happens when he comes to a red traffic-light? For answer, he demonstrated his method of stopping abruptly; he simply made a circuit of the nearest car, *however fast it was going*, swirling round in front of it (to the astonishment and horror of the driver) and thus going up the Avenue as he slowed his pace, leaving the final turn to face south until he had almost stopped. It looked appallingly dangerous, but he seemed quite unconcerned, and when the traffic moved on again, he caught up a bus and had a spirited conversation with the driver, though that was nothing to what happened a couple of minutes later, when he saw, at the wheel of a car, a former colleague, and turned right across the Avenue at right angles, as the thundering traffic bore down on him, to motion his friend to wind the window down and talk. Speeding along – I was now parallel to them, on the other side of the Avenue – they chatted casually for a while, then he nodded his friend goodbye, turned, and cut across the traffic in another right angle to rejoin me.

A few minutes later, as he was beside me, the cordless telephone in his briefcase rang; with unperturbed nonchalance he opened the bag, took out the phone and answered it, never ceasing to weave in and out of the traffic. He finished the conversation, caught me up again and said 'This is going to cost me money – all the currencies are down against the U.S. dollar.' He waved again, and sped on, intent on sorting out the troubled dollar at his office. I offered a silent prayer that he would not spot another red-head.

★   ★   ★

I suppose that most people who do not know New York, and a surprisingly large number who do, think of Fifth Avenue as made up entirely of shops, and very expensive and exclusive shops, at that. In fact, of course, from B. Altman to A la Vieille Russie (which is roughly the whole of Fifth Avenue's real shopping) is only twenty-five blocks. Yet the glamour of that stretch is such that it defines luxury and New York alike. There is a chain of European clothing shops called Fifth Avenue, there is a brand of cigarettes with the same name, indeed, the two words have become an adjective synonymous with fine quality the world over. (There is even a tiny, one-man shoe-repair shop in the heart of London, its name proudly displayed on the fascia: Fifth Avenue.)

The picture is a little faded now. First, some of the most famous shops, notably Saks, have gone a long way down-market since their days of glory; in London terms, they have ceased to be Harrods and become Selfridges. (In New York, I suppose, they hover uneasily between Macy's and Bloomingdale's.) Second, Fifth Avenue's native American-ness has been heavily diluted by the growing international nature of the luxury retail trade. There is nothing that seems particularly American, let alone Fifth Avenue, about Gucci or Bulgari, Louis Vuitton or Cartier, Van Cleef or Aquascutum, Benetton or Bally, Jaeger or Dunhill, and there is a great deal that is essentially English about Burberry and Asprey. (One day, I shall tell the whole truth about Louis Vuitton baggage. Oh, hell, I might as well do it now and get it over with. There is no doubt that it is made by the most skilful craftsmen to the highest specifications out of the finest quality materials. But it is hideous, vulgar and ludicrously overpriced. Hideous because the exceptionally nasty browns that persist throughout the range make it look, even in its perfect condition straight out of the factory and into the shop window, dirty; vulgar because of the LV logo in which it is smothered, so that it has the impudence to insist that the customers shall be a permanent advertisement for it wherever they travel, more fools they; and ludicrously overpriced because it is ludicrously overpriced. The proof that it is justice which rules the world, despite so much evidence to the contrary, is the existence of the cheap imitations which in recent years have flooded the market, and which are indistinguishable, at any rate to the eye, from the real thing.)

The international aspect of Fifth Avenue is accentuated by the way in which so many of the world's international airlines have felt obliged to have a showroom and ticket-sale office on it. And it is in the typical Fifth Avenue airline office that one of the most striking symbols of our world is regularly on display, without, as far as I know, anyone hitherto remarking on it. The customer is at the counter, the sales clerk is doing fine with the itinerary and the bookings, there is only the flight from Rio to Valparaiso to confirm, when there sounds – not just at that position, but throughout the whole place – an ululation like the cry of horror and matricide from within Agamemnon's palace which tells the audience that Clytemnestra has met her doom: 'The computer is down!'

The computer is down; if our world needs an epitaph, and it may, could there be a better? The computer is the apotheosis, or possibly the *reductio ad absurdum*, of the uses of technology; more exactly, the alteration in our lives based on those uses. The telephone and the aeroplane are the most obvious examples of the way in which advanced societies, provided with these undoubtedly transformative labour-saving inventions, have steadily allowed them to control us, rather than we them. Busy people everywhere think they are making use of the telephone and the aeroplane, and so of course they are; but they fail to notice how the telephone and the aeroplane are making use of *them*, by the way they find it necessary to structure their lives around these aids to less strenuous living. Suppose that, in the United States or one of the nations of western Europe, there was a prolonged and complete strike of key personnel in the airline and telephone industry, sufficiently successful to ensure that no telephone-calls or aeroplane flights could be made. The result would be a disaster on the level of the Black

Death — not just *perceived* thus, but actually like it in its paralysing, unmanageable, terror-laden nature.

And in this respect the computer has now replaced whole generations of technology. In thousands of ways, it has made life easier and more convenient for countless millions of people, and it is still relatively in its infancy; we can hardly guess at the changes in our world — changes for the better — that it has yet to bring about. But its vulnerability — 'The computer is down! The computer is down! Orestes has avenged Agamemnon!' — is less remarked upon.* It is not necessary to think in terms of science fiction, of mad professors sabotaging the world's economy or provoking a nuclear war; the vulnerability of the computer can, even on the most prosaic and modest level, cause havoc little short of such dramatic catastrophes. There is in London a theatre — built only a few years ago and equipped with the most advanced technology — with a curtain which acts as the safety-curtain — still, by tradition, called 'the iron', though it is a very long time since it was actually made of iron — as well as the ordinary curtain which signals the end of the Act. Its operation is governed entirely by computerised electronics, and it is indeed fascinating to watch it silently and smoothly slide into position and out again. Until, that is, it went wrong, one night, when the staff found that there was no manual means by which it could be moved, and after half-an-hour or so of fruitless wrestling by the management, a theatre spokesman came out on to the stage, apologised to the audience, and bade them go home. (I was there. I was also there — in one of London's biggest and best-known bookstores, Dillon's — when the central, computerised mechanism that simultaneously governs all the cash tills in the store went awry — 'Agamemnon! Agamemnon!' — and it was belatedly discovered that there was no way in which the tills could be opened, and business transacted, other than waiting for the computer to right itself or smashing the impenetrable safes with a sledge-hammer.)

B. Altman's is not the most elegant or beautiful store on Fifth Avenue, but it is without doubt the most handsome and dignified, and looking less like a shop than any of its competitors. It had to; when Altman opened his store at 34th Street, he was doing what today would be called breaking the zoning laws, for the Avenue at that point was still entirely composed of residences, and the mansion residences of the very rich, too. It was all very well when he was safely on Third Avenue and even lower down the island, but his move to Fifth caused shudders; I imagine him standing on the top

---

* We are now faced with what are called 'computer viruses'; these seem to be as incurable as AIDS, and are beginning to excite a comparable terror.

step, bowing and scraping as Astors and Waldorfs drove by in their carriages, eventually enticing them into his iconoclastic emporium, after which he was a made man. Besides, it was not long before Fifth Avenue had spread far further north, and not long after that it had begun its transformation from living-space to commerce. It is said that when Altman opened for business, he didn't even dare to put his name outside the building, let alone anything that would hint at what went on inside.

But here we are at 42nd Street, one of the only two subway stations on Fifth, and we must leave commerce for a while. London visitors to New York, whether for the first time or as seasoned travellers, come with one universal certainty: even though they take only one journey on the New York subway system, and even though they take it in the middle of the day, and even though they are surrounded throughout by hundreds of people, and even though on their journey they are going through terrain no more sinister than the route from Fifth Avenue to Grand Central Station, they will, in the course of it, inevitably be mugged, maced, shot, stabbed or robbed, or any two or more of these. And the truth behind this conviction is that it is held not in the way Americans in London ask, 'Is it safe to drink the water?', but because it is Americans themselves – indeed, New Yorkers *them*selves – who have painted the picture of travel on their subway as invariably fatal. Yet $3\frac{1}{2}$ million people ride it every day, and a clear majority of them survive the experience. I have always noticed that when New Yorkers are talking about the bad things of their city, whether it is traffic jams or crime or drugs or noise or rudeness, a certain relish can be heard in their tones, a sense of pride in the drawbacks of the place; other cities are awful, they seem to say, but in any contest of awfulness, *we* shall always come out on top. And on no aspect of the awfulness of New York are New Yorkers so united as in the belief that their subway is the greatest horror of all the horrors New York is heir to.

Let us begin, in our search for the truth about the subway, with two curious facts. First, more than fifty tons of rubbish are removed from the subway trains and platforms *every day*. Second, there is a continuing and substantial demand for ammonia and cayenne pepper from the subway guards. The first of these unrelated items is difficult to believe but easy to understand; the second needs explanation.

It is all the fault of the token-suckers. The New York subways do not use tickets, but metal tokens, about the size of a quarter dollar. Access to the platforms is via a turnstile, which will open only when one of the tokens is dropped into a slot. Tokens (which can also be used on the buses) can be bought at the token-booths that every station has, and the New York subway has a flat fare – currently one dollar – for any length of ride: one token, one dollar. Now for the token-suckers.

These are people who jam the turnstile slot with a pin or a piece of cardboard; the unsuspecting traveller puts his token in the slot, but it doesn't fall through to activate the turnstile mechanism, because the token-sucker has been at work. The legitimate traveller curses, and goes to another turnstile, having wasted a token, or appeals to a sympathetic official who will let him through the manually-operated gate. Later, when the coast is clear, the token-sucker, knowing that the token is caught only a little way below the level of the token-slot, sucks it out, and – voilà! – he has a token, value one dollar. It seems an exceptionally bizarre way of making a living, and a fairly thin living at that, but no doubt the token-sucker thinks it is better than nothing, besides being a source of harmless fun. But that, I admit, does not explain the need, on the part of the subway authorities, for red pepper and similar substances.

The solution is even more bizarre than the puzzle. In order to foil the token-suckers, the guards are in the habit of pouring into a turnstile slot jammed by a token-sucker a sufficiency of some evil-tasting matter, so that when the token-sucker comes on his rounds, he gets, before any question of a token arises, a mouthful of the horrid bait, and flees in search of repentance or a Coke, whichever he thinks will better alleviate the unpleasant stinging sensation in his mouth.

As I have said, O. Henry called New York 'Baghdad-on-the-Subway' (he also called it 'Yaptown-on-the-Hudson', but New Yorkers tend to remember the former designation rather than the latter); it was because of his conviction that at any moment a New Yorker can walk through a doorway and find himself in an adventure as exciting and romantic as anything in the *Arabian Nights*. The battle between the token-suckers and the providers of corrosive substances suggests that O. Henry was right. What novelist, what specialist in fantasy, would dare to invent the token-sucker? Indeed, where is the imagination lurid enough to do so? Yet Ralph Caplan's list of commodities and services available beneath New Yorkers' feet must be exactly the kind of thing O. Henry had in mind:

New York offers subterranean corned beef, pizza, souvlaki, calzone, salted pretzels, corn bread, kielbase, crunchy granola and oysters. You can also buy fresh flowers, Danish modern furniture, authentic kilts, fake furs, rare books, records and the stereo equipment to play them on, money market funds and investment advice. You can buy a knish, a Sony Betamax, or a hundred shares of IBM. You can bank, get your hair cut, your nails trimmed, your blood pressure taken, your fortune told, and your passport photo taken in case you want to leave.

But who would want to leave such a world? Would it not be the ultimate romantic thrill to live permanently in the subway?

The answer is that many people do, and it isn't. Jim Dwyer is the only – at least nobody seems to have heard of another anywhere, including him – subway correspondent, writing three times a week for *Newsday* about the New York subway, and nothing else. He spends some fifteen or twenty hours a week down there; he is plainly in love with it, and fiercely protective, carefully circumscribing the dangers and insisting that though they are real they are much exaggerated, and that in any case it is only at night that the passenger has anything to worry about.

Perhaps. But I asked about the whistle which sounds when a train is coming in, and he told me that that was to alert the people who will not wait on the platforms, but stay up at the top of the stairs, that they can now come down and board the train immediately. And I asked about the meaning of the sign on the platform reading 'Off hours waiting area', and he told me that that was a section of the platform that was always brightly lit and was also visible from the token-booth, so that help could be summoned. And I asked about the token-booth itself, which must acquire a good deal of cash in the course of a day, and he told me that the entire booth is encased in three-quarter-inch bullet-proof glass. And I didn't ask, because I hadn't noticed it, though he told me anyway, that the window where the tokens are sold has a gap at the bottom only a finger's breadth wide – just enough for the money to be slid through and the token slid back – because criminals, when the window was a real *guichet*, had got into the habit of squirting poisonous substances through it to stun the custodians and rob the booth.

Then I asked him about the real subway-dwellers, the troglodytes who never come up for air. There are two categories: the first consists of the vagrants, the homeless, who either kip down on the platforms or board a train late in the evening and sleep stretched out on the seats all night (the New York subway runs right round the clock); there is inevitably friction in the morning between the commuters and the troglodytes. (Expert train-sleepers pick the lines which never come up above ground, and therefore they don't get chilled on a cold night when the train stops and the doors are opened.) But the second category of subway-living sounded more like India than New York: people live in the tunnels, in the space between the sets of tracks. The police practise a live-and-let-live philosophy; every now and again they make a half-hearted attempt at a general eviction, and on one of these drives they found a man living in a tent, with a cookstove and a supply of candles, three feet from the rushing trains, and two cages, containing respectively rabbits and doves.

I accused Mr Dwyer of being not so much the reporter of the subway but its philosopher; he calls it 'the public commons' of New York, and insists that it is the most democratic experience the city offers; 'up there' are 5000 cars battling it out, horns blazing, while 'down here' the investment banker with millions stands shoulder to shoulder with the secretary, the student, the housewife and the shoeshine man. And it seems that there is a set of unwritten rules. Hear Jim Dwyer:

> If you put more than three million people in a confined space there's a very deliberate etiquette; there's a minuet that goes on among all these people who are crammed into the train every morning and every night. They have to respect each other's square foot of space and they have to keep their elbows and their newspapers out of somebody's face. There would be mass rioting if they didn't. This is the most civilised place you could possibly find. We're not talking about a homogeneous population like in Tokyo where everybody is one race. We have every race and creed under God's sun – out of God's sun actually – on the subways, so there has to be an extremely elaborate system of rules. You never meet another person's eye, you don't stare at another person without invitation, you generally carry a newspaper or a magazine, and this functions like the *chadour* in Muslim countries, it's a veil to keep our souls intact; the fact is that you can put 250 people into a subway car and in that kind of extreme intimacy you have to have rules. You don't talk to the person next to you because you don't know what you're sitting next to; you may be next to the most pleasant and amiable fellow, but you don't know that, you may be sitting next to Bernard Goetz.

Ah; I knew we had to come to that. But Jim Dwyer – since he had rejected my title of subway philosopher I had switched to subway poet, which made him less uneasy – approached the case from a very strange angle.

> If you go to the lost and found department – an absolutely fascinating room by the way, where they have artificial legs and dentures as well as the umbrellas and the gloves – there was a baby-carriage, because when Goetz opened fire that day everybody ran for their lives, and a mother just grabbed her child out of the pram and ran out of the train. Now the police held the baby-carriage for two years, because they figured that she'd come back to get it, and she

would be a material witness to the shooting and what happened. But she realised that, too, and didn't want to get involved, so she never returned to claim her child's baby-carriage. And that to me was the most important human symbol of the Goetz case, not the vigilantism we were told about, but the need for rigorous and, if unspoken, rules of behaviour. There is a sort of stone face that New Yorkers put up on the subway; they seem to be extremely cold and hostile. But that's a paper-thin façade really. Every ride for each person has its own character and shapes their day in an important way. There is a whole colony of retarded young people in New York, and learning a routine like the subway is an enormous advantage to them. They have in the subway system a passport into the riches of the city life it can bring to even the people who would not be able to function in a city without it. At every corner that you turn there's some bit of glory and light down there.

I asked him if he had ever been mugged or robbed on the subway, and he said he had, once, years before he became the subway reporter/philosopher/poet, indeed when he was a child; somebody had snatched his fishing-rod and run off with it.

But the policeman who was riding shotgun on the train we were travelling in as we talked told me that in Spanish Harlem, which was his usual subway beat, the cops patrol the platforms in pairs, and nobody pays the fare – they just vault the turnstiles. But then, Jim Dwyer told me of the Chinese cook who worked in a late-night restaurant, and was going home on the subway at three o'clock in the morning, and

... these four kids came in. She was an older woman, short, a little stout, and very tired. She was by herself, but she wasn't really worried, till they started hassling her and giving her grief; she very calmly reached into her bag, took out the Chinese cleaver that she used to chop the vegetables every night, and very slowly cleaned the finger nails on one hand and then cleaned the finger nails on the other hand, and the kids ran from the train screaming, 'It's momma Kung Fu'.

★   ★   ★

Half wanting to believe, and the other half believing, I came up for air, and to resume my march along the shops of Fifth Avenue. But at 42nd Street there is a shop with the unique property of satisfying every customer, however exacting, and of carrying a stock so huge and so varied that even the greatest department stores retire from competition with it.

Libraries are as old as books. But books aren't more than about 6000 years old, and printing less than a tenth of that. Literacy – not universal or widespread literacy, but literacy itself – is an infant, a seedling, an upstart. Who invented writing? Vain question, which yet must tantalise anyone with imagination. Hendrik Willem van Loon's charming introduction to biography, *Van Loon's Lives*, takes the form of a series of dinner parties with characters throughout history, all summoned up by some necromantic skill deployed by Erasmus. Likely and unlikely couplings at the table provide interest and amusement, and the biographical information is woven by the author into the talk. But for one of these evenings, Erasmus is bidden to invite not specific named individuals but 'the two greatest benefactors of the human race', and everybody is agog to know how that age-old argument will be settled. The result is a comic catastrophe, for a brace of apemen arrive, being respectively the discoverers of fire and of the knife; the one enabling the human race to survive, the other enabling it to progress. But the apemen know nothing of civilised behaviour at dinner, and smash the place up.

The hunt for the inventor of writing is just as fruitless, for all that he is a hundredfold nearer us in time. (I once tried to discover who invented what today we call applause – that is, signifying approbation by clapping the palms together. I had no success at all, and returned from my quest with nothing but one more item of unforgettable but entirely useless knowledge, to be stored with my vast collection of such morsels; the Romans, at any public spectacle, applauded by flapping the corner of the toga. If it is impossible to find out who first bid us clap, what hope have we of discovering who first taught us to write?)

There have been enduring civilisations, some of them with a considerable degree of sophistication, which had no written form of communication; the American Indians, for instance. Others have had similarly remarkable gaps in their knowledge; the Incas had a very advanced knowledge of astronomy, but never discovered the wheel. But for fully literate adults, illiteracy is one of the strangest disabilities imaginable, as is demonstrated by the fact that no-one who learned to read at the normal age can remember what life was like before the knowledge was acquired.

When 'Omer smote 'is bloomin' lyre, writing was far advanced, though the authorities now agree that he did not make use of it. (They also now agree that he wasn't blind. That, though, is about all they do agree on, apart from their unanimous rejection of Samuel Butler's weird claim that Homer was a woman.) If we go back to the Old Testament, we must be getting closer to our quarry, and beyond that there is Egyptian hieroglyphics.

And a little before that, the trail peters out in impenetrable darkness.

But of one thing we can be sure; the first book was at once followed by many more, and as soon as there were a dozen in the same place, libraries were born. The earliest great public library we know about is Ptolemy's in Alexandria, though most of us know about it only because it was burnt. But that is in itself significant; the feeling of horror and loss that the image of the burning library makes almost inevitable is based on the deeply-ingrained feeling that a book is more than knowledge, it is a kind of icon. I do not know of any civilisation which actually practised bibliolatry, but we look with disfavour at any society, or any individual, with no regard for books. And a lot of books together are recognised as far more than the sum of their parts; a library, public or private, specialist or general, ancient or modern, is understood, even by the most tenuously literate, as treasure.

Most advanced nations today have what is called a copyright library, a library in which *every* book published within the country's borders is included; in some, such as the United States and Great Britain, the law requires every publisher to provide a copy of every one of his books to such a central collection. (And of course such all-embracing libraries acquire huge holdings of books published in other countries.) The two biggest of these institutions, at any rate to measure by the comprehensiveness of the *omnium gatherum* within their walls, are the British Library (formerly British Museum Library) and the American Library of Congress. But it is probable that the New York Public Library has the world's third largest collection. And it is quite certain that it has the most ebullient, philosophical, passionate, voluble and Armenian library director anywhere in the world, certainly not excluding Armenia.

I shall come to Vartan Gregorian in a moment, when I describe what passed when I did come to him. But first, the only thing that is bigger than he is: the New York Public Library building itself.

Set back from the Avenue at 42nd Street, its noble frontage is decorated from end to end by the crowds of people who have draped themselves on the thirty steps from the street to the entrance to take the air and their brown-bag lunches, and read, talk or meditate in the sunshine. At each end of the mighty sweep of the steps there sits a lion, correctly a lion couchant. They have had a variety of names, these beasts, but for some years now they have answered to Patience and Fortitude; to tell the truth, they are, though undoubtedly well loved, not very leonine beasts. Landseer's quartet of lions in Trafalgar Square, set to guard Nelson's Column, look as though they would eat nothing but bread and milk, or even muesli, and Patience and Fortitude have something of the same timid air, not quite the Cowardly

Lion of the *Wizard of Oz*, but suggesting that they would take a knob of sugar from a friendly hand. Perhaps it is as well; such an institution must be ever-welcoming, and no ordeal, by fire, water or lions, should stand between the reader and the book. To anticipate a little, Gregorian, as we talked, put it well:

> We believe that this library is an extension of intellectual freedom, freedom of thought; we do not therefore invade the privacy of our readers, we do not keep tabs on them, we do not ask what they read. Our library is freely accessible – any citizen can come and use it as a right, not a privilege, without any identification card. We do not have photos taken, or letters of introduction written; we welcome everybody to come and use it, students and scholars and ordinary citizens, and the more we are used the better we feel we have been fulfilling our mission.

I stepped into the entrance hall; it was like walking into a Byzantine cathedral. (Later, Gregorian was to call his library 'a cathedral for learning – almost like a Gothic cathedral, where each person can contribute his share, where it will never end because learning, knowledge, culture and civilisation will never end'.) Immediately, a torrent, a waterspout, a cloudburst of statistics was poured over my head: the place took 14 years to build and cost $9,000,000; it has 31·7 million items, of which 9·2 million are books; there are works in 3,000 languages or dialects; it is open 57 hours a week; there are almost 90 miles of shelving, and work is in hand beneath the library making room for another 50 miles; it is currently displaying 14 exhibitions, it is running 56 public educational programmes, the annual total of such programmes run by all the Branch Libraries as well as the Central one put together is 17,537, attended by 459,918 people; the Central Library has 2,195 permanent staff, the average annual number of visitors is 1,189,483, the total number of cardholders for the branch lending libraries is 953,290; last year 309,156 items were purchased for the Central Library and 845,783 for the branch libraries; in the same period 121 foundations gave at least $1,000, as did 1,110 corporations and 1,300 individuals, while a further 38,000 individuals each contributed less than $1,000; the number of telephone enquiries answered last year was 237,550 and enquiries conducted by correspondence numbered 16,987, while personal and telephone enquiries answered throughout the entire network totalled 5·7 million. And in the De Witt Wallace Periodical Room, which is named after the man who founded the *Reader's Digest* (a solemn thought), and who 'spent many hours in this room reading and condensing articles for the *Reader's Digest*' (an even more solemn one), 10,000 periodicals in 22 languages from 124 countries are maintained by a staff of 15 people.

After the facts, the ornamental prose, as Byzantine as the architecture:

> After contemplating the façade the visitor goes to the portico and, through a bronze door, steps into Astor Hall, one of the city's monumental entrance rooms. High arched bays rise on all four sides to a segmental vault. Every surface is white marble, even the vaulting. The effect is quite overwhelming. The visitor knows that he is now in one of the nation's great classical buildings. Only within the classical tradition can such proportion, balance, penetration of space, judicious disposition of ornament be achieved. The design is grasped at once because Astor Hall bestrides a main axis that continues from the terrace steps through the entrance to a central arch leading into the Gottesman Exhibition Hall. Resplendent with white marble arches and walls ... Twenty-four columns of Vermont marble ... The ceiling of oak is beautifully carved in the manner of the Renaissance.

This place was now beginning to feel intimidating. I ducked into one of the smaller rooms where the effect was not overwhelming, and nothing was carved in the manner of the Renaissance, and where the Arents Collection was housed. The Arents Collection was collected by a Mr Arents; so far so good. And what did he collect? Two very different subjects: on the one hand, books published in monthly or weekly parts, like Dickens and so many other nineteenth-century authors, and on the other hand, everything relating to tobacco.

The part-works collection was extensive, but not especially interesting. But the thought of Dickens, and particularly of Dickens in America, roused a memory of one of the most astonishing facts of all literary history. Today, obviously, the success of a book is measured by the number of copies it sells. In the nineteenth-century, too, that was inevitably a test of a writer's popularity, and one which Dickens consistently passed with the very highest honours. But it wasn't the only one, nor the most dramatic. It has been established beyond scepticism, though incredulity rather than anything as modest as scepticism is apt to greet the fact, that when he was publishing *The Old Curiosity Shop* (one of the weakest of his novels, moreover), and had got to the penultimate chapter, there was a crowd on the quay at Boston when the ship from London arrived, shouting 'Is Little Nell dead?'

But it was the tobacco collection that was clearly Mr Arents' pride, and it was made more delightful for me by the thought of the uproar that he would raise if he were making his collection today. The first of the Arents

Collection treasures I examined was a beautifully preserved set of a weekly series about tobacco and smoking, which was full not only of advertisements for tobacco and tobacco products, but of articles and information extolling the wisdom of smoking tobacco in every form, on the ground that the habit was most beneficial to mental and physical health. Indeed, carved over the fireplace in the Arents Room was a rubric that could now lead to a lynching, or at least a tarring and feathering: 'The man who smokes, thinks like a sage and acts like a Samaritan'.

And then I opened a drawer, and the whole of my youth swam before me. Because, packed in neat compartments, all neatly labelled, was a glorious feast of cigarette-cards. (I suppose that I must pause here to explain to readers younger than fifty-five or so what I am talking about, for they certainly will not know without instruction. A cigarette card was a slip of pasteboard about $2\frac{1}{2}$ inches by $1\frac{1}{4}$ inches which was inserted into every packet of cigarettes sold by every cigarette manufacturer who had adopted the practice – which was virtually every cigarette-maker in the trade, and certainly all the makers of popular brands, except Woodbines, which were so cheap there was too little margin for the cost of the cards. (It was a popular belief that Woodbines were made from the factory-floor sweepings of other brands. A wicked libel, no doubt. Or possibly not.) The card, however, was not blank; on one side of the typical cigarette-card was a picture, and on the obverse was a text, referring to the picture. The cards were issued in 'sets'; a set normally consisted of fifty cards on one subject, and the manufacturers took care to see that roughly equal numbers of each card of a set were inserted in the packets. There was an enormous number of subjects: film stars, sporting heroes, historical themes, beautiful views, motor cars, stamps, famous buildings, statesmen, trains, popular authors, singers, ships, schoolboy howlers and hundreds more. The aim, of course, was to collect all fifty cards of a set; many of the manufacturers would give a free album in which the cards could be kept to anyone who had bagged an entire set. Naturally, it was children who collected the cards – we would hang about the doorways of shops selling cigarettes, and beg the card from the purchaser of a packet. Of course, this was a trap for the children-collectors, because it must have led vast numbers to take up smoking, and no doubt that was the intention on the part of the cigarette-makers: catch 'em young.)

But here before me were not only sets of cigarette-cards; there were *sets which I had myself collected*. There were cricketers, flags, even a set of items of 'Railway equipment' (why I collected those I could not imagine), and the years and feelings of my childhood came flooding back in the staid, ordered world of the New York Public Library's Arents Tobacco Collection.

The cards ceased to be made at the outbreak of the Second World War; paper, along with almost everything else, was strictly rationed, and this was an unacceptably frivolous use of so scarce a commodity. (Books had to be published in accordance with regulations which even laid down a maximum width of margins.) After the war, the companies tentatively decided not to re-start the practice, which had been expensive, and though it would have taken only one manufacturer to break the agreement for the others to be compelled to follow, none did, and the cigarette-card was relegated to history. But fortunately it was the history of tobacco to which it was relegated, and I offered up thanks to the late Mr Arents, for giving me an hour of such pure and mellow nostalgia.

All collectors strain the bounds of ingenuity to claim an item with only the remotest connection to their subject, and Mr Arents was plainly no exception. Preserved in a handsome slip-case was half the manuscript (the British Library has the other half) of *The Importance of Being Earnest*. I turned the pages; Oscar's hand was not artistic, nor even elegant, but very clear. With the Ellmann biography so fresh in my memory, it was a moving moment, as I recalled the terrible final years, and the fact that *The Importance* was his last play. But when I came back to reality I had to ask what it had to do with tobacco. 'Ah,' said the custodian, 'don't you remember – the denouement, when the mystery is finally cleared up, turns on an engraved cigarette-case.' So it does. But Mr Arents, the good soul, was no fanatic, and his eclecticism would shame the anti-smoking zealots of today, or at least would shame them if they were capable of shame. For he included items *against* tobacco as well as in favour of it, not least (in a first edition) King James the First's famous *Counterblast to Tobacco*. I don't know what had got up James's nose, apart, presumably, from tobacco smoke, but it had certainly got a long way up, and I couldn't resist reading the magnificent peroration aloud; indeed, I couldn't resist doing so in a Scots accent, while the staff gathered round, spellbound:

> Have you not reason to be ashamed, and to forbear this filthy novelty, so basely grounded, so foolishly received, and so grossly mistaken in the right use thereof; in your abuse thereof sinning against God, harming yourselves both in persons and in goods, and raking also thereby the marks and notes of vanity upon you; by the custom thereof making yourselves to be wondered at by all foreign civil nations, and by all strangers that come among you, to be scorned and contemned. A custom loathsome to the eye, hateful to the nose, harmful to the

brain, dangerous to the lungs, and in the black, stinking fume thereof, nearest resembling the horrible stygian smoke of the pit which is bottomless.

I began to explore this amazing place more thoroughly, and at once discovered one striking difference between it and the British Library. The issue hall, which is also the main Reading Room, has a window at which, when you have tracked down the book you seek through the computerised system, you hand in a slip on which you have written the details of author and title; you are then given a number and bidden to wait until it flashes up on a screen. I tested the system; ten minutes after I had handed over the slip my number came up and my book was handed over. Last time I used the British Library there was a wait, between handing in the slip and getting the book, of two-and-a-half days.

Notices and leaflets were everywhere; read very carefully, they could tell the reader slightly more about the Library than the Library might wish. Here, for instance, is a notice of a Library exhibition to be seen in Harlem; it is called 'Marcus Garvey: The Centennial Exhibition'. The description reads 'Over 250 photographs, paintings, prints, manuscripts and publications interpret the life and times of the pioneering social reformer'. Pioneering social reformer! That is a sign of the times, to be sure; Garvey was a mad and unscrupulous demagogue, of whom I shall have more to say when we get to Harlem. But I must say now that the Library's exhibition, or at least its annotation, is another item of nervous hat-doffing to contemporary susceptibilities, and the feeling was considerably strengthened by the principal short guide to the Library and its divisions. The account of the Schomburg Center for Research in Black Culture (which is where the Garvey exhibition was being held) runs like this:

> ... one of the finest research facilities in the world for the study of black history and culture. Containing more than 100,000 volumes, the Center's vast collections include such rare holdings as early editions of poetry by the American slave Phillis Wheatley, and the original manuscript of Richard Wright's *Native Son*. This nucleus is strengthened by microfilm files of more than 400 black newspapers, an extensive collection of over 1000 periodicals, as well as rare books, personal papers, manuscripts, sheet music, photographs and works of art that document black culture.

That took me back to the heady days of the Sixties, when the campus revolts led university authorities to set up bogus 'Black Studies' courses, and even courses in Swahili. God knows the treatment of human beings with black skin by those with white has been, over the centuries, one of the greatest abominations in all history. But nothing is gained, and much (such as historical truth) lost by the pretence that black American culture, rich and diverse though it undoubtedly is, has anything of the depth and breadth and historical continuity of white. Read through that paragraph describing the Schomburg Center again; does it not lack substance, scope, *bottom*? And there is an irony in the very same publication, when it comes to a description of the Library's Jewish Division. For all I know, this might be no less an item of insurance than the Schomburg Center, but there is a noticeable difference when it comes to what the Jewish Division holds:

> ... one of the greatest collections of Judaica in the world and the most accessible for both scholarly and personal use ... While the collection offers commentary on all aspects of Jewish life it also includes Hebrew and Yiddish language texts on general subjects. Here one finds a census in French of the Jews of Alsace taken in 1784 and a volume of essays examining eight hundred years of Jewish life in Munich written in German, as well as a Yiddish manual on stenography and a Hebrew text on aeronautics. About forty per cent of the Division's holdings are in Hebrew characters, and the remainder in other languages, primarily English, German, Russian and French. The Division is especially strong in bibliographies and reference works, Jewish Americana, history and social studies, Kabbalistic and Hasidic works, texts by Christian Hebraists, rabbinic responsa, Hebrew and Yiddish literature, and periodicals and newspapers.

When Jesse Jackson called New York 'Hymietown' he was betraying an instinctive anti-semitism buried only skin-deep and thus likely to break out with embarrassing consequences. But the affronted Jews ('What would be said,' asked one of them, 'if a Jew referred to Harlem as Niggerville?') might have reflected that they could make a handy compliment out of the insult, by a subtle set of comparisons. New York's racial diversity is such that claims to pre-eminence must always be dangerous, as well as useless. But it is those who are most anxious to please and placate who may be doing the worst damage.

No such dark forebodings can dominate a meeting with Vartan Gregorian, a rotund, bearded lover of life wedded to his library. He looks like the third New York Library lion, and his c.v. reads like a library in itself: nine professorships, thirteen fellowships, twenty-one honorary degrees, twelve other awards and four decorations, twenty-five current board memberships and another twenty-five past ones (including the 'Mayor's Commission for the Year 2000', though surely the year 2000 will arrive without the help of the Mayor?) and listings in *Who's Who in the World*, *Who's Who in America*, *Who's Who in the East*, *Who's Who in the Southwest*, the *Dictionary of International Biography*, *Men of Achievement*, *Contemporary Authors*, *Community Leaders and Noteworthy Americans* and *Current Biography*. And among his preoccupations he has found time to translate *The Poetry of Elia Abu Shabake*, by A. Bustanni, though there is no indication of what language it was translated from: presumably Armenian.

Gregorian was born in Persia, and surrounded by books almost from infancy, but when he came to New York as a youth, and first walked into the Library of which he was to become President, he was so intimidated that he walked right out again, unable to believe that anyone could walk into such a building without answering any questions, not even about what he wanted to find out. It was probably the last time in his life he was intimidated.

We talked in his office, which was naturally crammed with books from floor to ceiling and piled on every piece of furniture except a massive and handsome globe, presumably exempt because it was impossible to balance books on it. And at once it was clear that for Vartan Gregorian a library is very much more than a collection of information, even 31·7 million items of information including 9·2 million books in 3,000 languages or dialects stacked on 90 miles of shelves.

What is useful does not necessarily mean that it's valueless in the long run, or transcendental in the long run. The library *is* a centre of information – that's one of its functions. But more important than that, it's a centre for learning, a centre for culture. It embodies the spirit of humanity. It embodies the memory of mankind and the unity of civilisation, the unity of culture. In many ways a library is the only tolerant institution in the world's history. Because that's where you have the mistakes, the wrongs and the rights, the accomplishments and the failures of human endeavour. So in a sense a library must not be a passive institution, but rather an active one, in order to remind people, to instruct people, not only about unity, continuity, change, but also about tolerance, and the same time to provide a comparative approach to peoples and civilisations and institutions. Because we have reached a time when we are almost falling into a national Alzheimer's Disease – becoming a-historical, anti-historical, a-literate, not even illiterate, a-moral, not even immoral. The library has to remind people that there are five thousand years of recorded experience of mankind that is theirs to learn from and to contribute to.

I reminded Gregorian that when Henry Ford said 'History is bunk' very few people agreed with him, and certainly very few educated ones. Now that view is widely held, perhaps most widely among the educated. What has happened?

> Part of it is due to our educational system. As knowledge is fragmenting, as there is greater specialisation in our universities – however much needed for scientific and other scholarly purposes – the synthesis is missing. As a result, most of the knowledge seems to be disintegrated combinations of disintegrated items rather than a combination of unified forces. Therefore an interest in unity, an interest in some kind of dialectic, whether it's spiritual, materialistic or an understanding of historical forces, that interest in the unity is disappearing. Lewis Mumford warned us early in the nineteen-thirties about the barbarism of specialisation. And what is happening, as a result of the fact that available information is now doubling every five years, is that we have so many more new disciplines, sub-disciplines, breakdowns of sub-disciplines, that an interest in the continuity of civilisation, which is one of the strengths of history and historical knowledge, and in history itself, is receding. That is one of the reasons why biography as a genre is one of the most popular genres now because there's a beginning, a middle and an end, and somebody, through the biography, understands about the life and times of individuals.

Oh, but it is worse than that, I reflected, as Gregorian drew breath. Once upon a time it used to be true that any educated man or woman could understand any scientist who could explain articulately what his work was. The first edition of the *Encyclopaedia Britannica* was published in 1771, in three volumes, and there were men and women in London and Edinburgh, Washington and Paris, Weimar and St Petersburg, who already knew everything in it. Sixty years later, Goethe died, his last words a plea for more light. No layman can now understand the experts, the technicians, the scientists, the doctors, and that has been true for many decades. But the next stage was the divide among the experts: the physicist could not understand the biologist, and we have now got to the point at which one kind of physicist cannot understand another kind.

What has become of the 'liberal education' (a phrase which is now ominously used only as a joke)? I remember the experiment noble of Keele University, which was, under its first Master, Lord Lindsay, to offer a genuinely wide and – more important – *integrated* education, an education in breadth and depth at once. It failed; presumably (I have never read any convincing explanation) foundering on the rock of the needs of the new world, with its insatiable appetite for detail to feed science and technology. I can see no possible way of reversing that trend; indeed, it can only get narrower and worse. Gregorian feels the same, but naturally puts his trust in libraries:

> The libraries have to play a cultural and educational role, almost like the medieval monasteries did, but on an individual tutorial basis – to allow scholars to have their students and mentors in the libraries. But it is more important to show the connections; because a library for me embodies the connections of our culture and our civilisation; I usually quote T. S. Eliot's description of Dante's *Inferno* as the place 'Where nothing connects with nothing'. That's what we are driven to in many instances, and the library has to show the connections. In order to do that – this may shock you – we have 17,000 public events annually in the New York Library system, through the branches and main libraries.

I wondered for a moment what would have happened if I had tapped him on the knee and said, 'Actually, it's 17,537', but the torrent of passion and enthusiasm, the knowledge of the danger we are in and the way it is getting greater all the time, was pouring out of him in a longing to make the world hear, and act.

> We have nine literacy centres, where we teach illiterates to read and write, and also those who have problems with English as a second language – we do all this free. We also have exhibitions, public lectures, discussions. But all of this is intended to stimulate the public's interest, not in the library but *through* the library, about learning, about culture and education. Libraries must not abdicate their educational role, their cultural role, by becoming merely depositories of information and knowledge. That's one of the reasons that libraries, in our nation at least, have been neglected, because they have accepted willingly or unwittingly the role of an auxiliary enterprise. As a result they have been *treated* as an auxiliary enterprise, rather than a central enterprise of a civilised and cultured society. Ours is a logocentric society: we live by the word, but especially by the written word, and that has been one of the foundations of Judaeo-Christian civilisations, but it has also become a global phenomenon – the fact that the written word is the best means of providing the continuity of our accomplishments, our fantasies, our spiritual ecstasies, our suffering.

You make a library sound like a temple, I said to him; do you think of it as a temple?

13 The skater's waltz   14 Another acquisition …   15 … for the New York Public Library

Yes, I think of it as a temple. As a matter of fact, I am giving a lecture later this month, at Brown University, and the title of the speech is 'The Book and the People of the Book'. But the greatest challenge facing us now is how to transform information into structured knowledge, and not to allow people to deny us choice by inundating us with information. If I were George Orwell now, I would not say 'Deny information'; I would say 'Inundate people with undigested information', and the result will be they will be unable to make conscious choices, and therefore you can control them if you control the mechanism. And that's where education comes in; we have to have a methodology, to be able to understand, to ask the right questions, to be able to know that just because something is not in the computer it does not mean it doesn't exist, that knowledge is multi-faceted, that information is only one of the sources.

Then he played a card which I suspect he had played often before, and none the worse for that, as it made his point with dramatic force.

When I came here I was asking why they have the 1939 Warsaw telephone directory. In 1981 that is not information any more. And I was told that it was one of the most heavily used books in the post-war period, because it made it possible to trace Holocaust victims; it became a document, a legal document, a document of social history and economic history and national history. That is how, through proper guidance and questioning, the 1939 Warsaw telephone directory became knowledge, because information has to be transformed, to be given a structure, in order that we are able to control it and understand it, and not be manipulated by it. Nothing is useless, because we don't know what is useless temporarily, what is useless absolutely.

But *everything* is useless absolutely to a man who is not only unable to transform and control and understand information, but unable even to read it. And that secret, shameful, still spreading disease has infected no fewer than 25 *million* American adults; many experts on the subject suggest that the figure is even higher, and all are agreed that the pandemic is out of control. Hear the man of words, and of words in books, and of books in libraries, on the subject of those to whom even the hospitable doors of the New York Library are closed, since the 31·7 million items including 9·2 million books are of no use at all to men and women who cannot read them:

16 When in Rome . . .

In India and in other traditional societies, there is an aural tradition that replaces the role of literacy in some instances, but we do not have that kind of tradition. The number of our illiterates is compounded each year by some eight hundred and fifty thousand students dropping out from the school system, and therefore adding not only to the problems of illiteracy but also the problems of partial literacy. But literacy is a means to motivate people to participate in their system, their democratic system, to understand democratic institutions and so forth. That's frightening. On top of this, as immigrants come to this country, we don't have a fixed problem, we have an evolving problem; some are illiterate, some are literate only in their own languages, so you have a problem of illiteracy about America, illiteracy about democracy. Even the notion of literacy itself, which in the nineteenth century was a unified phenomenon, has been fragmented into civic literacy, technological literacy, scientific literacy, computer literacy, English literacy; we are an entire people who are partially literate, the worst being the functional illiterates, because they are denied the choice of being autonomous beings in their decisions, because they don't have the option to enquire further.

I left the building, its steps still bright, alive and noisy with the crowds exchanging words, in a troubled frame of mind, for all the vitality, optimism and relish of Vartan Gregorian. Literacy, to people like us, is not merely a tool, a means, a path; it *is* those things, but it is also, and far more importantly, an essential element in the make-up of a sentient being in our kind of society, second only to a soul. I thought of the legend of the man or woman who casts no shadow, of the Wandering Jew and the Flying Dutchman, those outcasts of the earth, doomed for ever to sidle through the darkness. Illiteracy is not like the losing of a limb, sight, hearing; it is closer to madness, and closer still to death. But beneath the almost meta-physical horror of the condition itself there lurked a greater horror still; of those among the millions of illiterates *who do not mind their illiteracy*. Never mind Gregorian's well-founded fears for a democracy in which so many cannot participate in any meaningful way; what about the troglodytes who will not come out of their caves? What about the man or woman who wallows in illiteracy with no sense of deprivation, loss or incompleteness? What kind of horizon, what kind of life, can such people have? What kind of human beings can they be? I suddenly remembered *The Island of Dr Moreau*, where the unhumaned keep telling themselves they are still men. But here, in America, is an island where the humans declare themselves non-men, and do it without shame, singing, not as the reproach Kipling meant it to be, but as an anthem: 'Brother, thy tail hangs down behind!'

The two lions, Patience and Fortitude, sat placidly on their pedestals. They looked unconcerned.★

★　　★　　★

But it was time to go round the corner, where Baghdad was indeed waiting for me, and not one Aladdin's cave but scores were ready to show their wares.

Diamond: the very sound of the word denotes luxury, wealth, fortunes, covetousness, love, beauty. (I have never trusted the German language, and hardly the Germans, since I discovered that the German for jewellery is 'Schmuck'.) I suppose that in a word-association test 'diamond' would often bring the response 'Amsterdam'. I don't know why the Dutch are so well-entrenched in the world of diamonds – their buying and selling, their cutting, their setting – but my lifelong conviction that Amsterdam is the world's centre of the diamond industry was severely shaken after spending a day among diamonds in New York – the Jewellery Exchange, the Diamond Club and the office of William Goldberg.

The corner of Fifth Avenue and 47th Street is New York's Diamond Alley, the Hatton Garden of America. I have always wondered how anybody in Hatton Garden makes a living, because with the street composed almost entirely of precious-stone and precious-metal dealers, the competition must shave margins paper-thin. Diamond Alley in New York must have the same problem; some of the kiosks that the dealers operate in are hardly the size of a telephone box; indeed, I asked one of them what the size of his was, and he said, 'It's five feet by four'. Asked what the rent was, he wouldn't answer, but when I ventured 'Five thousand a year? Ten thousand?', he laughed and said, 'More, much more – from here up to 57th Street is the highest-price real estate in the world beside Rodeo Drive in LA.'

So how do they make a living, let alone turn round in a space five feet by four? The answer was all round me; eager buyers thronged practically every booth. This is presumably the upside of the competition problem; the buyer finds safety in the sellers' numbers. One booth owner likened it to a flea market, but there must have been scores of millions of dollars' worth of jewellery in this crowded bazaar.

But that was nothing compared to the Diamond Club. It sounds like a

---

★ Shortly after our meeting, it was announced that Gregorian was leaving the Library to become head of Brown University.

less glamorous version of the *Folies Bergères*, but it is very serious indeed. (Starting with security; I lost count of the number of checkpoints I passed through – the last one was a turnstile – for all that I was accompanied by a senior member of the committee.) No jewellery-making is practised here, nor any diamond-cutting; it is solely for buying and selling, and the rules are complex and fascinating.

A long, meticulously clean and smart room; the walls, pierced by wide picture-windows, are lined by tables; on each table there are two very powerful fluorescent strip lamps, infinitely adjustable. My guide explained that only a north or east light is really right for examining diamonds, but the lamps help. The international nature of the trade was emphasised by a set of clocks running round a central fitment where the finest weighing-machines are fixed; the clocks show the time in Bombay, Tokyo, Israel, Antwerp. Almost all the dealers present wear hats or skullcaps; in New York, this is overwhelmingly a Jewish trade.

It is conducted almost entirely on trust; certainly no money or cheques were to be seen, and only the briefest scribble recorded a transaction. The trust principle means that there must be strict executive supervision and control; the officials of the Club are all elected by the whole membership, and have absolute power. The elections mirror real political ones alarmingly closely; they even use voting-machines, and canvassing and promotion can be done to any extent anywhere other than on the Club premises.

The Supreme Court of this democracy is the bench of arbitrators. When a dispute arises, the elected board rules on whether it should go to the arbitrators; if the board decides that there is no real issue, they refuse to send it for arbitration, which I suppose is the equivalent of a court of law refusing to hear a too trivial case. But if it goes to the arbitrators, their decision is final, and there is no Court of Appeal.

The procedures for buying and selling are positively Chinese in their formality. Across one of the tables, buyer and seller confront each other. Buyer examines the proffered diamond. Sums of money are bandied back and forth; buyer makes up his mind to buy, and states his price. He does so by putting the diamond in a tiny envelope; he seals it, and writes his 'bid' on the flap. Now the seller takes the limelight; until he has decided whether to accept or refuse the offer, he may not open the envelope or show the diamond to anyone else. If he accepts, he puts out his hand and the buyer shakes it; both say 'Mazel and broch'; this is Yiddish for 'Good luck or disaster', and symbolises the trust principle on which all such transactions rest – they are saying that, however the deal comes out for each of them, there is no going back.

Buying or selling, each dealer examines the goods with the traditional tiny magnifying glass called a *loupe*. There was not a bigger or more powerful instrument to be seen, and I felt that tradition could be carried too far. I sought my expert in the throng, and he explained. 'A big magnifying-glass is no good,' he said; 'it shows you the whole thing, and you don't want to see the whole thing, you want to see it facet by facet. It's a matter of focus, not of just magnifying.' He pushed a *loupe* into my eye, handed me a pair of tweezers, and bade me pick up a diamond he had casually thrown on the table. I approached the operation with the greatest care and delicacy, picking up the diamond with the gentlest possible touch; whereupon he roared with laughter, and reminded me that a diamond will withstand even the roughest handling, and that I could scrape the tweezers on them for a year without making the slightest mark: 'Diamond cut diamond,' he said; 'remember?'

I wandered about this most prosaic of Aladdin's caves, and came to the Club's notice board. The lost-and-found section was rather more interesting than most such appeals for the owners of mislaid umbrellas, fountain-pens or kittens to come forward. 'A parcel of 13 carats of fancy shapes; finder please return to security desk or executive office.' There were a couple of dozen such losses recorded; are diamond dealers even more casual than I had already discovered? Some of them are certainly more light-fingered than I would have believed; another section of the notice-board carried a rogues' gallery of photographs of members who had not paid their dues for 1988. I thought that was rather harsh, but the next section offered a display of firms which had been found to give certified cheques that had turned out to be counterfeit, and the final panel had another list of firms, introduced in each case with the warning 'Before doing business with ... please contact the Security Director'.

Most bizarre of all was a notice headed 'A New Scam'. Dealers were warned not to wear short jackets which left trouser pockets visible. The perpetrators of the new scam, who must be quite extraordinarily imaginative, have taken to homing in on those short-jacketed dealers whose exposed trouser pockets look as though they are stuffed with valuables, then pouncing on the pocket, ripping it down; the packet of diamonds, assuming that it *was* a packet of diamonds which was causing the bulge in the pocket, falls out, to be fielded by the thief, who then presumably makes off with all possible speed, leaving the dealer not only poorer by the value of the diamonds but also with the need of a substantial repair to his trousers. Apart from giving a new and more exciting meaning to the word 'pickpocket', the new technique must give dealers wearing long jackets, and passers-by in no way involved, a good deal of harmless fun.

Business had become brisk; the tables were filling up. I asked my guide, indicating the covered heads everywhere, why this was almost unanimously a Jewish trade. The first part of his answer was brisk: it isn't. There are, he said, half-a-million dealers and cutters in India, and they aren't Jewish. But in the west . . .? He agreed – New York, Los Angeles, western Europe. But why?

The answer was much the same as the one Isaac Stern gave when I asked him why so many violinists, including almost all the leading ones for a century back, were Jewish. Diamonds (like violins) are easily portable; they are readily negotiable anywhere (there is a vast literature for the violin, as opposed to, say, the flute); though very many trades were barred to Jews in eastern Europe for so many centuries, the diamond business (or music) was not; if you are fleeing from persecution it is not difficult to hide a packet of diamonds in your luggage (a violin is *ipso facto* innocent).

He broke off, beckoning me to come with him; at one of the dealing-tables a man had pulled out of his pocket one of the tiny paper packets. He opened it almost absent-mindedly, then tipped the contents onto the table; there must have been a hundred or more in the heap so casually displayed (and no melodramatic square of black velvet to show them off). My informant murmured, as casually as the dealer had poured out his wares, that the heap was worth about three-quarters of a million dollars.

Then I went to see William Goldberg, a former President of the Association. He has clearly done well; I gathered that his firm was in size and success only just behind the front rank of the Harry Winstons and Van Cleefs. But I said he had *clearly* done well; on his desk there was a champagne glass, constantly replenished, in his hand was an eleven-inch cigar, behind his head a humidor with a dozen more. He sat in his shirt-sleeves and braces, the two tufts of white hair at the side of his bald crown stood up in comfortable disorder, and he looked upon the world, and particularly the world of diamonds, and saw that it was good.

It was particularly good at the moment. For nine years he had been pursuing a tiny, beautiful pink diamond, in an exquisite pear-shaped tapered cut; he had been beaten at an auction for it all that time ago, and had waited patiently for it to come on the market again. When it did, he was not going to lose his nerve again; it was knocked down to him for $600,000. I asked him if he had already got a purchaser for it, and he looked horrified: 'I'm not going to *sell* it,' he said, as though I had been talking about his wife; 'I'm going to keep it.' I believed him; he couldn't stop picking it up and putting it into his huge hand, a tiny point of pink light sparkling and glowing; it wouldn't have taken him much more to kiss it.

He, too, was amazingly casual about his stock. He pulled open a drawer – not a safe, nor a strong-box – and poured on to the desk a heap of diamonds even bigger than the one displayed before me at the Diamond Club (and of better colour, too – those had been rather yellowish). Then he opened another drawer (neither had been locked) and pushed across to me, in the most off-hand manner, a diamond, pure white, the size of a large quail's egg. As I turned it this way and that between my finger and thumb, looking into it to see the icy fire, he mentioned that it would go for a million dollars.

Ah, but his greatest triumph was yet to be related. It happened some years back; a gigantic diamond, one of the biggest the world has ever seen, had been found in a South African mine. It was deeply embedded in the ore – the 'rough' – and very little could be discovered about it other than it was very large indeed. Months of work in the cutting-rooms would be needed before the quality of the stone could be properly appraised. But in its present state, it weighed 353·9 carats. Goldberg didn't hesitate; he put up several million dollars for the stone, sight unseen. Then the work began.

Slowly, the cutters revealed the pure diamond, and announced that it was flawless. The work of cutting went on, and in the end the 'Premier Rose' emerged, cut into a pear shape and weighing 137·02 carats. (The original also yielded the 'Little Rose' at 31·48 carats, and the 'Baby Rose' at 2·11. All three received the very highest rating that a diamond can have: 'Flawless D'.) From then on, Goldberg and his firm were accepted as serious dealers in the biggest stones. He sold the Premier Rose to another dealer for $10,000,000; he believes that the buyer had a Middle East customer for it, but he has never seen it again, or heard of its whereabouts.

Obviously, I had to visit the cutting-room; along the way, I noticed that not only Goldberg's outer office door, but every door along the corridor, carried a *mezuzah*. In the factory itself, another surprise; it was staffed almost entirely not just by Jews but Hassidic Jews, with the traditional ringlets and long black coats. There must have been some fifteen or so operatives, each with his wheel and his tools, grinding away, following a meticulous geometrical pattern, at the hardest substance on earth, and the rarest and most precious, too.

I asked Goldberg if anybody could become a skilled cutter, given enough patience and determination. He thought yes, but made an exception for himself, claiming to be too inept; indeed, he had been told sharply, in his apprentice days, to get out of the workshop after ruining a valuable stone. One of the workmen, engaged on the cutting of a tiny stone, told me that it would have about a hundred facets when it was finished, and all, of course, perfectly symmetrical. I looked at it through the *loupe*, and saw facets so tiny that they could hardly be seen, let alone cut, yet perfectly regular.

Goldberg, who is approaching seventy, has clearly never lost his zest for the business: 'I can't wait', he said, 'for the bell to ring in the morning when our vault opens so I can come here.' I asked him the obvious vulgar question: did the fact that the thing nestling in his palm cost hundreds of thousands of dollars add to the thrill?

> Let's put it this way; we all know how important money is, it does a lot of things for a lot of people, and I personally have great satisfaction in being able to earn it. Yes, after having said that man does not live by bread alone, there is still a certain pleasure in earning money. I enjoy earning it, not only for the money's sake, because there is a certain ego-pleasure in being successful. I like it when we buy an interesting rough, or buy an estate and recut the stones; then people smile because they have created something beautiful; this is a *smiling* business.

I asked him about buying diamonds for investment, and he said he wouldn't advise anyone to do it. First, it's a risky business; there was a huge crash in 1981, and a lot of people got badly hurt. But, more important,

> Diamonds are meant for beauty, for pleasure. They do have an intrinsic value which goes on, and if you bought them at the right time you'll find that they're worth considerably more. But to think in terms of 'I'm going to buy a diamond for $10,000 and trade it for $11,000 six months later', that's ludicrous. If you want to do that, buy securities or real estate, but buy beautiful jewellery to give yourself aesthetic pleasure.

'But you make it sound', I said, 'as though to speculate in diamonds is not only unwise, but actually sinful.' 'That's right,' he said, 'I've never thought of it with that word, but you're quite right, I do feel that. I guess I think it's wrong to speculate in beauty.'

I left with the glitter of these astonishing things still shining before me. I noticed that security was markedly more relaxed for the departing than for the arriving. Presumably, it was reckoned that if anyone had been passed respectable on the way in, he would be very unlikely to turn nefarious while inside.

A few more steps, and I was at the Algonquin Hotel, a most friendly, charmingly inefficient establishment (though it must be said that the cock-roaches are *very* small), which would never be heard of, and rarely patronised, if it were not for the legend of the Algonquin Round Table, at which the wits of the town would gather every day at lunchtime, to be witty. The fame of this institution has, over the years, grown to be thought of as a giant contribution to an imperishable art, a combination of the Abbey of Thélème, Wilde at his epigrammatical best, the laughter of the Homeric gods, the Mermaid Tavern when Shakespeare and Jonson presided over the revels, and the repertoires of all the sophisticated comedians of history.

The trouble with this legend is that, closely examined, it turns out to be about as funny as Yorick's skull. Although the First Gravedigger implies that Yorick's jokes had the table on a roar, the only one of the master-wit's witticisms he recounts to Hamlet is the one that consisted of Yorick pouring a flagon of wine over the Gravedigger's head, which is probably not the funniest thing that has ever happened in the history of the world. (It was Rhenish wine, but I don't think that makes a significant difference.)

The same is true of the Algonquin Round Table. The Table and its hangers-on included many of the most assiduous memoir-writers in American literary history, yet none of them has recorded for posterity any catalogue of the scintillations that flashed back and forth across the celebrated board. There is a clue to the hollowness of the legend in the person of Dorothy Parker, who was, by common consent, one of the very wittiest of all that witty company. Well, *two* biographies of her have recently appeared, and neither of them can come up with any more of her witticisms than the four on which her reputation has always rested, and which (e.g. 'Mr X played the King as if someone were about to play the Ace') have been reprinted hundreds of times. The conclusion is that the famous Round Table, though it undoubtedly existed, and was no doubt surrounded by New York's cream of wit, was a myth. And there is an item of circumstantial evidence that to me seems conclusive. The Table was a lunch table; the wits ate as they wittered. But how could anybody say anything truly funny over the Algonquin's food?

★   ★   ★

At 48th, though, I had found Mr Schwartz the furrier (if we are playing Happy Families) and found, too, that he was as much the philosopher of fur as Jim Dwyer was of the subway. I have always maintained that 'shop' is the most interesting conversation there is, provided only that the man or woman talking shop does so in a manner intelligible to someone from another trade. I have sat at dinner-parties next to lawyers, jewellers, painters, bankers, academic experts in anything from electricity to mathematics and Egyptology to the Kabbalah, athletes, theatre directors, publishers, dressmakers and soldiers, and with the proviso above (and somehow, the more recondite the subject the more clearly the expert speaks about it, presumably from long practice in the art of making himself understood) I have never been bored, not even by the shop-talk of a ballet-dancer.

Mr Schwartz had no obstacles to overcome; he talked with remarkable eloquence, and had every detail of his business at his fingertips, but his shop and showrooms were at once made warm and inviting by reason of his goods, and I was wallowing in them before a word had been spoken.

Along with 'diamond', the phrase 'a fur coat' has the extraordinary quality of instantly summoning up the idea of beauty and luxury, together with the feelings attendant upon such ideas. But why, I asked Mr Schwartz? Because, he said, not only is the business of finding furs very difficult and arduous, and the craft of making them rare and slow, fur is primitive, elemental. Because it came off a living creature?

> No, because it's not something artificial. There aren't very many things that we relate to these days that aren't fabricated, out of some chemical or other process that we can't really understand or relate to. All of us can understand the exact origins of something made of fur and the way it came about, and we can relate to it.

I pranced about the racks, draping myself in one luscious garment after another (I was surprised at the number made for men), demanding the name of every fur I tried. The first was beaver, and Mr Schwartz's patter triumphantly bore out my theory of listening to experts; he explained that since the beaver was indigenous to the United States, it had contributed substantially to the settlement of the country; because there was so much demand for it from Europe's rich, and particularly Europe's royalty, the traders pushed on into the interior in search of more skins and more Indians to produce them. Now how else would I have ever known that?

In addition, I learned that the raising of one ranch mink costs the farmer $35, so that at forty to sixty skins for a coat made entirely of female mink the answer to the next question – why is mink so expensive – was obvious; that the crown prince of furs is sable (huddling into one, I could well believe it) and that only the Russian variety is really luxurious; that the top price for a really fine fur coat – say Russian sable or Canadian lynx – is about

$225,000; that most furs will last their wearers from ten to thirty years, and that they should be cleaned every year and stored in a cold-vault; that fur is cleaned by brushing sawdust very lightly into it to collect the pollutants which in our cities' atmosphere inevitably seep into the garment, and that racoon suited me because its grey matched my hair (information I could have easily done without).

There was one other question, but Mr Schwartz couldn't answer it for me, because everyone who thinks about fur coats must devise an individual answer. Mind you, Mr Schwartz – the subject, of course, was cruelty – did enliven my thinking about it by telling me that the more extreme sects now parade in front of McDonald's denouncing 'the breakfast of cruelty', because people eat bacon and eggs.

All the same, all the same. I know that, apart from some endangered (and therefore protected) species, the animals bred or captured for fur are everlastingly renewable in the ordinary course of nature. Some, indeed, such as racoon and beaver, are growing *more* prolific. Which reminds me that I learned some time ago that the walrus – I am not suggesting that walrus coats are about to become fashionable – increases in numbers the more it is hunted. (For its ivory, incidentally.) I know that every such animal is going to die sooner or later, and that the ranch-bred ones at any rate are humanely killed. Have we, though, the right to take animals not for food nor for survival (presumably the wearing of animal skins goes back far into prehistoric times as a form of protection against the elements), but simply for adornment?

I don't know. I come back to the uncomfortable feeling that there is nothing between eating *foie gras* and vegetarianism. Yet I know that the people who denounce the customers of McDonald's for eating bacon and eggs are absurd. But I also know that nobody *has* to wear a fur coat. But I also know that Mr Schwartz's wares are things of remarkable beauty, made by outstanding craftsmanship. I gained time in discovering that, so far from the campaigners making headway with their campaign, the demand for fur coats is bigger than ever; but the problem remained. If I were rich, I think I would adorn my lady with diamonds rather than fur (though I dare say that somewhere there is a movement for Diamonds Lib), but what if she asked nicely for one of Mr Schwartz's sables? I postponed the struggle to another day, and walked out of Mr Schwartz's showroom into a torrential downpour. Perhaps a sign of heaven's disapproval; to be on the safe side, I took it as a penance, and having got soaked, I decided I was absolved.

A moment or two later, I decided I wasn't; for what am I doing now, trying on *hats* in Fifth Avenue? I don't wear a hat, I never have worn a hat, except for a fur one in cold winters, especially cold winters in New York. But here I am, surrounded by hats of every style, shape, material and colour, and just to make the situation even more weird, I have learned that the firm – Bullman, it's called – started out 120 years ago making hats for the Amish communities. Now the Amish think it sinful to wear any kind of adornment, so the hats made for them were always of severe cut and invariably plain black, which could certainly not be said about many of the hats in this showroom, for all that the firm was still in the hands of the descendants of the founder as late as 1973.

Mr Stein – no Amish he – was as knowledgeable about hats as Mr Schwartz had been about fur. When I said of one – something of a cross between the Amish hat and a bolero – that I felt it was a little old-fashioned, he said crisply that no hat is old-fashioned, and any hat gives personality to the wearer, so that in addition to its practical use, the wearer gains in confidence. Indeed, he said, the hat-wearer can change his personality, his look and his manner simply by changing his hat. Headwear, he said firmly, is classic. And how, I asked, do you see the future of the hat?

> I think today that the fashion-conscious man is looking for something to identify with just as he chooses his belt or his necktie, he's looking for an image to present. And we look for many images; think of the Robert Redford movie 'Out of Africa', and the safari hat he wore – that's an image, it evokes an image whether you're wearing it with a suit or a leather jacket. And think of the 'Crocodile Dundee' hat; the second movie is coming out soon, and we have a licence for the hat – that's another hat that gives an image, a novelty image, to headwear.

'And me,' I said, 'which of all these hats would you feel would represent my image, or make an image for me?' 'Oh,' he said, 'I think you would look great in a cowboy hat like *this*, very wide-brimmed, a real image there. A real outdoors man who can get things done, a man of the West, an action taker.' 'And that', I asked, 'is how you see me?' 'Absolutely.'

I made an excuse and left. And found myself, at 48th, talking about elevators. Well, there are 60,000 elevators in New York City, some of them big enough to take an armoured car, and more than half of them in Manhattan.

There'd better be. It is a strange thought – strange for a Londoner, anyway – that without them it would be impossible, not just difficult but impossible, for millions of people in New York to get to their homes or offices. In a city where the average residential building is not more than four or five stories high, and most places of business a similar size, if there is no elevator, or it is out of order, nothing but mild irritation and a vow to take more exercise from now on would be the entire reaction, and the stranded would begin the climb. But if you live or work sixty floors above the street, you cannot climb the stairs, or for that matter descend them. It therefore follows that buildings do have elevators, and that they are checked for safety and functioning not less than twice a year. The elevator inspectorate in New York numbers hundreds, and each of their biannual visits is recorded on the certificate which every elevator must by law have; if it is not displayed in the elevator itself, there must be a notice in the elevator saying where it may be found.

So what happens when the elevator *does* break down? Or rather – since there must obviously be an emergency squad to deal with a rogue elevator that has got stuck – what happens when *all* the elevators break down simultaneously? Obviously they don't, at least this side of science fiction. Not all that obviously, though; once, they did. In the famous electricity 'crash' of 1965, when much of the eastern seaboard of the United States was without power for several hours, with the epicentre of the 'earthquake' in New York City, many thousands of elevators instantly ceased to run. If they were on the ground when the plague struck, there was no problem other than making emergency arrangements for the people who were scores of storeys above or below where they needed to be; if they had stopped at a floor reasonably close to the ground, people could at least get down, and if the floor wasn't too far *below* their destination they could get up. But what about the people who, when the engine spluttered and stopped, were between floors?

There were hundreds of elevators, that night, hung between Heaven and Charing Cross. The British, who not only pride themselves on facing adversity but actually enjoy it, would have risen to the occasion; to the surprise of many, including many New Yorkers, so did New York. As far as all the evidence shows, nobody died, nobody had a heart attack, nobody went mad, and almost nobody panicked, though some trapped elevator-passengers had to wait a good many hours for rescue. (The legends that were spawned that night were many and lurid; they include the story of the Englishman who, staying in a hotel, plugged in his electric razor, whereupon the lights in his bathroom instantly went out. Embarrassed by, as he thought, having fused the bathroom wiring, he went into his bedroom to phone, apologise and request help; he became much more embarrassed to find that he had killed the bedroom lights as well, and when he found that the phone wasn't working either, embarrassment turned to horror, which got much worse when he put his head out of the door and found that the entire corridor was in darkness, too; evidently he had wrecked the hotel's entire electricity system. Then, high above the streets of New York, he looked out of the window.)

If the elevator inspector, then, is the unsung but essential hero of New York, I thought it would be a good idea to talk to one; he was John Ryan, and was just about to retire after thirty-eight years in elevators. How does a man get to be an elevator inspector? Was it a childhood ambition, like the traditional yearning to be a train-driver? Nothing so romantic; when he came out of the Navy at the end of the Second World War he had had some electrical training, and thought he would put it to practical use.

What is the first thing you think of, what do you look for?

I look for the certificate, I want to make sure that my men have signed the certificate. Then I watch to see if the car stops level, and then I look round to see if there is anything that is going to disturb anybody who gets into it.

Is it dangerous work sometimes?

It is when I'm working on top of them, and particularly when there's another elevator passing in the shaft, because if you're in the wrong place at the wrong time you're going to be hurt. Elevators are merciless.

Do they sometimes fall out of control?

Fall is a bad word, because the brakes will stop them; but they sometimes overspeed. Oh, sure, sometimes they crash into the pit, but there we have what we call buffers, wire buffers – a huge spring like you have under an automobile, it takes a tremendous amount of pressure, and it takes it slowly. It catches the car, that's what it does.

Does anybody ever get killed in an elevator?

Not unless they're on top, and even then only if they do something silly. Or if people don't follow the instructions that we give for getting out of a jammed elevator; we've had terrible experiences with people who should have been safe – once, an elevator stuck in a court building, and two attorneys climbed out and then helped another lawyer, a lady, out, and she fell clean down the shaft. You always stay put and wait for expert help.

What should you do if the elevator starts to fall? Do you jump off the floor?

No, you don't, it doesn't make any difference, because the elevator keeps you going at the same rate she's going herself. And anyway, whatever is going to happen is going to happen in seconds, no, in tenths of a second.

When you're out, socially, do you talk elevators?

Yes, silly as it sounds, we do. Went to my daughter's wedding, sat at a table, was busy talking elevators. I don't think she ever forgave me.

It's time for lunch. There is no outstanding restaurant on Fifth Avenue. On the other hand, there is a considerable number of good ones, or at any rate well-known ones, scattered very close to Fifth, many of them only a few paces from it; the Côte Basque, Le Cirque, the Chalet Suisse, La Réserve, the Gotham Bar and Grill, the Caravelle, Lavin's, Prunelle. But the very list provokes enquiry into one of New York's greatest mysteries. Very few New York restaurants, in any part of the city, would rate two stars in Michelin's Red Guide, and I think it unlikely that any would be thought to deserve three; possibly that is part of the reason why Michelin has never contemplated a Guide Rouge for the United States, or at any rate has never got further than contemplation. Still, you can eat very well indeed in New York if you choose your restaurants with care. But here comes the mystery.

Why are so many of them, including an extraordinarily high proportion of the very best, run by men who are not only unpleasant, but who clearly pride themselves on their unpleasantness, so much so that a more suspicious restaurant-goer than I might easily conclude that there is some kind of annual competition for unpleasantness, with a trophy for the winner? Seasoned New York diners-out will recognise at once what I am talking about, and will certainly be able to list half a dozen leading restaurants which would have a good chance of the citation every year. But the diners I refer to also know, as do I, exactly why this state of affairs persists. It is because the unpleasantness to which I refer is invariably confined to lunchers or diners *who are not known as regulars, and more particularly as socially prominent regulars*. Those who are known to the maître-d' and the gossip columns will receive the kind of fawning that I imagine the Emperor Tiberius insisted upon and got; I have never seen the greeter at the Côte Basque actually lick the shoes of Mrs Brooke Astor, but I am sure that if it happened nobody would be surprised (apart from Mrs Astor, presumably). I *have* heard the lout who runs (and owns?) Jam's – indeed, I was sitting beside the lady it happened to – walk off with that year's prize in the highest Category for Offensive Behaviour Outside the Line of Duty; taking the orders, he discovered that she has a naturally quiet voice, and he remained where he was at the other end of the table and shouted 'I can't hear you' at her. (I did toy with the idea of telling him that she was the wife of a member of the British House of Lords – which was true – if only to watch him come and lick *her* shoes.)

There is a social *naïveté* which is one of New York's most amusing absurdities, and for some reason it shows itself at its most marked in the city's restaurants. In Europe, the rich and famous, apart from the *lumpen* nouveau-riches (pop-singers and promoters, stock-market yuppies, dress-designers and the like), do not advertise themselves or their presence; when booking a table at a restaurant, they are quite likely to give a nondescript name rather than their own. Not so in New York, where the *gaucheries* of the rich are such as to make any sophisticated European gape with astonishment. In one way, the desperate eagerness, on the part of the rich and famous, to be seen at the most 'fashionable' restaurants, and their terror of finding themselves in an unfashionable one, is endearing, even touching; but beneath that silly façade, and the extraordinary social insecurity it demonstrates, there is the corrupting effect on the quality of the restaurants they patronise, and – worse – on the behaviour of the staffs. Whence the unpleasantness of the latter towards the clients they don't know, and the far nastier fawning upon those they do. (Nor is that by any means the limit of their *naïveté*. It is my frequent habit, when I am lunching or dining on my own, to start with a half-bottle of champagne as an aperitif. Some wine-waiters seem slightly bewildered by this not wholly unreasonable practice, but the worst that happens is a shrug; the champagne is provided as required. But then, almost literally without exception, the waiter takes away all the other glasses which have been laid on the table. Nothing very terrible happens, because when I have chosen my meal I ask for the wine-list back and choose the wine, and naturally they bring a glass as well as the wine. But the assumption is that nobody could do anything as bizarre as have two different kinds of wine at one meal. And the most extraordinary thing about this custom is that it takes place not only in simple, unsoph-isticated establishments but also in some of the grand temples of New York gastronomy.)

But to return to the fawning of New York restaurateurs on the social élite, it must be said that even if it were less repulsive it would hardly excuse the lack of the simplest politeness to the rest of the customers. The 21 Club used to practise this rite with remarkable assiduity, and Mortimer's, not only in the person of its horrible owner, still does. But it could be said that those who went to the 21, and those who go to Mortimer's, for the food rather than the social recognition, respectively deserved and deserve what they got and get. (Which was even more true of Sardi's. Does it still exist?) But what astonishes any European is that in New York it is practised by many restaurants which serve genuine and consistent *haute cuisine*, which in London and Paris, Rome and Munich, Brussels and Salzburg, is *invariably* accompanied by perfect courtesy to every customer. (Perhaps *that* is the reason Michelin would rather not compile an American restaurant guide; their tests include the quality of the reception.)

There are, of course, exceptions: the people at the Gotham behave as though they are pleased for every customer, and that attitude cannot be caused by anxiety about trade, because it is almost invariably full, and quite rightly; La Régence, in the Plaza-Athenée Hotel, is staffed by faultlessly trained and courteous sophisticates; and of course, anyone who has ever set foot in Le Chalet Suisse (which, in geographical fact, is the nearest very good restaurant to Fifth Avenue, being only half a dozen strides round the corner) will know just how warm, effusive and wholly genuine a greeting can be. But for the most part, strangers to the senior staff and the newspapers must resign themselves, in most of New York's best restaurants, to enjoying the food alone, since there will be very little else for them to enjoy.

The restaurant guidebooks, of which there is a growing number (particularly since the Gault-Millau organisation★ has at last brought out a new edition of its own New York guide) are increasingly drawing attention to this unpleasant phenomenon, especially the splendidly iconoclastic Seymour Britchky, whose restaurant reviews could be read with enormous enjoyment by a toothless vegetarian teetotaller with a stomach ulcer. Some of the guides have started also to rebuke greedy restaurants which crowd tables together in uncomfortable and sometimes embarrassing proximity, though one defended the practice at Le Cirque (which does serve quite good food), by saying 'Would you prefer Woody Allen six feet or sixteen away from you?' That question, at any rate, I can answer with absolute certainty: given the choice, I would like him sixteen miles away. Kingsley Amis, not long ago, suggested that the worst thing about being a member of the human race was that Allen was also a member of it, and I know what he means. His obsessive portrait of the cringing Jew is so revolting, even to an exceptionally assimilated Jew like me (the self-pity is positively more odious

---

★ And 'organisation' is the word. To start with, Gault has gone; the partners separated some time ago. Moreover the new edition, though it calls itself Gault-Millau, is described as being no more than 'supervised by Christian Millau', and lists an Editor-in-Chief, an Editor, and a host of other participants in its compilation. It seems that the outfit has been leasing out its name and reputation (the latter justly high) while exercising no more than an ultimate control; the Swiss and German versions, though they bear the official imprimatur, seem to have been compiled entirely by the natives. Possibly this is the penalty, or at any rate the consequence, of success. Gault-Millau, Gault-Millau, wherefore art thou Gault-Millau?

than that of Sammy Davis Junior), that I almost feel impelled to cross the street when passing a cinema showing one of his films.

But this is beginning to take me far from the habits of New York restaurateurs. You think I am exaggerating, importing my London propensities and expecting them to be treated the way they would be on the other side? Hear Julie Baumgold, surely a streetwise New York lass if ever there was one, describing, in *New York* magazine, a characteristic scene at Mortimer's, a favourite for the Award in this and any other year:

> Two well-dressed men walk into the totally empty restaurant and are given the Table O'Shame in the rear. 'Do you have something less in line with the kitchen?' one asks, looking out over the field of white cloths. 'This is ridiculous', the other man says, even as they are hanging their overcoats and scarves on the pegs. 'Let's go.' 'It's ridiculous', echoes the woman in the black cape and checked Valentino suit who has been invited to temporary purdah, the bar. 'I say,' says Glenn★ with that certain smile, 'it's *my* restaurant and I hold tables. It excludes the boisterous overdressed element ...' It's late when a patrician couple blows in. After a lifetime of headwaiters leaping forward, of the beckoning arm and opened palm, they stand waiting, but no-one comes. Six minutes, twenty minutes. Their chins go up. The lady suggests the bar, but the man gives her a poisoned look. Now it is principle. But what is principle if, despite the shoes, the noses, the gentle manners, the good coats, they are invisible, two ciphers in the void, two victims of whim. 'This is ridiculous', the woman says softly. But no-one at all is listening.

★　　　★　　　★

The Rockefeller Center is one of the more architecturally distinguished places on the Avenue, though the competition is not extensive. The extraordinary finger to the sky that the central, tallest skyscraper makes is only the heart of the complex, not the complex itself, which is said to comprise almost twenty such reachings for the stars. (It is impossible to count them all, or at least it is impossible to count them more than once and get the same answer.) But the point of the Rockefeller is that although it fronts onto the Avenue, it immediately flees from it; it is one of the very few spots on the entire thoroughfare that makes it possible for a Fifth-weary traveller to get out of the hurrying hell of the roadway and the bad temper of the sidewalks. A dozen strides into the Rockefeller's heart, and peace

---

★ Birnbaum.

descends; peace, that is, for New York, since there is an interior bustle, produced by those who have fled from the one outside. There is a fountain, a massive statue of Prometheus, even those most rare Manhattan objects, benches on which the heavy-laden may sit them down and rest (and having rested, visit the French bookshop that is housed in the handsome promenade).

One of the bitterest and most justified complaints against central Manhattan's grid system, at any rate from those who come from less regular lands, is that there are no alleyways, not even a crooked street to inject life into the regularity. Well, the Rockefeller Center is the nearest thing to such European asymmetry, and in addition its central tower, the seventy-floor RCA Building, which has much of the same aura as the Empire State, possesses an elegance and proportion that in itself soothes the spirit. Of course, the name must send shivers down the spine of anyone who knows anything about early industrial society in America, for the first John D. Rockefeller, founder of the dynasty and of Standard Oil, was perhaps the biggest swine in that amazing rogues' gallery – a very considerable claim – and a miser to boot. (The family has worked assiduously ever since to expiate their ancestor's sins, and, on the whole, very successfully.)

And less than a block away, at the corner of 48th, is the handsomest bookstore in all Manhattan, let alone on Fifth. Scribner's started life as a publisher, and at first the shop displayed only Scribner's own wares. That ended long ago, and now it carries a vast range of everything. It is beautifully laid out, and faultlessly staffed, but its greatest attribute is its magnificent wrought-iron Beaux-Arts façade, which is echoed in the lofty interior, fully two storeys high.

Which is all very well, but the moment I turned my back, the building was sold (the business had been sold earlier, but to another book-store/publisher, Rizzoli, which is as thorough, well-stocked and choosy as Scribner's, but not so beautifully housed) to a clothing store, and a chain clothing store at that: Benetton. The new owners insist that the interior will remain untouched, but we have all heard such promises, followed by the splintering sound when they are broken. Have I really looked my last on that lovely shop-front? If so, I am glad that my final glimpse was of those four ornamental seals that grace the building – indeed grace the Avenue – and contain the images of the four great printers: Gutenberg, Caxton, Manutius and Benjamin Franklin. If the new owners are sincere, let them show their sincerity by leaving the whole thing in place, and adding a fifth seal for the fifth great master of printing: Froben.

★   ★   ★

Murder knows nothing of no-go areas; the homicide map of New York no doubt shows thicker clusters in some places than in others, but there are no completely empty spaces anywhere on it. Still, you might think that one or two spots might be spared, and if you were to draw up a list of such immunities, it is very likely that St Patrick's Cathedral would be on it, and probably right at the top.

St Patrick's is the oldest building on Fifth Avenue; it was begun in 1858. The Gothic Revival now sets teeth on edge, but that is because so much of it was bad, yet too solid to knock down. In itself, unless you hold implacably to the severe principle that *no* imitation can be a work of art, the neo-Gothic can be considered dispassionately, and the best of it genuinely praised. St Patrick's is not quite the best; it has the shape and appurtenances of buildings with flying buttresses, but omits the flying buttresses themselves, while the pinnacles to crown them float uneasily in the air. It has had the misfortune to find itself in the crammed and threatening midtown, whereas when it was built it was accused of being too far away for New Yorkers; now it is inevitably dwarfed by its surroundings, particularly the towers of the Rockefeller Center across the road. To get any feeling from St Patrick's the visitor has to enter it. (Hardly an unacceptable requirement; it wasn't actually built just to be looked at.) The stained glass is not thirteenth century, but the architects cannot be blamed for that, since by the time they broke the soil, the thirteenth century had come and gone. But at least they got many of the windows made at Chartres, and although very few Fifth Avenue buildings can ever get enough natural light, packed as tightly as they are, that matters less in St Patrick's, and the windows glow quietly and peacefully.

Any church must be peaceful, or it has missed its vocation. Inside, its neighbours being invisible, there is nothing to shrink its size or majesty. It isn't the biggest church in New York; that title goes to the Cathedral of St John the Divine. But its huge vaulted space and arches make it seem even larger than it is. Experts say it resembles Cologne, and indeed that it was consciously modelled upon that eternally unfinished creation; I have never been able to see the likeness, unless it is that both of them, for all their size and august form, exude a wholly benign atmosphere, with nothing severe, demanding or harsh in their tone. But as I say, any church should feel welcoming. It does, too; any sunny mid-day, its steps are strewn with people having their lunch from brown bags, exactly as they do on the steps of the Public Library, though the library has more steps.

This is perhaps a diversion, but there is an added horror in what is to come; the more you know St Patrick's, the greater the shock. I had walked past St Patrick's, as I subsequently realised, only a few minutes before the catastrophe. A man of Cuban origin, Joseph Delgado, ran into the Cathedral, shouting madly. He tore off his clothes, screaming and lashing out at anyone near him; he started to beat a woman with his belt. One of the Cathedral ushers, John Winters, a man of seventy-seven, moved to restrain the obviously insane man, who thereupon drew a knife and repeatedly stabbed Winters, who died of his wounds a few minutes later. A policeman – it is still not clear whether he was already in the Cathedral or had been alerted by someone seeking help and rushed in – pulled out his gun and shot Delgado dead. Cardinal O'Connor had been told that some kind of disturbance was going on inside St Patrick's; he arrived just in time to see the two dead men sprawled in the aisle. 'I didn't see a pool of blood,' he said, 'I saw a river.'

O'Connor, like the Archbishop of Canterbury, was in the Second World War, though Runcie was not then in orders, and fought as a soldier; O'Connor was a naval chaplain, but had therefore anyway seen violent death a-plenty. At the time it happened, there were only a few people in the building, engaged in private prayer. O'Connor gathered them together and prayed with them, while the bodies lay in defilement; afterwards, he said, 'I couldn't remember a thing I said.'

It transpired that Delgado had had a long history of derangement; he had been in and out of mental hospitals and prisons for years. John Winters, the man he killed, was an Irish-born immigrant to the United States. He had worked as a security guard, and when he retired, being still fit and active, got the job as a Cathedral usher.*

The son of the dead man was himself a Catholic priest; a few days later, he conducted his father's funeral service, which O'Connor attended. Next day, the killer was given the Church's rites; he, too, had been a Catholic. The decision to give him Christian burial raised some eyebrows, but the priest who officiated said that it was a 'sign of forgiveness', since the man was plainly mad; 'I wasn't going to let him go to the Potter's Field.' O'Connor did not attend, but approved the decision.

Then it got worse. O'Connor, troubled by the Police Department's insistence that he should have guards about him, and still shaking from the horror of St Patrick's, was returning from the Requiem Mass for the murdered usher, when, in the car, he got a message which said that one of his priests, in the Bronx, had been violently murdered. He told his driver

---

* A curious cultural puzzle arose next day. If this had happened in London, every newspaper would have had the same headline the following morning: 'Murder in the Cathedral'. Not one of the New York papers, or anyone else, used the reference.

to change course, and went at once to the home of the murdered priest, who had been beaten, shot and strangled; he said more prayers.

The week, however, had not yet finished. On Staten Island, vandals broke into the Synagogue and set it on fire. Nobody was hurt, but the Holy Ark was reduced to ashes; the Ark is the most sacred object in a synagogue, holding as it does the Torah – the scrolls of the Law. Jewish rites dictate that if the Torah is destroyed, its remains must be buried, in a coffin, with a burial ceremony; since the Torah is the heart of the Jewish religion, its 'death' must be treated as would a human being's. O'Connor sent a message of sympathy, and went on the news to denounce this outrageous crime against Judaism. Next came a service to cleanse St Patrick's. It wasn't exactly an exorcism, though it presumably came to the same thing – removing the defilement of murder from a holy place.

Perhaps he should have done it as a full exorcism. We know that mere anarchy is loosed upon the world, that the best lack all conviction while the worst are full of passionate intensity, even that things fall apart, the centre cannot hold. Satanic possession is today not very often diagnosed as the cause of crime; schizophrenia and social conditions are more usually blamed. Perhaps we are wrong, altogether wrong; perhaps the Devil exists and sends out his spirits into the bodies of poor wretches like Joseph Delgado. It seems unlikely that if the policeman had commanded the devils to come out of him, rather than shooting him, there might have been a different outcome, particularly if he had done so before Winters was stabbed; perhaps, though, it would have depended on the strength of the policeman's conviction.

No, let me be serious; I *am* being serious. There is evil in the world, is there not? Some of the evil around us comes in a simple form; you have a wallet, I want it, I have a club, now I have your wallet. Then it becomes more complicated: you are a Jew, I am a Nazi, I spit upon your Jewish gaberdine. Then it becomes more complicated still: God has told me to cut off the heads of all red-headed children under seven years of age (he gave me the instructions in a dream), so please pass me that hatchet. Then the complication reaches its height: I am Joseph Delgado, and inside my head torturing fires are consumimg me, while my limbs writhe in sympathy with my brain; this is hell, nor am I out of it.

Unless the universe really is a bunch of random atoms and occurrences, which is absurd, something *happened* to Joseph Delgado, and none of the usual explanations explains anything at all. But one of the *un*usual ones explains a great deal. If evil exists, why should it not have an embodiment? And if it has an embodiment, why cannot the form in which it manifests itself enter into a man or woman? We titter nervously if somebody speaks of Satanic possession; well, we ought to roar with laughter if somebody purports to explain what Delgado did by saying it was the result of a psychopathic disorder.

The Devil will not win the war; of that I am quite certain. But I see nothing strange about his winning a good many battles, with very heavy casualties ('The Pope, how many divisions has he?') on the other side. With the events that crowded in on New York, their focus, by a dreadful irony, right in the middle of Fifth Avenue, he routed the forces of good and danced in triumph on the battlefield. Be of good cheer; the fight-back had begun before the dance was over. The son of the murdered usher, conducting his father's obsequies, ended with an exhortation which demonstrated that Satan's victory can never be complete: 'Leave not', he said, 'in anger or hatred.'

No-one knows where madness, evil and pollution will strike next. But the horror of the defilement (will anyone, ever again, be able to enter St Patrick's without a shudder?) was curiously eased only two blocks further up.

Is there another city anywhere to rival New York in the number and variety of religious, quasi-religious and even anti-religious faiths it offers? There must be hundreds, and dozens of them unknown to all but the few initiates; England after the Civil War spawned a huge gallimaufry of sects, though all but a handful were, however tenuously, Christian. (As is demonstrated, a cynic might say, from the way they hated one another.) But America in general, and New York in particular, is festooned with all the religions not only of North America and Europe, but of every corner of Asia and Africa as well; from the most rigid Catholicism to the most primitive animism anything is available, and it would not be in the least unlikely to come across a human sacrifice cult. (I suppose that sado-masochism, however far the definition is stretched, cannot be classified as a religion; if it could be, New York would indeed harbour such a sect, since more than one eager victim has died in the course of such activities, one or two of them in the most fashionable circles.)

But even if we concentrate entirely on the Christians, the number of their rites must run into scores. (The Jews, it occurs to me, have no such fission other than the loose categories of Liberal, Orthodox and Reform, with the Hassidim forming the shock troops of the Orthodox. Certainly there is nothing in Judaism to compare with such gnawed bones as the Real Presence or for that matter the Tridentine Mass. Have Jews ever persecuted other Jews? I hope not, if only because the irony would be unbearable.)

Which brings me to the corner of 53rd Street, where stands New York's chief Episcopalian church, St Thomas's. Built just before the First World War in the then prevailing version of Gothic, it is a noble pile, though for fully a year it has been practically invisible beneath the scaffolding that has enshrouded it. Inside, it is gloomy in the dusk, largely because of that same scaffolding; it is, however, well worth waiting for the eyes to become accustomed to the murk, if only for the reredos, which is enough to make Tilman Riemanschneider look to his wooden laurels, particularly because St Thomas's is of stone. Stone or no stone, it fills the east wall from floor to ceiling, a distance of some 120 feet. It is covered with figures in the most amazing profusion and the most remarkable catholicity (if that word will not be misunderstood in an Episcopalian church). There are Christ and the Virgin, three angels and thirty-two saints, not all of them well-known (St Polycarp, for instance – when did anybody last erect an altar to him?),★ as well as all four Evangelists, SS Paul, Augustine, Francis, John Chrysostom (a frightful anti-semite, but let that pass), the beastly Athanasius, Stephen, Gregory the Great and of course the church's patron. In addition, though, there is a notable selection of appropriately holy figures, including the Venerable Bede, Wesley, Cranmer and Laud, Wycliffe, Hooker and Bishop Butler (the one who said 'Things and actions are what they are, and the consequences of them will be what they will be – why then should we desire to be deceived?'); all sound folk, though Cranmer and Laud were executed and Wycliffe was lucky to be spared that fate and Wesley would have shared it a century or two earlier. But then the visitor is startled by two notable figures who can claim neither sainthood nor a place on the bench of bishops nor an aura of sanctity except in the most secular sense: George Washington and – of all people – William Ewart Gladstone. This is a broad church indeed.

Its pastor is the Reverend John Andrew. I don't know whether the practice of subscribing, for a modest fee, to a clergyman's sermons is widespread in the United States (or in Britain, for that matter), but it seems it is done at St Thomas's, at the reasonable rate of $12·50 a year, or 25c a time. Anyway, I put my quarter in the box and went away with the latest issue, a most profound and revealing discussion of death, sparked off by a letter he had had from a child, which ran – *sancta simplicitas!* – 'Dear God, What is it like when you die? Nobody will tell me. I just want to know, I don't want to do it. Your friend, Mike.' Mike got his 25 cents-worth, and a bit over.

★ I take it back; I have discovered that he had the distinction of being martyred under – of all philosophical and unfanatical Emperors – Marcus Aurelius.

... the basic fear remains. It lurks at the back of every Christian head. The fear of being forgotten by God, uncared for by God. The fear that God's control ends at death's gate. The fear that for all the brave words, there is extinction ... Beneath the serenity of the face of Christ as he accepts the welcome and the proclamation of his Kingship, there is an acceptance of another kind; acceptance of human apprehension as the dark clouds gather round him, the loneliness which the approach of death brings with it to the solitary soul, for dying is not a group activity, and nobody can shoulder the burden for you; its quiet inevitability, its certainty, its deliberate speed and its effectiveness ...

And he goes on to say something else, about you and me. For true life in him there has to be true death, the solitary grain of wheat has to fall into the ground and die, it has to experience that solitary experience so as to be solitary no more. There has to be the last surrender, there has to be a falling, we must allow ourselves to be dropped from the hand of a faithful and loving Creator into the good earth of his caring, knowing that all things are in his hands, grain and resting place alike. When we allow it, he can act mightily. For herein lies his promise, that remarkable promise Christ makes precisely at this point: 'Where I am, there will my servant be' ...

I stood in the vestry and read the whole thing, and concluded that the Reverend John Andrew, rector of St Thomas's, was an interesting man. Then I sat awhile in the dark church, which somehow seemed less dark, perhaps not only because my eyes were now attuned. Lead, kindly light, amid the encircling gloom ... outside, Fifth Avenue's hurrying thousands seemed to be wasting their time in an even greater hurry than usual.

*   *   *

And here I am at 699 Fifth Avenue, where a great deal of reflection is provoked, absolutely none of it about God. The seeds of the thoughtfulness were sown a little earlier, as I was browsing through a magazine called *Go*, which is subtitled 'For the modern man'.

One of the advertisements was for an item in one of the enormous range of what were dubbed (and the name has lasted) 'Men's toiletries'. (There are signs that 'fragrances' is making headway, and may ultimately dislodge the earlier term.) This was from Clinique's collection, and the ad is worth printing in full, and worth, even more, discussing when printed.

His face will wake up to something dermatologists have known for years: To look healthy and trim over its bones, skin needs a step beyond cleansing. It needs exfoliation.

Exfoliating skin means removing the layer of dead, skin-dulling flakes that accumulate every day – and even more every night – on the surface.

Shaving helps a little, but to remove flakes completely it takes a unique product: Clinique Scruffing Lotion – three strengths for three skin types. Find yours, plus a fast, free skin analysis, at any Clinique counter.

To look its best, your skin's freshest layer should show. With Clinique Scruffing Lotion, it does.

I peer in the mirror, for signs of dead, skin-dulling flakes, the tell-tale *stigmata* of one who has not practised exfoliation this morning. To my relief and delight, I find none – unless, to be sure, they cannot be seen except by those who man the Clinique counter and give enquirers a fast, free skin analysis, ending, to the surprise only of the most naïve, in a recommendation for one of the three strengths of their Scruffing Lotion to remove the invisible flakes and reveal the skin's freshest layer. (The old rule goes: Never ask the barber whether you need a haircut.)

'Men's toiletries' are a very recent phenomenon. When *haute couture* could no longer survive on dressing individual clients, it did two things, one obvious, one less so. The obvious course was to turn to mass production; the less obvious, indeed not obvious at all, was the invention of a need for men to be perfumed and groomed in a way which had until then been confined to women. It was an instant, colossal success; the annual turnover of the industry must by now be billions of dollars, and there are scores of firms competing for what seems to be an infinitely extendable market. What started out with deodorant and was followed by after-shave has now ramified into dozens of potions, unguents, spirits, creams, for the hair, the face, the body, the hands, the eyes, the skin. I had not previously encountered Scruffing Lotion by that or any other name (the entire theory on which it is based, incidentally, is imaginary, as human skin is self-exfoliating), but it will certainly not be the last of its kind, and if it catches on rival manufacturers will move into the production of scruffing lotions of their own.

And the number of such rivals is extraordinary. In that single issue of *Go* (it was further subtitled 'Grooming and Fitness edition'), wherein were advertised clothes (including underwear), cigarettes, liquor, cars, watches, hi-fi equipment, shoes and 'accessories' (also, not only sun-glasses but ordinary – or rather, extraordinary – spectacles), there were 'toiletries and fragrances' by Aramis, Armani, L'Oréal, Lagerfeld, Calvin Klein, Tuscany (with a view of Florence), Krizia Uomo, Vintage Gruene ('The first vintage Cologne – a number of collectors' bottles bear the inscription "1988 Première Edition"'), Giorgio ('VIP Special Reserve Shave Foam and Spray Deodorant'), Kouros, Halston, Cruzon, Right Guard, Antaeus, Royal Copenhagen, Polo, Quorum and Musk. Some of the fragrances were physically present in the advertisements; readers were invited to pull a tab fixed to the page which would unleash a breath of the precious ichor, but although all of these were pleasant enough, it was impossible to detect any difference in scent, let alone quality.

Somehow, when I had worked my way through this list, it seemed less surprising to meet a 'Lonelyhearts' column in the magazine, though one of a rather special kind ('How can I get the most out of my cycling workout?', 'I like to wear boutonnières, but I'm afraid they're out of fashion', 'My hair is extremely thin, and no matter what styling aid I use, it seems to stay flat and lifeless' – 'Whether he's a banker, a baker or a highway toll-taker, a man's hairstyle is essential to his image – see "Six Hairstyles That Work", page 254').

All this was by way of preliminaries – the preliminaries, that is, to 699 Fifth Avenue and its tenant, Bijan, or Bijan Pakzad in full. The glass door bears the remarkable legend 'By appointment only'. Since I had an appointment, I approached the door, but before I could touch the handle a white-jacketed, white-gloved butler – there is no other word – swung it open from the inside, and I marched in and gazed around.

> In Xanadu did Kubla Khan
> A stately pleasure dome decree . . .

It has been estimated that the staircase – a double-branched one in brass and glass sweeping up to where the business is transacted – cost almost as much as the entire building did when it was erected early in the century. I could quite believe it; in fact, by the time I had made a couple of circuits of the place, there was very little indeed I couldn't believe, even much of his publicity ('In 1981 Bijan made an innovation in the concept of male elegance by creating the first concentrated perfume for men . . . in signed and numbered Baccarat crystal flacons, the deep-toned and mysterious scent is compounded of 23 rare essences and priced at three thousand dollars for each six-ounce bottle . . .'), which is presided over by a man who gave up a successful practice as an ophthalmologist to help build the Bijan legend, not that Bijan seems to need much help in that particular department, though if he did it would be forthcoming promptly and in lavish quantity:

'Bijan has an unerring memory for details ... carried the color of a sweater in his mind for two years until he finally found a piece of cashmere that matched it ... Bijan staggers his associates by creating every theme and detail of his work ... he is the only menswear designer in the world who creates the shoes, shirts, scarves, ties, jewelry and watches his clients wear, plus their crocodile briefcase, luggage and now fragrances as well ... plans and personally installs his famous and provocative window displays, conceives and totally supervises his witty and often startling advertisements' (in which case somebody should tell him that Château Margaux is not spelt Margeaux).

The tide of nonsense swells higher; a new fragrance, we are told,

> ... is contained in a patented bottle of hand-blown quality, completely unique in design, created by the designer himself. It incorporates an open circular center with an internal 'web', which divides the inner space of the bottle into two separate sections, while sharing a common neck. The swirl design of the cap is a replica of Bijan's original Baccarat bottle, adding a sculptured effect ... The result is a flacon that is softly rounded in sculptured form. It has a timeless familiarity, yet is a revolutionary breakthrough in the art of automatic glass production; an unprecedented combination of modern technology and brilliant design.

And that's only the bottle; the cardboard box it comes in has a verse of the anthem all to itself:

> Working closely with packaging experts, Bijan's creative ideas led to the invention of an unprecedented new design ... the wrap box! Constructed without any glued seams, lined with a beautiful graphic design and secured with only two ingeniously placed interlocks, the box unfolds gracefully to display the precious Bijan perfume within. The presentation is unique and lavish. It creates a gift-wrapped effect that accentuates both the fragrance and the dramatic flacon that holds it.

'No man is a hero to his valet'; no man is safe from his press-agent, who in this case is as likely as not to quote George F. Will's description of Bijan as 'the Bernard Berenson of the fine art of success', without noticing that the latest biography of Berenson has the melancholy task of revealing that Berenson was the most frightful crook.

I found myself struggling not to drown in the absurdity, the suffocating atmosphere of self-worship and aesthetic fraud, the fanaticism (I put my tape-recorder down on a table, and returned a few moments later to find it had disappeared – into, I discovered, the office, banished because it spoilt the perfection of the showroom's design, *even though there was nothing else on the table*), the air of hokum that pervaded the place like incense (perhaps it *was* incense), the implausibility of everything and everyone in the place, starting with the 'By appointment only' rubric on the door, continuing with the prices – two or three thousand dollars for a suit, seven hundred and fifty for a pair of slacks, five hundred for a shirt – and finishing with the attitude of reverence displayed by everyone in the place to their employer, which would have made the Emperor Domitian uncomfortable and Stalin positively embarrassed.

Almost drowned, and not waving but sinking, I decided to make one great effort to ignore the calculated decadence of it all, and examine the goods on sale. Sniffing hard, I began to open cupboards and drawers. And then the wonder grew.

Bijan is a flamboyant and absurd showman, and the nature of his promotion material is such that it might almost have been *intended* to make him seem vulgar, ignorant and ridiculous. But the almost incredible truth is that, beneath it all, he is a genius of design and good taste. The more things I pulled out, the more racks I riffled through, the more wool and silk and cashmere I ran my hands over, the more colour schemes I came upon, the more arrangements and displays I considered, the more certain I became that as a designer of men's clothes and all that goes with them, including the scent bottle of timeless familiarity and the swoon-making cardboard box secured with only two ingeniously placed interlocks, I have never come across his equal.

The clothes are not spectacular in the literal sense; indeed, they are for the most part conservative in design and colour, though clearly made from the finest materials and made to a very high standard indeed. Bijan winced when I used the phrase 'off-the-peg', but that is the correct designation; he gets his woollens from Britain and has them tailored in Italy – 'Because British cloth and Italian tailors are the best' – but the solemnity of fittings – including the absurd rite of the ripped-off sleeve – is unknown *in diesen heil'gen Hallen*. Yet the fecundity of his imagination as a designer is quite extraordinary; after a time, I began to believe almost everything he told me, including his claim that he has designed four thousand ties, all different – indeed, if I had stayed much longer, I would have begun to believe his publicity.

Good taste cannot be defined; some of Bijan's advertisements, including the one with the Château Margeaux, include parallel lists of taste good and bad, but they are tired and witless, and could be transposed at random without making any difference. But in the showroom, once the visitor has passed through the ordeals of reverence and smugness, everything he sees and touches is in apparently effortless good taste. Given that, it doesn't matter, if it ever did, that he claims to have flowers specially flown in daily from Holland at a cost of $10,000 a week (flowers are automatically, in the ordinary course of commercial business, flown daily from Holland to New York, and, having arrived, can be bought at any good florist's, and in bulk at the wholesale markets), because such breathlessness cannot affect, in any impartial observer, the realisation of the talent and quality of everything around.

A series of massive wardrobes was flung open before me; the furniture, like its contents, is all designed by Bijan, and the handsomeness and ingenuity of these closets reinforce the admiration, which – for the same impartial observer – gets less grudging as time goes by. Each wardrobe is based on a single theme of dressing: one is for evening wear, another for business, another for casual dressing, but though the basic suits are the keystone of the collection, everything else is included, too – ties, shirts, shoes, pyjamas, sweaters, scarves, cufflinks, handkerchiefs, *everything*. (Well, everything except underwear – presumably even Bijan cannot make boxer shorts in good taste.)

Nor does that exhaust what the unerring eye of Bijan can achieve. As each of the cupboards was opened, my first impression was not of the calculated variety and comprehensiveness of the contents, indeed it was not of the contents at all; the eye and feelings were ravished by the composition of what was seen. The various fitments and racks and shelves holding the clothes, and the colours and shapes and textures of the clothes that were held, were composed into a painting, and a painting, moreover, that breathed a harmony and grace that Pieter de Hooch would have recognised and welcomed – and painted.

Bijan himself is a gnome of a man, ebullient (very expressive hands, constantly used), voluble, passionate, with no more than a slender grasp of English grammar and a slightly weird vocabulary, yet making himself clear with the very force of his conviction. Self-taught, shining with confidence that wavered only once, when he felt obliged to tell me that he was a multi-millionaire and didn't have to go on working, always hovering on the edge of absurdity but never falling over, discreet about his clients, at any rate to the extent of never attaching a name to an anecdote. The outfits he makes are 'my babies'; clearly, so are his customers. He is naïvely proud of the number of heads of state he dresses, the captains of industry, the prominent politicians, the men of immense wealth (they'd better be), who must buy ready-made (another wince) because they haven't time to go back and forth for fittings. And then:

> I study that person; his size, his weight, his profession, what he could like, what he should not wear, and after that I study my fabrics, I put the whole thing together – say for example fifty outfits with the right ties, right shirts, right shoes, raincoat, topcoat – what to wear and where to wear it. Very much those gentlemen are much respected, very powerful men in the world, sometimes with twenty-five thousand employees in their own field. Lots of trust, and that trust makes me so proud, that trust makes me definitely know not to take advantage. I really don't know anybody that doesn't trust me through those fifteen thousand customers that I have.

Then I asked him if he wanted to change people, to make them abandon their habits of dressing and re-design them.

> Very much, very much. But before I change him I teach what he wears, how bad that could be. First I study him, first I see why he do not like to be changed. Recently, I had a very famous artist/singer in the world – you know him and I know him, the name is not important, because I don't like to talk about the names of my customers, he had the tendency to wear a short trouser. I insist that he should not wear. He is a lovely man, beautiful voice, but his pants is always too short. I told him I do not agree, well the reason was 'I feel more comfortable, I can sing better'. I said 'I don't understand, shorter trousers, three inches, *had no statement*'. He said no, I said yes, he said no, I said goodbye, but in a nice way.

I said goodbye, but in a nice way, and went on my way up the Avenue in a complicated frame of mind. It was Ruskin who coined the term 'Illth'; he was not much given to puns, but wanted a striking word for what he was condemning, and chose a back-formation from 'Wealth'. But what was he condemning? Not just ugliness, surely; not bad taste; and in any case he couldn't have found Bijan's designs guilty of either. Nor was it just conspicuous consumption, though that certainly affronted him. It was the profusion of possessions that existed only *to be* possessions, and were made for that purpose alone.

Our world today is full of illth. The Scruffing Lotion which removes imaginary dead skin-cells, the gadgets and 'executive toys', the new craze, almost at once to be superseded by a newer one, and that in turn by a newer still, the mechanical fingernail-dryer (yes, it exists, as does the device for testing the soil of your garden for dampness, so that, if it registers danger-ously dry, you will be alerted to water it), the constant revolution of 'fashion', that *ignis fatuus* which has drawn so many women, and not a few men, into the quicksands of illth from which bourne no traveller returns – these are not the equivalent of Henry Clay Frick's pictures, and the reason is obvious: the nature of Frick's pictures is entirely independent of the reason he bought and hung them. No doubt he did so to flaunt his wealth, and no doubt he was damned for it, but the pictures work their magic on visitors to the museum who have never heard of him (or the artists who painted them, for that matter). Can you say as much for the 'Ear-ring caddy covered in real leather with the owner's initials embossed on the lid for a trifling extra charge'?

Here is another advertisement, presumably aimed at women's equivalent of the Scruffing Lotion. It is called 'Skin Caviar', and is made by La Prairie:

> Skin Caviar is an intensive skincare treatment in a totally new encapsulated form. This new technique of encapsulation allows unique combinations of ingredients in a high-powered concentration. It is just this intensive con-centration of vitamins, humectants, emollients and plant naturals that gives the skin the look and feel of a more perfect texture ... a firmer brighter tone.

Or in other words, La Prairie are now making their face-cream in little pellets. Perhaps, I thought, I should get a little closer to this curious world, fascinating and repellent, absurd and serious, despised and envied.

★   ★   ★

So I went to the Tiffany Feather Ball, at the Plaza Hotel. The Plaza Hotel is not what it was. Its style, or rather the name of its style, is, or should be, a source of amusement to the British, for all the guidebooks insist on calling it 'Edwardian'. So it is, literally, as it was built in 1907, when Edward VII was on the throne. But after all, he was only on the throne of Britain and the Commonwealth, and few Americans, I imagine, felt that they had owed him allegiance since 1776 or thereabouts. This matter of nomenclature runs deep in the United States: 'Edwardian' can mean little to most people, but 'Victorian' is understood almost everywhere, though she, too, was hardly America's monarch. It goes further: 'Georgian' is a perfectly respectable American adjective, applied obviously to silver but also to other things that need locating in time, and not even the name of the great enemy is

18

19

barred from the American dictionary. Why has no patriotic American lexicographer or philologist devised a series of terms that denominate historical periods without being forced to use those of the, er, Mother Country? (While he is about it, he might do something about the 'English muffin', which is neither English nor a muffin. Mind you, few of the Danish pastries sold in either America or Britain have ever seen a Dane.)

Anyway, the Plaza is not what it was, which was something like the Savoy.* It still follows its old rule of hanging out the flag of a country whose head of state is in temporary residence, or indeed any notable figure from overseas, and its Edwardian architecture – *very* Edwardian – has lately been renovated and restored, and its green roof is as handsome as ever, but my *dear*, the clientèle! The functions! The crowds! The noise! The food! The old peace has gone, to be replaced by the now almost universal bustle that characterises hotels which have lost their character, and although its splendid feeling of space is still as strong as ever, the space is filled with new sounds, new demands, new people, many of whom were at the Tiffany Ball.

This is an annual event, held to raise money for an organisation called Just a Break, which helps disabled people by finding jobs for them. A worthy enterprise, then, and what could be a more harmless way of raising money? Tiffany provides the venue, the decorations, the music and the dinner (the decorations were hideous and the dinner dreadful, but that is by the way), so there were no expenses to be deducted, and every cent raised went to the cause.

Glittering scene though it was, the guest-list suggested that these people were not quite the indisputable 400. Mrs Reagan was the Honorary Chairman of the Ball, but she wasn't there; there was an International Committee which included three HRHs, two HHs, an HSH, a Duke, an Earl, two Duchesses, seven Countesses, three Counts, three Baronesses and two Barons, but only one Countess and one Baroness turned up, and even most of the National Committee (which presumably did the work, or some of it) were no-shows (Donald Trump was on the committee, but sent his brother). I don't think Norman Parkinson and Estée Lauder are quite enough to make a visitor feel that he is surrounded by the town's most august and aristocratic citizens.

The programme was an amazing document; apart from listing the names of all the people on the committees and displaying some photographs of the previous year's Ball, it consisted entirely of advertisements, which is

---

* But is the Savoy what it was?

18 Surely you wouldn't miss a little *one?   19 The pool on the roof   20 By appointment only*

presumably where most of the money came from, apart, of course, from the $1000-a-plate entrance money. Many were of well-known shops and firms – Revlon, Lincoln Cars, Calvin Klein, Pepsi-Cola, Manufacturers Hanover, *La Côte Basque* (the second most expensive restaurant in New York, and they took only half a page!); many were in the form of thanks or tributes to the organisers; many were simply the names of the donors, who presumably did not know that Pride is one of the Seven Deadly Sins; a few were from 'Anonymous', who presumably *did* know.

The stretch limousine is probably the most ridiculous, not to say ugly, vehicle ever invented, and that would still hold true if it were only used in the steppes of Siberia rather than central Manhattan, which must have the highest concentration of traffic in the world. I stood on the steps of the Plaza, watching them roll up to the kerb one after the other; upper crust or no, there must have been hundreds of billions of dollars passing me and going on in through the revolving door. One of the limousines remained at the kerb after disgorging its passengers; the chauffeur sat waiting. Curious, I peered in; on a tray-table there was a large plate of smoked salmon sandwiches and a bottle of champagne; presumably the owners had feared that starvation might set in between 87th Street and the Plaza, and were taking no chances. (It hadn't set in, because the feast had not been touched. Possibly they had heard about the food inside.)

Bijan and the Tiffany Ball; I imagine that many of the men at the latter were dressed by the former. (Who the women were dressed by I couldn't guess, but whoever it was had omitted, or had not dared, to tell the client that something a little *mature* – say thirty years more mature – might be more appropriate; rarely, anywhere, have I seen so much mutton dressed as lamb.)

The wealth of this town is in itself one of the wonders of the world. Not many years ago, American business magazines used to announce, annually, the number of millionaires in the country. They gave up the practice when the number became so large as to be meaningless; now they count the *billionaires*. With that wealth goes an immense charitable distribution; you can list it under guilt or self-imposed obligation, though whichever category is chosen it would be as well to remember that O. Henry, facing the same problem, concluded that tainted money buys just as many boxes of chocolates as the other kind.

L'argent ouvert aux talents: very well. I believe in the spoils to the victors; among the billionaires of New York a very high proportion indeed made it themselves, rather than inheriting it. (The list of the richest four hundred Americans changes each year by 15–20 per cent.) And I know that the bag-ladies of Fifth Avenue (and there are even worse open-air doss-houses) are not the victims of the rich, and that it is impossible to make the poor richer just by making the rich poorer. The unease I felt at the Tiffany Ball was of a different kind altogether, and I was astonished to realise just what I was thinking. Have these people no fear for their souls? Are they quite *certain* that there is nothing beyond death for them, or that if there is it will not take the form of a searching set of questions? If they wonder, do they feel sure that their charitable offerings will be accepted as a defence of their lives?

But why should they have to defend their lives, assuming that they did not get their gains by grinding the faces of the poor or evicting widows and orphans? Many of the very rich, after all, are puzzled to the end of their days at the paradox they live with – the realisation that although they can have anything in the world that money can buy, they find themselves still unsatisfied, and some even wake in the middle of the night, and hear their hearts beating, and stay awake till dawn, wondering what can be wrong. But is that puzzled and disappointed yearning going to be enough on Judgment Day? It would take a finer set of scales than I possess to weigh the billionaires at the Tiffany Ball, the manufacturer of the electrically-operated fingernail-dryer, and Bijan, and tell each of them, with real assurance, that when they were weighed in the balance they were, or were not, found wanting.

But the Tiffany Ball, and the uneasy questions it provoked, was not the only public display of New York's combination of entertainment and philanthropy to which I was appointed spectre at the feast. If Tiffany can set the town's feet tapping, shall Saks be far behind? By common New York consent, the Saks fashion show is the event which opens the new season (this year there will be six designers showing their wares); it is followed by Bloomingdale's shindig, then by the opening of the Metropolitan Opera's season and the New York Philharmonic's, after which the season is considered in full swing.

Having committed themselves, Saks were not going to be accused of half-heartedness. (On the whole, very rich New Yorkers could never be accused of that particular failing.) Eschewing hotels, convention centres and skating rinks, Saks threw its party in an immense marquee; they had entirely covered the Seagram Building Plaza in a white tent with a transparent top, so that, blurred but visible, the moon and the stars and the neighbouring buildings could be seen, come wind or weather, by the guests snug under the plastic.

The rich of New York, then, are not half-hearted. Nor, however, are they three-quarter-hearted. The lobby of the Seagram Building was the obvious venue for the cocktail hour, and since Seagram's is a liquor business, they had devised six new cocktails in honour of the six designers, respectively the Bill Blass Blazer, Geoffrey Beene's Kir Nina, the Adolfo Plaid Mixer, Carolina Herrera's Golden Jockey, Oscar de la Renta's Classic and Mary McFadden's Green Kimono.

Each guest was presented on entering with a set of six cards, each of which, presented at the bar, would produce the appropriate drink. Some of them seemed instantly lethal; I wondered whether anyone in the crowd, some seven or eight hundred strong, would try the death-defying feat of sinking the lot. But who would try mixing the Mary McFadden (gin, lime juice, crème de menthe) with the Carolina Herrera (vodka, peach schnapps, orange juice), and following the result with the Bill Blass Blazer (Crown Royal – whatever that might be – lemon juice, tomato juice, Tabasco, Worcester sauce and pepper) multiplied by Geoffrey Beene's Kir Nina (more of the peach schnapps, this time with champagne). Much better stick with Oscar: Glenlivet on the rocks.

Then the press-agent prose takes over:

> At 8, guests will relocate to the tented plaza to begin an elegant American dinner prepared by Glorious Food. A gracious ambience will be created by Robert Isabell, with tables covered with travertine marble colored cloths, surrounded by black ballroom chairs, and topped with hurricane lamps with beeswax candles and crystal vases filled with full-blown American garden roses in shades of white and cream.

But before we relocated to the elegant American dinner in the gracious ambience, I had time, with a Bernard Levin Bloody Mary (make a Bloody Mary and put it in a glass) in my hand, to tour the crowd. It seemed younger than the one at the Tiffany Ball, and – perhaps in consequence – livelier. Naturally, a fashion show would inevitably put the ladies on their mettle, and there were some startling creations, the most remarkable looking like a parodic version of the already parodic part of Count Orlofsky in *Die Fledermaus*. But as I moved in and out of the throng, a strange impression began to rise; so strange, that I began my tour all over again, and continued it with growing intensity. To disprove my almost incredible conviction, I began to hurry, lest I should be obliged to relocate without making sure; some of the guests, as I came skating through their group for the third or fourth time, must have thought me mad.

I came close to thinking that I *was* mad. It is notoriously difficult to disprove a negative; as philosophers have pointed out, the statement 'All swans are white' is immediately falsified by the discovery of a single black swan, so that the proposition can never establish a claim that it is proved, even if the black swan never turns up. As it happens, the homely illustration which the sage used in his argument was appallingly apposite at the Saks gala; apart from the waiters and barmen, *there was not a single black face to be seen anywhere among the hundreds of guests.*

I forbore to ask why; I was myself, after all, a guest in every sense. Perhaps, guest or no guest, I *should* have asked. There are, after all, a considerable number of black designers and couturiers; there must be, also, many black people interested in fashion, rich enough to participate and guaranteed not to spend their time rolling their eyes, playing banjos and calling for cornpone. (Some of them must be customers of Saks.) How and by whom the attendance–list was drawn up I never discovered; but the phenomenon chilled even the gracious ambience, white and cream roses notwithstanding. Thank God there were some Jews at the table to which I was guided, or I would have become paranoid before the evening was out.

★   ★   ★

Yet my meetings with money and what it can and cannot buy were still not finished. If, in New York, you want to know how the other half lives, you would do well to start with Mrs Cornelius Vanderbilt Whitney, whose name demonstrates not one but two of the great rich dynasties of America. Americans find quaint our system of hierarchy, in particular our peerage with its strange pyramidical structure. But they forget that they have such a hierarchy themselves, except that it doesn't go back nearly as far. The dynasties of America are based not on titles but on wealth; it must, however, be made clear what those words mean. They do not mean that the more money you have the higher you stand in the social order; such a notion would be greeted with horror among the upper classes in the United States. But perhaps this is the most appropriate point to establish the difference between old money and new money.

To start with, new money does *not* buy, in any quantity at all, many things that old money does. The point at which old money becomes new is not precisely marked. Roughly speaking, money made before the First World War is old, though a few families who made theirs in the twenties have qualified for the club. But it is not so easy to say that all the rest, made later, is new money. Take, at random, one of the designers who participated in the Saks fashion show, Bill Blass; take, equally at random, one of the guests at the Tiffany Ball, Estée Lauder. They are both very rich, but their money is certainly old within the terms (I am coming to the terms themselves shortly) which govern the categories, for in certain businesses, like theirs, money can be retrospectively classified as old, however recently it has been made. But only certain businesses; Steven Spielberg, say, has become immensely rich through his very successful films, but his money, however much of it he piles up, will never grow old; Leonard Bernstein's money, on the other hand, has long been, in the jargon of the reproduction-furniture trade, antiqued.

Now; what follows? What follows is the American class system, which is not determined by whether your ancestors robbed churches for Charles I, but whether they robbed everybody for themselves. You and I would be ashamed to admit that we were descended from John D. Rockefeller, whereas in the United States such a fate is the greatest social *cachet* you can have.

Let us not be high and mighty about it; having a title to your name because your forebears robbed churches for Charles I is no more admirable than getting a social *cachet* from the fact that your (much closer) forebears made stupendous sums of money by the most blackguardly business practices. Both have led, quite illogically, to a high place in the social order; an English Duke may today be a scoundrel, a drunkard, a bore, or all three, yet his place at the top of the social tree is secured for him and his descendants to the remotest posterity. *Exactly* the same is true of the American aristocracy, except that they do not have titles. They do, however, tend to be unintentionally comical about stressing the age of their roots, which mostly go back a mere eye-blink compared to British titles. (It's rather like Major Petkoff, in *Arms and the Man*, boasting that his family goes back nearly two generations.)

Yet that does not end the investigation of the American class structure, and the most important aspect of it – the results – is yet to be discussed. First, though, I had to discover how the other half lives; true to my own recommendation, above, I did start with Marylou Whitney, and after these musings it would not have seemed in the least odd if someone had entered to say 'Her Grace will see you now' rather than 'Mrs Whitney will see you now'.

Her Grace the Duchess of Whitney came into the room, which instantly flooded with charm. (Doctrinaire egalitarians make the mistake of believing that the very rich can't be nice.) She is sixty-five, and does not go all coy about the fact; nor does she need to, since you would have to be very close to her indeed, and to have exceptionally sharp eyes as well, to conclude that she wasn't a woman in her thirties. One of the ways you know it is old money is that it doesn't boast about it. (Conversely, one of the ways you know it is new money is . . .) She was beautifully and tastefully dressed, though presumably only an expert would know that the clothes were very expensive (if indeed they were), and she certainly wasn't draped in diamonds, though presumably she has plenty. In other words, would you know that she was very rich if you met her walking in the Park and didn't recognise her?

The test cannot be made. Though old money does not boast, it takes for granted that everybody else is rich. When she mentioned, with an entirely genuine casualness, that she and her husband had seven homes (actually, I think she said seven *other* homes), she clearly had no idea of the effect such a statement might make. The apartment on the twenty-first floor at 825 Fifth Avenue, where we were, was enormous, with the most astounding view over the Park and beyond it (one way you can see the arch of Washington Square and the other way you can see Harlem), but when she took me out on to the balcony, pointed to the next building and said 'We used to have an apartment there, a really lovely one, but this one is so small', I blinked almost audibly, let alone visibly. When, as we were talking about her parties (they are famous throughout society), and she talked, again without any realisation of the effect, of regularly having four or five hundred guests to dinner, I was about to make the obvious point, when she rendered me incapable of making *any* point by saying 'But tomorrow's is a very small one, just a little dinner-dance for sixty.'

I asked her what *she* got out of her parties, which must, however many staff she has, involve her in a good deal of hard work. The answer was enchanting:

> I don't know, I think it has to do with the child in me or something. I always loved having birthday parties and since my birthday's on Christmas Eve it was always a difficult time to have a party. So my mother said she had to make up for it and I could have parties all through the year. My sisters were very jealous because I had all the parties. Whenever I give a party I feel the same as I did when I was a child when I had a birthday party – dress up and have a lovely time and give a lot of people pleasure. I'm somebody who likes to look at the sun in the morning.

There was no boasting, either, about the sums she raises for charity, though that must be even harder work than the parties. Well, it *is*:

People look at me, and I say 'Would you come over and have a cup of tea?' And they say 'Cup of tea! What you mean, Marylou, is "Bring out your cheque-book".' I'm having a hard time convincing people that I would just like to have a cosy chat and a cup of tea.

One sadness was clouding the little dinner-dance for sixty on the following night; the fact that her husband would not be there. He was in their Kentucky home, and not very well, at any rate not well enough, at ninety, to travel. She talked of him very tenderly and lovingly, as well she might; he has said (though she didn't tell me) that just before he met her (she is his fourth wife) he was planning to kill himself: 'Why', he would ask, 'have I made such a success of my professional life and such a mess of my personal life?' It is not an uncommon question in our world; he answered it by marrying Marylou, and the marriage has endured for, so far, thirty-one years.

I have said that the stretch limousine is the most ridiculous means of transport ever devised; I have also said that it is one of the ugliest. But for my journey to Mrs Whitney's little dinner-dance I was provided with the longest stretch limousine made. There is a longer one in existence, but it was only built in order that the owner could get into *The Guinness Book of Records*; mine was the biggest in commercial production.

It was white. The curious ill-proportioned look of the 'normal' stretch limo was absent; it was positively handsome, though I did rather wonder whether it would collapse in the middle, because although it had wheels fore and aft, fore was separated from aft by twenty-nine feet; it really needed another pair half-way along. On the other hand, I was strongly reinforced in my view that nothing more absurd in the way of getting from one place to another had ever been devised, most particularly in the traffic of Manhattan, and I could not stop giggling at the absurdity of it. (I stopped giggling abruptly when the chauffeur overshot the street we were going to and, since it was rush hour and it would therefore take a considerable time to go round the block again, backed straight up Fifth Avenue, with the traffic roaring down all round us.) The windows were transparent from inside, opaque from outside, which gave me the opportunity of watching, while I was waiting to set off, the bystanders' reactions. They were, I was relieved to see, the same as mine: hilarity. After a time, they began to photograph it, and then to summon their friends and photograph them standing beside it. The interior was as ludicrous as the outside; it had two television sets, independently adjustable, so you could watch two programmes at the same time if you were so minded, a video-recorder, ice cabinets to keep the drink cool, rows of concealed lighting in the ceiling *and the floor*, cushions covered in the finest, softest suede, and of course everything controlled by the touch of a button.

And so to the party, where the final piece of the old money/new money fell into place in the jigsaw. The money, with a few ex officio exceptions like Walter Cronkite, who is presumably *hors concours* as an intellectual, and the gossip columnists (said to be invited because they can be very helpful in spreading the word for the charitable causes for which so many parties, though not this one, are held), was all old. But it was while I was talking to the assistant of the head of the PR firm engaged for the party (and what did Mrs Whitney want a PR firm for, rather than an anti-PR firm to keep her out of the limelight?) that I discovered what new money, however much of it is available, cannot do.

The girl knew practically everybody at the party – well, it was her job to – and annotated my guest-list most helpfully. We were talking about the old and the new, and she rattled off some *names* of people who would be guests at one or another of Mrs Whitney's parties, and some *kinds* of people who would not. With a target as inviting as that, I had to loose off an arrow: 'By the sound of what you're saying', I murmured, 'it seems that Donald Trump would be most unlikely to get an invitation.' Her assent to my conclusion was instant and unambiguous: 'Oh, no', she said; 'oh no.'

Is that not, I reflected, exactly the same as the ancient aristocracy of Britain, however far come down in the world, refusing to entertain people *in trade*? For it is almost a definition of being 'in trade' that those in it cannot have aristocratic family trees; likewise, the American old money would not care to rub shoulders with the new, which not only has great riches, but boasts about them. It was an instructive occasion, and it was destined to be more so before the night was out.

I harked back to the gossip columnists. True, they could lend a hand in boosting the alms-giving. Still, *gossip columnists*? At Mrs *Whitney's*? I was, of course, thinking in terms of the British ones, of whom it could be said – indeed, it is a definition of them – that they spend their lives cadging drinks off people who despise them. New York ones are rather different. First, they mostly avoid sleaze, and second, they are so many Caspar Milquetoasts when it comes to giving offence. Almost invariably, the New York ones gush rather than sneer – to the extent, indeed, that when I have been more than a week or two in New York I almost hanker for the bitching of our own. Ours, mind you, spend much of their time these days quarrelling with one another in their own pages, denouncing their rivals for getting things wrong, though they *all* get *everything* wrong, and claiming that some uninteresting item recently published elsewhere had already been published by them.

Anyway, William Norwich and Suzy were of the company, and nobody thought it odd. At least, they know not to eat peas off their knife, which is more than some of ours do. But after Norwich had made the round of the table I was at, one of my fellow-guests offered me a reminiscence. It seemed that, when Norwich was getting started, he got a job with the man who was telling the story. It was a lowly job, but no doubt welcomed by a beginner, and evidently offered a springboard. 'Yes, there he was,' my neighbour went on, 'I'd just hired him, and he was our junior employee. *And now he is one of the three or four most powerful people in this city.*'

Those seemed to me sixteen of the most amazing words I had ever heard, and they still do. A gossip columnist, however knowledgeable, with, of all things, *power*? And not just power, but as much power as the words implied? Can it be true, or even nearly true, or even slightly true? It's an alarming thought if it is, and it is also an alarming thought if it isn't but people like the man who told me think it is.

But suppose you weren't one of Mrs Whitney's friends, or a gossip columnist (incidentally, they prefer the term 'social columnists'), but you wanted to go to Mrs Whitney's party. Gatecrashing and false beards ruled out, how would you go about getting an invitation?

I don't know whether it would work with Mrs Whitney (though I don't know that it wouldn't), and in any case it would cost you $10,000. The man you would be paying the money to is a Social Publicist, and you would be paying him for a six-month period of tuition on How to Make Your Way into New York Society (it is billed more discreetly, of course). And from this he makes a living.

An odd living, surely? Our Social Publicist shrugged. He explained that if a couple comes into New York, knowing nobody in the social swim, they need guidance. He gives it.

But surely, I said, you can't just ring up some glamorous socialite who's giving a party and say, 'I want you to invite Mr and Mrs Whosit from Hicksville, Ohio?' 'Well,' he said, 'if the hostess is a close friend you sometimes can.' How else, though?

For the most part they start differently, they start on the charity circuit. They become members of various charities, they do various work for them and then they get on the committees; and that way they meet a great many people through the charities and they develop their own friends. That is probably the classic way of doing it – it would involve the Metropolitan Opera, the Boys

Clubs – anyway, one of the leading New York charities. That way you meet a great many very prominent people. But of course they themselves have to be reasonably attractive.

And reasonably rich?

That's right, you're perfectly right because you have to entertain, you have to have a certain wardrobe and all that costs money. You have to decide in advance that it can't be done on the cheap, it has to be done with a definite budget in mind.

He was modest in his claims; he said that many of his clients could have broken into the social circuit without his help, but it would have taken them five years; with his bunch of keys, the doors would swing open in one.

Then he made a claim which must strike a chord for anybody who has ever been to a big party.

Say they want to go to a particular charity party. OK, we can get them invited. But we can go a step further. We take care of our clients: we see who's going, and we see what would be suitable for them, or where they would enjoy themselves, and I can see that they are placed at a table with people who will interest them.

I reached for my cheque-book; never mind people who will interest me – can you guarantee to keep the bores away from the table I am at? Imagine the usefulness of *that* service. I warmed to him, and believed him instantly when he said that in New York there are about ten thousand hard-core (his word) party-goers, and he has the list, though depression set in when he said that most of them, when they go to a party, are working, which is why there is less drinking at New York parties than elsewhere: 'They go because they're meeting people, they've got ideas and projects, and it's really a business event under a social guise. It's not necessarily enjoyment.'

This town never stops surprising me. I had a terrible vision of huge crowds at monster parties, all drinking Perrier and hating it, and doing business in corners with other people just as depressed, and Mrs Whitney bursting into tears because none of her guests were enjoying themselves. I cheered up very slightly when he said he didn't include etiquette in his course; he assumed that his clients would know which fork to use before signing on. Then I asked him if he would take on a client who only wanted to keep his name *out* of the papers; was there, I wondered, an anti-social publicist in New York? He laughed; clearly, he thought it a very quaint idea, that anybody would not want to be in the limelight. And did *he* go to parties? The depression returned: 'Only the ones my clients are at.'

★   ★   ★

But it is tomorrow morning, and I am at Tiffany's at last, though not before making an important discovery about New York. All cities spawn madmen; the countryside only harmless village idiots. And a madman has just gone past me, at the corner of Fifth Avenue and 57th, shouting unintelligible comminations against the forces that have conspired to do him down. Since I have always held in mind my mother's profoundly significant rubric 'There's more out than in', lunatics have never troubled or alarmed me. But on this occasion I realised that *all* the lunatics I had ever encountered in New York had been very noisy, whereas London lunatics are quiet. The New York ones shout; the Londoners mutter. Why is this? Surely it is not a matter of traditional London understatement against traditional New York brashness? Possibly – a more practical solution – the general noise level in New York is such that it is essential for a lunatic to shout his lunacies if he wants them to be heard over the general din, whereas London, though noisy, is not nearly as noisy as New York, so that the *sotto voce* imprecations of the crazy Londoner can still be heard. I made a note to monitor the noise-level in London, and to see whether, as it rises, the lunatics begin to shout.

Tiffany's, then. I nerve myself for the exhausting battle to buy something in that justly famous but hopelessly inefficient emporium. This time it is a wedding present, and something in china or glass seems suitable. Taking a deep breath, I ascend to the floor where the china and glass are to be found.

Now there are many beautiful things in Tiffany's, and not only the diamond necklaces on the ground floor with price tags of a couple of hundred thousand dollars. Indeed, the china and glass department is full of tasteful and unusual things, which is why I shop there. I wandered about, untroubled by the staff asking if they could help me; this, as regular customers know, is not a matter of tact, as was demonstrated the moment I found something sufficiently beautiful for Janet and Bill. For the next stage of the Tiffany customer's ordeal is to find an assistant. But there are no assistants to be found. This is not, as it would be in many shops, because the assistants are lazy or indifferent, chatting to one another in a corner or painting their fingernails. On the contrary, the Tiffany staff are most assiduous about their duties. The problem is that every transaction takes about an hour and a half; all round the floor you can see desks at which patient customers, and presumably equally patient sales staff, are going through the ancient and infinitely prolonged ritual called buying something at Tiffany's.

First, then, you sit down. Nobody is allowed to buy anything at Tiffany's standing up. The next thing that happens (well, the next but one – the preliminary stage is the wait for a sales assistant to join you) is that the assistant pulls a form towards her and asks you for your name and address. Those unfamiliar with Tiffany's procedures are likely to make the mistake of saying that they don't want the purchase delivered, they will take it with them, so the name and address will not be needed. Oh, but they will. You'll be lucky if you aren't asked for your birth certificate or fingerprints, and I would not be in the least surprised if I were asked for two references, one of them from an ordained clergyman. Then she writes out, in duplicate, triplicate, perhaps decuplate, the details of the transaction. Then she asks how you wish to pay. Let us say that you will do so by credit card, as I did on this occasion. The girl takes the card and goes away; I should have mentioned at the outset that a book – preferably a thick one – is always useful for whiling away the hours when shopping at Tiffany's. For the girl does not come back for a very long time. She has not been kidnapped, she has not gone off for her tea-break, she has not even gone to check that the credit card or its transaction-limit is valid. She has gone on some Tiffanesque errand, part of the ritual, probably to Nebraska.

Eventually, she returns, with no explanation but with her charm undimmed – the girls at Tiffany, though you can die waiting for them, are meticulously trained. She then asks you to sign your name, and she gives you your card back. Then, the inexperienced will assume, she will produce the item you have bought, handsomely wrapped. No, no; she tears off a piece of the bill, which has a number on it, and tells you that the purchase will be found over in the corner. You go to the corner, where you find a counter with a dumb-waiter behind it. You present your numbered docket, assuming that you will be given your merchandise in return. By no means; it has not come up yet. You wait; you stroll round the shop, returning from time to time for news of your goods. You go to lunch, and linger over coffee. You return, and wait some more. Eventually, there is a rumble from the dumb-waiter, and lo! there is your prize. Then there is nothing but a sworn affidavit, a careful check of your fingerprints by the custodian, to see that the item matches the docket you have handed him, and you can leave. You may have to wait quite a long time for the elevator, in fact you will quite certainly have to wait quite a long time for the elevator, but you can leave.

That, I may say, does not exhaust the mystery of Tiffany's. They have a bizarre habit of abruptly ceasing to stock items which are attractive, popular and unaffected by fashion. They used to sell a small glass cube, some $3\frac{1}{2}$ inches square, with a single letter of the alphabet beautifully cut into one side, and frosted; the letter, in a most attractive 'face', with handsome serifs, almost entirely filled the space. They were, I suppose, paperweights, but they were handsome enough to adorn any occasional table or mantelpiece or bedside. You would tell the assistant (going through the regular ritual, of course) which letter you wanted, and some hours later you would have your purchase. One day, I asked for X. (Unlikely though it seems, I have a dear friend whose name begins with X, and I wanted a present for her.) Tiffany's, alas, could oblige me with any other of the twenty-five letters of the alphabet, but X was not stocked. I goggled, but held my peace. A year or so later, I wanted another of these delightful items, this time with a more familiar letter, but I was told that they had discontinued the entire line.

Baffled, I found another glass paperweight, unadorned by an initial but in a heart shape. As I recall, I bought it and brought it home; not long after, wanting another on another visit to New York, I went in search of it. I couldn't find it displayed, and by an astonishing chance I found an unoccupied saleswoman; I described what I was looking for and was told that she knew exactly what I meant, but the item had been discontinued. Perhaps Tiffany's are better for breakfast.

They are, as a matter of fact. There are tiny croissants, with a variety of sweet and savoury fillings, biscuits and vol-au-vents, rivers of tea and coffee, and monster strawberries proffered in abundance every time one blinked. Also a lethally delicious orange-juice cocktail, after four or five of which the absurd proceedings around me became quite endearing.

The breakfast was to celebrate the publication of a book called *The Tiffany Wedding*, by Tiffany's Director of Design, John Loring. The book covers every aspect of the nuptial process – well, all those which can be designed, though that definition can be stretched quite far, for this matrimonial guide not only includes the style of invitation cards, but etiquette itself. (The card for the invitation to the breakfast ran to twenty-two engraved lines.) To mark the book launch, Tiffany's had invited eight designers (I had actually heard of *two* of them) to design a wedding scene;

the result included *The Entrance of the Bride, The Bride's Table, The Farmer Takes a Wife, Behind the Scenes at the Wedding,* two *Morning Afters* and *A Casa de Campo Honeymoon.* There was a profusion of glass, china, silver, pots and pans, bedding, rugs, furniture, tablecloths, a splendid rural cookstove, and of course bridal gowns. I wandered lonely as a bachelor among these feasts of splicing, my ears ringing with the gasps of admiration (one or two slightly implausible) all round me, and was enjoying myself tolerably well when I turned a corner and saw The Cake.

There were several, of course, among the settings, but they were undoubtedly cakes; this one, and this only, was a Cake. That it stood four feet high and was stepped like a monument to a successful general was nothing; wedding-cakes often go higher. What gave it its unique quality was the fact that without being told nobody could have guessed that it was a cake at all. It was roughly pyramidical in shape, and covered – so thickly that only one or two gaps were left to peer through – with flowers made of marzipan, spun sugar, praline and other triumphs (if that is the word) of the confectioner's art. Greens, blues, reds, pinks, yellows, whites – every shade of every colour of the broadest imaginable spectrum was represented. It was magnificent in its stupendous awfulness, dazzling in its unashamed vulgarity, wonderful in its unrepentant 'Here stand I'. Examining it more closely (I longed to part the foliage, but didn't dare, lest moving one bloom should start a chain-reaction that would bring the whole construction to ruin), I could just see the nature of the cake itself, whereat my astonishment redoubled, for it looked – colour, texture, everything – exactly like the finest Strasbourg *foie gras.* Maybe it was. It was made by Becky Sikes of Ida Mae Cakes, and I forgot to say that each lower section of the four-fold monster was carved with sculptured patterns, and strewn with more mock flowers; in addition, equally edible lovers' knots were fixed at regular intervals right round. Surely, I thought, *surely* there cannot be a nouveau-riche family in all the country, however nouveau *or* riche, that could plumb such depths of hideous vulgarity far enough to buy it for their daughter's wedding? One thing was certain: if there were such a family, its money would be the new kind, not the old.

Reeling, I turned away, and came face to face with history. Before me stood a woman, instantly recognisable from a smile which must have been reproduced more often than that of the Cheshire Cat; ironical, too, that it should be the smile by which she is known, for her life contains a tragedy that is itself history, and will remain so. She had married two men who, for very different reasons, have a place in the world's hall of fame, and with neither, though again for different reasons, did her happiness endure. It

was like meeting one of the great mythopoeic heroines of the world –
Andromache or Brünnhilde – and I had a strange impulse to touch her.
Instead, I introduced myself.

Jacqueline Kennedy Onassis is still a most striking woman; there is something eternal about those ageless beauties like Diana Cooper and Elizabeth
von Hoffmansthal, signalled by the very fact that their beauty lasts. This
one had felt, one way or another, enough pain to wipe the smile permanently
from her face, yet there was nothing fixed or false about it, and the few
sentences we exchanged were not, at least on her part, only pleasantries.

How old *is* she? It would be ungallant to guess, let alone work it out.
Yet I challenge anyone to meet this complex, fascinating woman and not
feel the pain of her tragic life: the first, fairy-tale, marriage destroyed by
the hideous chance meeting of a madman, a window and a gun, and the
second, inexplicable, petering out amid the prurience and cruelty of the
world. One touching moment sent a stab of compassion through me;
though she paused, uncomplaining, before every photographer, she
declined, with a slow, smiling but decisive gesture, to let the television
cameras look at her. Ichabod! Ichabod!

★   ★   ★

But while we are up that end of the Avenue, there are other shops to be
visited, though without expectation of more such haunting encounters.
Here, for instance, is Bergdorf Goodman, which has had a good, and
generous, idea. Each of its windows – very striking for the most part – has
the name of the window-dresser on it; one of these is a fascinating surrealist
design, recalling both de Chirico and Magritte. And here is F.A.O. Schwarz,
which New Yorkers fondly believe to be the biggest toyshop in the world,
though it has nothing approaching the quantity or the variety of Hamley's
in London. But Schwarz has one claim which outweighs Hamley's pre-
eminence, and indeed every other claim made by any other toyshop; it has
the finest and noblest collection of stuffed toy animals anywhere. There are
life-sized lions and monkeys and St Bernard dogs and even giraffes, and
every animal has a benign and welcoming expression on its face. I don't
know how many twelve-foot giraffes they sell; possibly none. But I have
never yet been able to pass Schwarz without going in to feast my eyes and
feelings on these friendly beasts. And here is Steuben Glass, which behaves
as though it is a cathedral rather than a shop. The visitor enters, and is
immediately struck blind, a most unsettling experience. After a time, he
realises that there is nothing wrong with his eyes, but that the shop is always

---

*21 Who will open the ball?   22 Why, Mrs Whitney   23 The carriage waits, my
lord   24 The butler has been delayed, my lord   25 Your time is up: it's a* cake

1

2

23

24

26

27

bathed in stygian darkness, the better to show off the glass objects gleaming in their show-cases. Some of these are very beautiful, some – the larger glass sculptures, for instance – are as ugly and tasteless as the modern glass in Venice. (The prices are as crazy as Vuitton's, though I believe them when they say that their glass, as a substance rather than as design, is the finest in the world; measured by lead content – which, it seems, is the way to measure ornamental glass – it beats all rivals.)

The best is very good; fruit, birds, animals, abstracts – the gleaming glass springs at you as you wander the shelves, shimmering as though a touch would break it, though such glass, with its exceptionally high lead content, is very sturdy indeed. It is another of the stores that sells only one product, like that curious shop in Bond Street – Sac Frères – that offers nothing but amber (however many times I have passed it – certainly thousands – I have never seen anybody going in or coming out), and presumably thrives *because* it is the only one.

And here is that admirable tobacconist Nat Sherman, brother-in-arms of Mr Arents who made the Tobacco Collection in the New York Public Library. It is one of the friendliest and most charming stores anywhere along the Avenue, and Nat Sherman is without doubt the leading cigar-store in the United States, perhaps – indeed probably – the world. Certainly he sells cigarettes; for that matter he sells tobacco and gifts such as miniature alarm clocks and brooches. But cigars, cigars, and again cigars are his real stock-in-trade and his love. Ironically, the anti-smoking fanatics have boosted his business enormously, for all the studies have shown that if you must smoke the least unsafe thing to smoke is a cigar. But a visit to his shop on Fifth Avenue at 55th is like a visit to a very special Aladdin's cave. Everywhere there are boxes, bundles, humidorsful of cigars, from the most modest cheroot to the vastest, foot-long monster. Every variety, every brand, is kept; the staff are more knowledgeable than in any store or even specialist shop along the Avenue, and above all, everyone there – salesman and customer alike – plainly loves cigars. The cedarwood which makes the best containers for cigars has itself a lovely, crisp-sweet scent; the lovingly-rolled cigars a more powerful one which blends with but does not extinguish it; and an air of tranquillity pervades the store even at its busiest times.

And another thing: I once wanted a cigar-holder as a present for a friend who smoked them, but liked the little miniatures as well as the real thing. I wondered if there was a cigar-holder which was adjustable according to what size of cigar was being smoked, and went into Sherman's to find out. I described what I wanted, and added diffidently, 'I guess I've just described the impossible.' Nat looked at me reproachfully, and said 'Nothing's impossible'.

26 Face to face with history   27 Tiffany's-sur-Loire

From the Tiffany Ball to Nat's vastest Havanas; that is how one half lives. Now let us see how the other half does. Let us speak of beggars. *Beggars*? In New York, the richest city on earth? This needs examination; let us start at the bottom and work up.

Practically all cities, in nations rich or poor, have beggars. (I cannot remember ever seeing one in Copenhagen, or, come to that, Dakar.) The greatest concentration is in the cities of India, but it is not just poverty that has made Indian begging a gigantic industry; it is also we, the westerners, with our pity and guilt. Any western hotel in any Indian city has to have doormen to sweep the steps of beggars as they would of litter or leaves, and a taxi with a white face in the passenger seat, should it stop at a traffic light, will instantly be covered by children crying out for alms. (On my early visits to India the slogan invariably chanted – it was probably the only English the children had – was 'One rupee, one rupee'. Now it is 'one dollar, one dollar'. There are about nine rupees to a dollar, so the change may be attributed either to inflation or to the greater proportion of American visitors to India, whichever seems more convenient.)

Still, we are not in Calcutta, but in New York. The flip-side of America's success culture, of her enterprise and rational economic self-regard, is the penalty for failure – harsher, I think, than anywhere else.

First, let me describe the effect of such a penalty imposed upon the particular miscreant who had incurred it. I was walking down Fifth Avenue, on the Park side, towards my dinner. It had been raining heavily most of the day, but it had paused for the moment, though the thick cloud suggested that there was more to come. I came abreast of one of the benches that line the eastern edge of the Park. Somebody had stacked a row of bundles or sacks on it, and covered the lot with a couple of black plastic sheets, which would clearly not be voluminous enough, when the rain returned, to keep it off the sacks, which I had assumed was garbage, left tidily for the trash-wagons.

I wasn't all that far wrong, for as I passed the bench, the bundles moved. The instant of horror – was it snakes? – was succeeded by a realisation hardly less horrific. A human being, who had no bed but the bench, and no bedclothes but a few scraps of plastic, had settled down for the night, hoping, undoubtedly in vain, that the rain would keep off. This, then, was one item of garbage that the trash-wagon would not collect on its rounds.

Very well; London, though no New York, is also no mean city, and there are homeless people in it. Some of these sleep in cardboard boxes under the railway arches of Charing Cross, and an American on the defensive might say that we are more hypocritical, confining our homeless to such an area rather than allowing them to take shelter in the doorways of Piccadilly or Bond Street. Nor is it satisfactory for London to say – though it is true – that there is accommodation available for the troglodytes in their cardboard caves, and that many of them refuse, to the point of violence, to accept any roof over their heads other than the thundering of the trains, for a now celebrated law-suit in New York ended with a homeless woman in exactly the same situation, insisting on her right to sleep under the stars, and having that right upheld by the law itself. Nor, incidentally, is London's point met by saying – though this is also true – that the person on the bench (I never did discover whether it was a man or a woman, having been brought up never to enter anyone's home uninvited) was living in the soft comforts of unimaginable luxury compared to the homeless of Calcutta.

The debate continues. For many years, I have seen a beggar in Fifth Avenue – a black man, always upright and squarely in the middle of the pavement, facing downtown. He is accompanied by a sleepy black dog, always curled up at his feet, and he has a tray on his chest, with a sign attached to it reading 'I am blind. Buy a pencil'. The invitation, obviously, is rarely accepted; people put money in his tin cup without taking a pencil. 'One dollar, one dollar'; but here is where we part company with the Indian beggar, corrupted by our hush money, and also with the bag-ladies and the bench-dwellers, corrupted in a different sense by our indifference, and finally with the blind black man in Fifth Avenue with his pencils and his upright stance, which suggest that though he has lost his sight and his living he has not lost his self-respect.

For there is another class of New York beggar, the beggar-by-choice. I counted them in a stretch of some forty blocks; for every two down-and-outs, displaying cards with such messages as 'I am homeless and hungry', there were three who were, almost without exception, young, fit, clean, decently – almost smartly – dressed; *and begging*. Their patter did not take the form of telling their woes – unemployment, eviction, disability; it took no form at all, being restricted to a standard, unambiguous appeal for passers-by to give them money.

Two of them have stayed in my mind. As I was about to cross East 55th Street I saw a young woman – in her early thirties, I guessed – standing at the kerb on the other side of the street. She was dressed in a clean white blouse under a clean, un-holed sweater, and a no less clean blue skirt. Her shoes, though not, perhaps, of the latest fashion, were smart and not down-at-heel. If it had not been for the fact that I was stopped at the roadway waiting for the traffic-lights to change, I would have walked straight past her. My pause meant that I noticed her consciously, because I heard what she was saying. She was saying, in clear, untroubled tones, 'Has anybody got any pennies, or change?' She did not look ill, or haggard, or starved. She did not look happy, but she did not look unhappy either; she was matter-of-fact almost to the point of being bored. But above all, there was not the slightest trace of embarrassment in her appearance or her voice.

An image rose instantly to my mind's eye. In Vittorio de Sica's film *Bicycle Thieves*, there is an elderly teacher, out of work and without means. After a struggle with himself, he realises that he has no other course but to beg. He goes out, takes up a stance under a shop-awning, and waits. Along comes a man who looks sufficiently prosperous to be a potential alms-giver. The old man puts out his cupped hand, palm upwards; as the passer-by draws level, sees the beggar and puts his hand into his pocket, the old man is overwhelmed by shame; he turns his hand over and looks up at the sky, pretending that he was only putting his hand out to see if it was raining.

That was not all. One evening, I had been to La Réserve for dinner (an excellent one), and I was walking up Fifth Avenue; it was a fine night. There was a young man walking briskly the other way; as he stopped in front of me, I saw that he was dressed in clean jeans and a clean white shirt, and clean sneakers. I noticed his hair; it was fairly long, and blond, and had clearly been very recently washed. He was also clean-shaven. More to the point, he was smiling, and there was nothing strained, ironic, crazy or aggressive about the smile; it was the innocent, friendly smile of a pleasant, carefree young man out for a walk on a warm evening. Then he said 'Have you any change?' I was so astonished that, without thinking, I took a handful of coins out of my pocket and gave them to him. He said 'Thank you', not perfunctorily but with real warmth, and added, no less warmly, 'Have a nice evening'.

I went on my way; before I had time to weigh properly what I had just experienced, I realised that I was going in the wrong direction, down the Avenue instead of up. I turned round and retraced my steps; a few moments later I met the young man again. He recognised me as the benefactor of a recent encounter, and said again, as heartily and pleasantly as could be wished, 'Have a nice evening'.

I had already had a nice evening; the rest of it was to be a puzzled one. The sturdy beggars constituted a phenomenon that I had not previously encountered; the two I have described were only two of a considerable number. And only one conclusion was to hand. I suppose some of them were out of work, some perhaps, though their neatness surely belied the possibility, were homeless, some, though here credulity retires, were hungry (none, incidentally, looked or sounded in the least drunk or drugged); most of them were manifestly not labouring under any of those disabilities. They begged because they wanted to beg, because they had decided that that way of getting a living was preferable to the more usual ways, such as working.

It was clear that New Yorkers have ceased to notice the beggars, even those who beg from preference; indeed, one man I met at a party insisted that I was imagining it all, and I went to the extreme lengths of suggesting that he should walk down Fifth Avenue with me the following morning and count the sturdy beggars with me. (He said he was too busy.)

I had been watching the begged-from as closely as the beggars, and the pattern was the same whether the plea was answered or ignored; not only the broken down-and-out beggars with their piteous placards, but also the able-bodied ones with their clean clothes and casual bearing, were treated with almost universal absent-mindedness. If a passer-by, appealed to, walked on, he did so without embarrassment, guilt or anger, as though he had literally not seen or heard the beggar; more striking was the response of those who did contribute, for it was identical – the money was tossed into the proffered receptacle or passed from hand to hand, and the giver walked on exactly as if no such transaction had taken place.

People's lives can change dramatically from good fortune to misery, from confidence to fear, above all from riches to poverty; that knowledge is as old as the last line of *Oedipus Rex*. (Older, in fact, because Sophocles was quoting.) It is, of course, possible to envisage men or women, hitherto independent, reduced by some catastrophe to begging; but the memory of the days when they stood on their own feet and earned their own bread would stab them with pain and horror every time they held out their hands, like the old man in the film. Then there are those – I saw many of them, too, in Fifth Avenue – who had fallen through the final hole; they begged without shame because they were without feeling – hopeless, exhausted, uncaring. I can envisage myself, with some difficulty, brought to ruin and forced to beg; with even more difficulty, I can think of myself as sinking beyond shame; but by no stretching of the imagination, though I were to stretch it till it twanged and snapped, can I think of myself willingly embarking upon a life of begging without being forced to, only because it seems easier than digging holes in the streets, serving in a shop or delivering the mail.

New York is a city of live and let live; if young and capable men and women *want* to beg, nobody is going to try to stop them. No-one, after all, is obliged to contribute. (I gave the young man money, but thereafter gave only to the needy; it didn't do any good, though – every time I refused and walked by I felt guilty.) But surely *thought* has not been banished from Fifth Avenue? Does nobody stop to reflect on the meaning of this strange practice? It is certainly of recent origin, and I have never encountered it in any other prosperous country. Perhaps the American way has two flip-sides, or flips back, as in a conjuring-trick, to reveal a new side altogether. If anyone, by hard work and determination, can succeed (in monetary terms, anyway) and be admired, and anyone who fails to become affluent is of no regard and can be ignored, then perhaps those who have decided that they can succeed in this very curious vocation are tolerantly accepted into the ordinary and unsurprising ranks of ordinary and unsurprising entrepreneurs.

Israel Zangwill wrote a short story called *The King of the Schnorrers* ('schnorrer' is a Yiddish word meaning beggar), and certainly the hero feels no shame in his profession; rather, he takes great pride in it. He pledges £100 for his daughter's dowry – a huge sum at that date even for an affluent family – when he has nothing at all; having put up the promise, he has to schnorr the entire sum, and succeeds in doing so, amid the admiration of all. And perhaps we shall see a modern version of the tale; perhaps business magazines, after recording the fortunes of the twenty richest men in the United States, will list the incomes of the most successful beggars. At any rate, I shall not be surprised if one day I am browsing in Doubleday's on Fifth Avenue, in the section devoted to the vast variety of ways to become rich, and come upon a manual called *How to Beg*.

I come back to a question more obvious but less bizarre, than that of the sturdy beggars. I was shocked by the latter; but I was shocked, for other reasons, by the more conventional pleaders for alms, and more lastingly shocked, too. Poverty is always relative; the man who lives on the pavement in Calcutta does not say, when a millionaire in a Rolls-Royce goes by, 'I wish I was a millionaire with a Rolls-Royce.' But when a man with two crusts of bread goes by he does say, 'I wish I had one crust of bread.' At the same time, he knows that his father was worse off than he is, and his grandfather worse still. And that is why I am shocked by the number of *in*voluntary beggars in New York; they are everywhere, and they have no relativity to measure themselves against. They have only the affluent who pass them, and they know that not one in a thousand who go by, whether they give or not, will murmur those echoing words, 'There but for the grace of God, go I'.

I forgot to mention that the bench on which the human rubbish sacks had settled down for the night was exactly opposite the Frick Museum. I don't know whether that makes the matter worse or better.

*   *   *

I emerged from my hotel into a sunny morning. Parked a few yards along the kerb was a car. Fixed inside the window was a sign reading 'No radio'. I had frequently been seeing this message on parked cars – the point of it was that it was no use breaking into the car to steal the radio because there wasn't one. Hitherto, however, the messages had all been on pieces of paper or cardboard, taped or stuck to the window. This one was different. It was a grey metal plate, some nine inches by four, screwed to the window-frame, with a neat black line for a border, and the message to thieves embossed in red on the body of the plate. Hardware and office stores stock such things, which say 'Knock and enter', or 'No smoking', or 'Manager'. If some entrepreneur is making them, to read 'No radio', in this very permanent form, then this city is in trouble.

This city *is* in trouble. Any city that has had thirteen bank-robberies in one day (four of them in one hour), or has eighteen hundred *serious* crimes reported every day, five of them being murder, is in trouble, serious trouble. No bones about it, either, are made in this passage:

> Every year 500,000 purses [handbags] and wallets, and 100,000 cars, are reported stolen in New York City ... Your first line of defense is to be well informed. If you thoroughly familiarize yourself with the city, you are ... less likely to accidentally get into a trouble area ... Walk on well-lit streets and near the curb. Avoid dark doorways, loitering groups. If confronted, step (carefully) into the street ... Stay away from parks and park entrances after dark ... plan your route, then walk with confidence, never hesitating or wandering into unfamiliar areas ... If you are alone and you think you are being followed, go into an occupied place immediately. If confronted by a mugger ... it is probably best to co-operate – hand over your valuables ... If a suspicious-looking character gets onto your elevator, get off on a busy floor and wait for another ... When driving through a dark neighborhood, keep doors locked, windows rolled up (actually a good idea in *any* neighborhood) ... Carry as little cash and as few credit cards as possible ... *Never* display money in public!

That was from a perfectly ordinary guidebook, one of its functions presumably being to encourage people to visit New York. It is argued in defence of New York (when, that is, it isn't adduced as an extra condemnation) that New Yorkers, though their city is not top of the American crime rate list, have talked themselves into the conviction that it is the most dangerous place on earth. As Saul Miller, in his *New York City Street Smarts*, puts it:

> It seems unlikely that in Phoenix or in Seattle ... it would be considered the norm to have three locks on your door ...; to have metal bars on all ground-level windows and steel gratings on all other windows that face onto fire escapes; to make access to an apartment building more difficult for visitors than entry to maximum security wings of prisons ... to have cab drivers separated from their passengers by bulletproof ... barriers ... Where else but here do you take out your keys a block before you reach your apartment? ... Can it be possible that elsewhere parents give children 'mugger's money' each time they leave the house as a matter of course?

Well, whether they do all that in Phoenix and Seattle (both of which have crime rates *higher* than that of New York★), they certainly do here. After the Tiffany Ball, I announced my intention — it was a fine, warm evening — of walking back to my hotel. It was unanimously agreed that I was mad. I explained that my hotel was on 76th Street (the Plaza, where the Ball took place, is on 59th), that I was going to walk up Fifth, that I knew enough not to walk on the Park side of the Avenue, and that I had done such a walk at such a time of night quite frequently, with no untoward consequences. Their belief in my insanity was based on an unshakable belief that what I was proposing to do was quite unacceptably dangerous, and that I was inexcusably irresponsible, even if not suicidal.

And yet there *are* five murders every day in New York City. There are roughly 650 murders a year in the whole of Britain. Multiplying for population, we arrive at the conclusion that the murder rate in New York alone is 1600 per cent higher than it is in Britain.† That needs explaining. Particularly, I may say, because New York's gun laws are among the toughest in the nation. And I know, because I visited a shooting-range, and was told that I could not practise shooting, with a hand-gun, even in a properly-run, authorised, shooting-range, without a licence. And the granting of the licence, I learned, was not just a formality. The people in charge of the range were polite but implacable; that was the law. On the other hand, they said, if you really want to practise shooting, all you have to do is to go over to Connecticut, where you can just walk in, get a gun and blaze away.

★ I am sorry about Seattle, a most charming and friendly town.
† The British total *includes* the sectarian and terrorist killings in Northern Ireland.

I wandered about the range. It was plastered with what might be described as recruiting posters for the National Rifle Association. The NRA, of course, has for many years been one of the most effective and successful lobbies in the United States; again and again, when gun control legislation was under discussion, either in particular states or cities or federally, the NRA has marshalled its troops, its tame congressmen, its TV advertising, its letter-writers and its lies, and succeeded in blocking the legislation every time. (The posters said 'I'm NRA, and I vote'; 'Never disarm'; 'Register to vote – your gun rights depend on it'.)

And yet, though the people who run the NRA must make any dispassionate observer think lovingly of the ancient practice of lynching, the laxity of gun laws, appalling though it is, and enormous though its contribution to American murder rates is, cannot be the whole explanation, cannot be even most of the explanation, of the level of murderous violence in the cities of the United States.

Then what is? The next line of defence for New York, and the United States in general, is, of course: drugs. It is well known that addicts of hard drugs will do anything, including robbery and murder, to get the money with which they can buy the next fix. Much of the violent crime, then, is directly attributable to the drugs epidemic, which is certainly worse in the United States than anywhere else on earth. (What caused *that* is another important question which doesn't seem to have an answer.) Yet even the drugs explanation cannot be the correct one, since the drugs epidemic itself is of comparatively recent origin, and the murder rate, though it was lower before the drug wave, was still far higher than in any other fully civilised country.

But that leads me to another, and much more dramatic, debate going on in the United States. There is now a body of serious opinion which advocates legitimising the hard drugs. The argument goes as follows: the drugs are now very expensive, and there is an enormous amount of crime that can properly be attributed to those who rob or kill for the money to satisfy the craving. If the drugs were legally available, the price would fall dramatically, and no-one would need to commit crimes to be able to buy them.

This is, in a sense, a very loud echo of the British system of 'registered addicts'; these can get their drug on prescription; and at a comparatively trivial cost, so that no-one on the register has to murder his grandmother for it. But what is now proposed in America (the argument has been raised in Britain, too, though it has made little stir as yet) goes much further. The counter-arguments are obvious: though heroin may become cheaper, it will still not be within the reach of many who will still have to commit crimes to get it, and many law-abiding citizens who are now deterred from trying illegal drugs might turn to legal ones. I think it is inconceivable that such a reversal of policy could be made, or that the American legislature (let alone the British) would countenance it. But I have no solution to the drugs problem, which now affects practically every country in the world. For that matter, I have no solution to the mystery of how and why it happened, and I have never come upon any solution to that mystery, any more than to the other one.

Next, 'organised crime', a quaint euphemism. 'The Mafia', a phrase to strike a chill in any heart, kills not only by contract but in the course of its less spectacular business; in addition, intergang-warfare not only improves the chances of gang members getting shot, which is greatly to be welcomed, but ensures that a substantial number of innocent bystanders get shot too, which isn't. Yet the gangs cannot solve the problem, either, if only because most murders are plainly not the result of gang-crime or gang-warfare.

The figures suggest that murder is much more often than not a family matter, or a matter among neighbours, or among casual acquaintances and passers-by. Lately, Americans, while driving, have taken to shooting other drivers for incommoding, overtaking or bumping them. This, though, is only an extension of the 'family and neighbours' slice of the cake. Much newer are the gangs of young people whose *only* wish seems to be to kill members of rival gangs; this seems to have begun in Los Angeles, and spread to other cities. But although that kind of warfare will again put the rate up, it suffers, as an explanation, from the same logical defect as all the other possibilities: the murder rate was unacceptably high before the new casualties began to be counted.

Then there is the belief that the 'frontier spirit' still operates, so that Americans keep and use firearms because they are likely at any minute to meet a grizzly bear, a herd of bison or a squadron of hostile Indians; unlikely. For that matter, the decline of religion is widely believed to be a cause of crime, and no doubt it is also blamed on sunspots, the predictions of Nostradamus and the Jews.

It was time to stop theorising and find out what crime actually means on Fifth Avenue. The Holmes Detective Agency seemed the best place to start, and when I learned that it hires out bodyguards, there seemed an appealing symmetry in talking first to one of them and then to one of their clients: the bodyguard and the bodyguarded.

Jack O'Reilly was not at all like a television detective; he had been a policeman, and when he retired from the force he found that going fishing every day got to be boring. So he used his experience (he had been assigned to guard duty, as a policeman, for the New York visits of the Pope and the Emperor Hirohito) to set up as a private bodyguard. Do you carry a gun? Yes, this is a Smith and Wesson 38; I carried it while I was with the Police Department, so I am more comfortable with it than with anything else, though I do carry a nine-millimetre, and sometimes a shotgun, depending on the job. And have you ever had to use them? No; and if I did, I would feel that I hadn't done my job properly, because I think it's a preventive job, being able to spot the bad guy in the crowd before anything happens.

But you may get shot?

The possibility is always there, but I could also have been shot any time when I was a policeman for twenty-two years – I did undercover work in vice and narcotics and organised crime. If I was asking for trouble, I would be maybe walking a tightrope or swinging from a trapeze, but my training with the police is such that I don't think anybody is going to get me. And I am living and working with people that are usually very wealthy, so I'm living their lifestyle and they are picking up the tab for it. What makes the work interesting is not the possibility of getting shot, you know. And I get top dollar. Anyway, it was much more dangerous on the streets of New York as a police officer than it is being a bodyguard. You're not hanging out in the neighbourhoods where people are throwing bombs or shooting people in the streets, or throwing cinder blocks on the tops of the radio cars and setting them on fire; in this job, you're maybe looking for somebody who is mentally ill and looking to hurt the person you're guarding, or maybe you're looking to a kidnap. It's safer than being a cop. But not anybody can hire me. First, they have to be able to afford me. Second, I have worked all my life fighting crime, so I am not for hire as a bodyguard for anyone who is doing anything that is illegal . . . And I'm a non-violent person, if I use my gun I know it will be because I have to. I know the law; if I had to do it, it would be because I was doing it to save someone's life. At some point, maybe, I will become scared one day and wake up and think 'Wow, this is a pretty dangerous job and I am vulnerable', and at that point I will probably just call up and say 'That's it'. And go fishing.

And the client? Malcolm Sheppard was an expatriate Englishman, with an international business and an office in New York. And why did he need a bodyguard?

One of my employees, on hard drugs, tried to extort money from me, with a gun at my head. My secretary called the police, and they came; he had the gun in a folded newspaper, and they frisked him and found it, and they threw him in the back of the police car. He was taken down and booked, and that night I got a call from him – they're allowed a phone call – and he actually called me to ask would I bail him out. He had an extensive record with quite bad felonies – armed bank robbery, assault, drug charges. And he was bailed before the Grand Jury, and that's where it started. He threatened to kill me, turned up at my workplace, turned up at my wife's workplace, phone calls day and night, kept calling the office, saying 'Drop the charges or I'm coming down.' So that's how I got involved with bodyguards, from the Holmes Detective Agency.

And what was it like, living with a permanent bodyguard?

Horrible! It's not that comfortable, having someone with you twenty-four hours a day, in your own house, especially when you have a family, a child, and some guy you don't know sitting in your living-room, because there's someone might come in and try to kill you. They are dedicated guys, I mean, I felt safe with them, but I kept saying to myself, well, like, this can't go on for ever, it's not cheap, you know. We contacted the police several times, but they weren't really concerned. Something has to happen for them to do something. So if I'd been murdered, they'd come. But that would be too late, right? And till then, it would be Legal Aid saying, 'Well, that's against the guy's civil rights, he hasn't actually done anything.' It went on for six months, and eventually he got sentenced – not just for my thing but for several others. He could be on the streets in about a year's time. And I'm very visible, he knows the name of my company, it's pretty easy to find me in the Yellow Pages. But in New York this isn't a major thing; what happened to me happens to hundreds of people every day. It's out of control, it's getting scarier every week. There's no respect for the law, so the law doesn't care. I was scared for my life, I wasn't going to die for this guy, just by saying 'I don't need anybody'. I had the sense to protect myself, because the police weren't going to do it. Trouble about two weeks ago; my partner fired a guy, he'd smashed a van up, he was continually late, you know, and the guy went for my partner. 'I know where you are,' he says, 'I'm going to burn your car, I'm going to burn your building down.' We called the police, and they said 'Nah, let us know if something happens.' What are you supposed to do? They're all out of their minds, no discipline, their schooling's disgusting, no respect, and this is the most corrupt city in the world. The city is totally corrupt. Twenty of its highest ranking city workers have been indicted on fraud charges. I pay outrageous taxes, and there's people on welfare with three different social security numbers, claiming for five different kids and the dog – they'll get away with whatever they can get away with, and if they get caught it's just 'Don't do it again'. The

West Indians fight with the Italians, the Italians fight with the Puerto Ricans, all the dirty work is being done by the minorities now, running around with the drugs. I'm a big guy, I mean, like physically – one on one with a guy without a weapon I wouldn't be too much concerned. But you don't know, these people are crazed. The bodyguards cost me thirty dollars an hour, twenty-five, twenty-eight thousand, it's a lot of money. And when the guy gets out, what's he got to lose? He'll come back again. And there was another thing, one of the bodyguards, he was a weirdo, he *wanted* something to happen, he wanted someone to go down, you could see it in his mind, he wanted to hurt the guy, and he called up and actually said to him, if you come down here there's only two ways you'll leave, one's in handcuffs and the other's in a pine box. And he would have gone for the pine box scene, right off. He was a brilliant bodyguard, sure, but he wanted something to happen. He thought he was still in Vietnam.

The cool words of the bodyguard, professional to the tip of the barrel of his Smith and Wesson, contrasted luridly with the stifling rage of the guarded. From him, there poured out a flood of resentment, the inevitable resentment of the law-abiding and hard-working citizen against the criminal and the wastrel. The minorities, the poor on Welfare, the corrupt rulers of the city (he even said that Koch was corrupt, whereas even the Mayor's enemies agree, even as they count the indictments of his appointees, that Koch is one of the few mayors of this marvellous and terrible city who has never been on the take) – these are the cause of his misfortune. The harassed and overworked police, accused of indifference; the law which offers a multiple felon the protection of his civil rights and legal aid to protect them all the better; the lenient judges who will let his implacable pursuer out very soon now; 'they' and 'them' and 'those'; the enemies who thus collude with the criminals have conspired to do him down.

In a sense he is right; they have. New York is out of control, and his boiling anger is the anger of a man who, because he believes in order (see how disturbed he was at the attitude of the trigger-happy bodyguard), believes that there must be a visible causal reason for the condition of the city, and he lashes out at every passing possibility. His accusations are unjust, of course, or at least only accidentally justified – criminals among the ethnic minorities are not criminals *because* of their origin, and the fraudulent welfare claimants are not siphoning off so much money from the city treasury that there is none left for the maintenance of law and order. But if his cure is meaningless, his diagnosis is faultless: New York is a city in which, because jogging-for-health is widely popular, the guidebooks give helpful information about the best kind of running-shoes to wear, urge runners to check the weather forecast, remind their readers to run facing oncoming traffic, and then lay down this no less important principle:

> Run with determination; it may discourage muggers, attackers and rapists.

And so it may, for all I know.

But there are other variations on the theme. There is, for instance, an advertisement for a rape-counselling service; their posters, which are very striking, are everywhere, particularly on the buses. At the top it says, in quotation marks, 'Rape only happens to other people'. A variation on a familiar cliché; but the cliché was at once wrenched, starkly, into a different and unforgettable form. Beneath 'Rape only happens to other people', the other people were listed, without quote marks or comment: your sister, your mother, your grandmother, your girlfriend, your daughter, your wife. Then it summed up with the rubric, 'Arm yourself with awareness'. On the poster I was looking at somebody had crossed out 'awareness' and written above it 'a 38'.

It was time for me to handle a 38, and see what it felt like. I returned to the shooting range, this time with clearance from the police. First, I talked to the owner, Jerry Preisner, a friendly, eloquent figure (I would say disarming if it were not inappropriate) with no touch of the fanatic. I asked him how easy it was to get a licence to carry a gun in New York, and how easy it was, licence or no licence, to get hold of one. His answer was crisp:

> The City of New York is probably the most difficult city in the world to get a licence from. Unfortunately, only the rich and the famous get pistol licences, like Donald Trump and Arthur Sulzberger and Winthrop Rockefeller.

Come, come, I thought, and indeed said. Isn't this the familiar grouch about the rich? Who says that these august figures have guns, when poor Honest Joe can't get one? I had forgotten about the admirable American Freedom of Information Act; the gun lobby had used it to discover who in New York had a gun licence, and it turned out that by and large it was the people who, surrounded by security every minute of their lives, needed it least.

Though, as I have indicated, I feel that the best and most fitting treatment for the leaders of the National Rifle Association (a fraudulent title anyway) is a public and collective hanging, Preisner made a good case for the citizen with a gun. For one thing, misuse of a *licensed* gun in New York is so negligibly small that the authorities have given up collecting the data. For another, it seems that the background check for anyone who applies for a licence is very thorough. And again, there was the 'Orlando experiment', in which the police of that town, after a series of gun crimes, worked with a selection of some hundreds of innocent citizens, training them in gun use. The crime rate fell abruptly and substantially. Hear Jerry Preisner again:

> A criminal is not seeking to go against someone who can defend himself. They seek the infirm, the aged, the young, the helpless. They're not interested in someone who has the ability to give them back what they are trying to do. I'm not advocating that everybody have a firearm, but when you have more civilians that are trained and have the guns and it's publicised the criminals will just have to do something else.

And he summed up with the most plausible defence his case has:

> All the bad guys already have the guns. The good guys are unable to be licensed. So you have disarmed the legitimate citizen and you have made no impact at all on the criminal community.

The same views were expressed, more subtly, by Larry Wilson, who has the advantage of being one of the world's leading experts on guns ancient and modern. Like all real experts, he was in love with his subject and modest about his accomplishments; a slim, elegant figure, he complemented Preisner, the bluff, typical Jewish New Yorker. I felt that if those two set up in business as a debating-team against gun control the other side would be hard put to it to match them. (As it happened, I was in New York when the gun world, pro and contra, was in the throes of a delightful tragicomedy. An unarmed young man had been shot, not fatally, while apparently trespassing, without, it seems, criminal intent; the householder had opened fire. A common occurrence in the United States, of course, but on this occasion worth all the headlines it commanded, for the householder, who had blazed off, without a gun licence, was Carl T. Rowan, the liberal newspaper columnist, one of whose most constant and vigorous campaigns was for more gun control. Naturally, the gun lobby was having a high old time, especially as Rowan was defending himself on gun-lobby terms – protect my family, right of all law-abiding citizens, etc., etc.)

I asked Larry Wilson whether it was valid to say that the history of the gun was to some extent the history of the United States, and he said 'Yes, it is; one way to look at it is if we didn't have the firearms we'd probably be weaving Indian baskets today', a remark which I realised only later was quite extraordinarily ambiguous. Wilson went further than Preisner on the need for legitimate citizens (interestingly, he too used the world 'civilians') to undergo some kind of formal training in the use of the guns he believed they should have a right to possess. He also put two startling figures on the problem: he estimated that there were 200 to 250 million guns in the country in private hands, and that 50 million households held firearms.

Had he himself ever been mugged? I *think* he blushed slightly as he said he had been mugged in the Lady Godiva chocolate shop at Christmas time; fancy the world's leading expert on guns having his pocket picked amid the pralines, the truffles, the orange creams and the liqueurs!

He was holding a box as we talked, and plainly couldn't refrain from opening it; when he showed me what it held I was transfixed by its beauty. It was, he said, built to an antique pattern of a gun called a 'dragoon'; the original had been made by Colt in his London factory. (I said I didn't know that Colt worked in London, and was delighted to learn that the factory was where the Tate Gallery stands today. Why is it that these tiny, accidental details of history remain in the mind for ever while the great currents that make the world become hazy? I have always maintained that the only two dates that *everybody* in Britain knows are November the Fifth – though few could fit the year to it – and 1066. But I got a nasty shock when a survey revealed that today some 40 per cent of schoolchildren *don't* know the date of the Battle of Hastings.) Anyway, the gun – long, slim and perfectly proportioned – was a miracle of steel, silver and gold. Larry explained that it was a present for Gene Autry, the old cowboy film star, from his wife; Autry, who preceded John Wayne in the role of the sheriff who rides off into the sunset at the end of the film, having shot the bad guys and saved the good guys, was to be eighty-one in a few days' time, and the whole thing had been done in secret, with letters in plain envelopes sent to Mrs Autry marked Personal.

The gilding and decoration had been entrusted to Tiffany's, and they had made it into a stunning work of art. It was encased rather than inlaid, with fantastic decorations in gold and silver – patterns, pictures, devices, whorls and curlicues, with Gene Autry's signature reproduced in a fine line of silver on the butt. I held it, and nearly dropped it, surprised by the enormous weight; Larry explained that that was the quantity of gold and silver that had been used. I could imagine the pleasure with which the old cowboy star would open his birthday present. Larry, incidentally, mentioned that Tiffany, who had been making and decorating swords and guns in the middle of the nineteenth century, had designed a pair for General Custer. A fat lot of good they had done him.

28 The bag lady settles down for the night

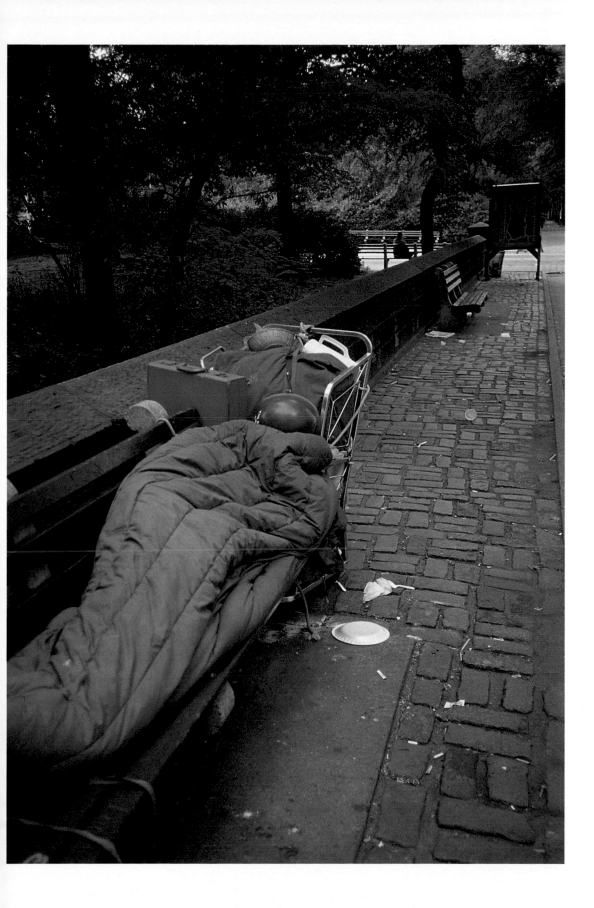

29

31

I handled the beautiful gun once more, and murmured that it would almost be a pleasure to be shot by it. 'Well,' said Larry, 'I do have some silver bullets.'

★   ★   ★

And now, at last, tethering his horse at one of the posts outside the saloon, Sheriff Levin, fingering his badge thoughtfully, enters in search of the badmen. Preisner's shooting range is clearly run very well and very strictly. Everywhere, there are signs and posters – a score or more in one form or another – repeating the safety rules: what you must *never* do in any circumstances and what you *must* do at all times. It could be said, of course, that this is no more than commercial prudence; if people were shot there through carelessness the place would be promptly closed down. But why should not commercial prudence rule? The result, wherever the impulse came from, was clearly a rigorous, almost fanatical, attention to safety.

'Now', said Jerry Levene, my teacher in the art of shooting, 'the first thing you do when you pick up a gun is make sure that you keep your fingers well away from the trigger. The next thing is to make sure it is always pointing down-range, and the third thing is that you open the cylinder.' He demonstrated the action, and the revolving magazine swung open. 'You push it right out', he said, 'and you look to see that there is no bullet in any of the six chambers. *Then*, you are ready to load.'

He showed me, with great care and three times, how you push each bullet firmly into the chamber. 'Now you shut the cylinder back into its housing, and turn it till it locks. It locks with a distinct click, and you don't do *anything at all* until you hear that click.' I followed his instructions, and the click was audible. 'Right,' he said, 'you now have a loaded gun, which is a lethal instrument, and you've got to obey all the instructions *exactly* from this moment on.'

Things were getting quite exciting, but the air of calm that Jerry exuded was wonderfully reassuring. He showed me, on an empty gun, how to cock it, how to keep my fingers away from the trigger until I was ready to fire, how to apply the pressure which would shoot the first bullet.

The weapon was a 38, the standard issue for the New York Police (I was soon to see one drawn for real); I was now almost ready to fire it. One more instruction from Jerry: 'When you're shooting on a range like this, you count the shots yourself, for obvious reasons – if you miscount, you could leave a bullet in the chamber, something could go wrong. So you count up to six.'

29 Demonstrating   30 Demonstration   31 New York's finest

The shooting point at the range resembled nothing so much as a row of British election polling-booths; the shooter entered one, from which he could not see the voters on either side of him. The ledge on which he marked his ballot was there to rest his elbow on if he wanted thus to steady his aim. Then he – I – pointed my gun at the target, and pulled the trigger.

I have gone into such detail, though I realise that many of my readers will be well acquainted with some kind of firearms and the drill for using them, for a purpose. I had, in my schooldays, been taught to fire a rifle, using ·22 bullets. I retained no clear memory of the training, and I had not held any kind of gun in my hands except when, on my journey *To the End of the Rhine*,* I fell in with the Black Forest huntsmen who, having kitted me out in their uniform, thought they might as well supply a gun, too. (Though, being unlicensed, I was forbidden to fire it, and didn't.)

The world had changed, in some ways by no means for the better, since I was a schoolboy. The level of violent crime in Britain, never mind the United States, had risen beyond anything that could have been imagined only a few decades before. The idea of a gun, if not the object, is familiar to millions; so, now, is the idea of its use, even in Britain. It is no longer strange to think of law-abiding people wanting guns; it is no longer impossible to believe that Britain's police will one day carry arms on the beat. It is no longer very unlikely that most of us will sooner or later face a criminal who is willing and able to do violence in the course of his crime.

I am a man steeped in the arbitrament of words, an advocate of free speech even for villains, a believer in persuasion rather than force, of armed deterrence rather than armed conflict (*si vis pacem, para bellum*). But I had in my hand an instrument that would, if I pointed it at another human being and pulled the trigger, kill him. You may say that every time I pick up a knife to cut my meat I have in my hand an instrument that would do the same, even though more messily. Yes, but the knife is not *made* to kill, even though it has often been pressed into such homicidal purpose, and the gun has no other function; it is a lethal weapon and *only* a lethal weapon, whether used for aggression or defence. How did I feel before I pulled the trigger, and how after?

Before, nothing; I was too busy concentrating on the rules, the safety provisions and my tuition. But then I pulled the trigger, felt the mild kick of the recoil in my hand, and heard the shot. As I blazed away at the target (I did not prove myself an overnight champion shootist, but I did get four of the six shots on to the foot-square target), I cannot deny that I felt the

---

* Cape, 1987.

excitement. The recoil heightened it, proving as it did that I was using real ammunition, not blanks; there was a distinctly recognisable feeling of power, inextricably entwined with a slight feeling of guilt.

Not surprising, I suppose; urban and peaceful man is at a loss (and a damned good thing, too) when a killing instrument is put into his hand. Urban and peaceful man is *always* at a loss when he faces, or even suspects, that he is capable, in certain circumstances, of becoming less urban and even less peaceful. I did not begin, even slightly, to see myself as Gregory Peck in *High Noon* (or even Gene Autry twirling his birthday present by the trigger-guard), and I am quite certain that I do not want to own a gun of any kind, much less carry one, even if I were to live in New York, crime level or no crime level. But I did have a very slight, but unmistakable, feeling that if I *did* live in New York, I might find myself signing up at Mr Preisner's shooting-range and going along on a Saturday afternoon, say, and spending a couple of hours popping away at the target.

Or possibly I wouldn't. The ingenious Jerry Preisner has devised a form of indoor warfare that might be designed for people like me, troubled at the thought of enjoying the feel of a gun. He sells it under the title of 'Paint Pellet Survival Games'. For $17 an hour you can hire 'Combat City'; there, up to six players are equipped with protective helmets and visors, all-enveloping clothing, and pistols which fire not bullets, nor even blank cartridges, but pellets of paint. No licence is required, no-one can get hurt, presumably the winners are the ones with fewest paint marks on them, and in case the players want something more structured than a simple contest of paint pellets, Mr Preisner offers a series of 'Combat Scenarios', which include 'Walk Off Duel', 'Blackout', 'Hostage' and 'Save the President'. And if all those pall, 'Players may bring their own opponents and settle differences the old-fashioned way.'

Meanwhile, what of the law? (The men, that is, not the courts.) If crime is out of hand, what are the hands doing? To find out, I thought I might shake a few, and find out how goes the fight. So I went out on patrol in a police car, late one night, high up on Fifth Avenue in Harlem, and saw how the other half lives.

The other half lives by dealing in drugs. The cops in the car (if you begin to think that the *New York* policemen look young, you really *are* getting old) were hard-headed rather than cynical; they knew, and said, that the drugs war is being lost, even has been lost. Until crack came on the scene (crack is a more intensely addictive form of cocaine) it was possible to think that there could be a solution; no longer. 'Why they take it I don't know,' said one of the cops; then he smiled at his own *naïveté*. 'People here', he said, after a pause, 'are poor. They have no jobs, no education, no nothing, yet some of them are driving around in thirty-, forty-, fifty-thousand-dollar cars. When you stop them, they can have two, three thousand dollars on them. The profit from crack is phenomenal; they've got kids here, eleven, twelve years old, running it for them. You can get any kid around here, anybody. I mean, he doesn't work, he has no money, he wants a few things, and the quickest way to make a dollar is by selling drugs.'

Not even the thought of the judiciary let the bitterness off the leash; Officer Krupke kept the same even, casual tone when he explained that the law was a revolving door:

> The problem is when we do make the arrest, two-three days later you'll see the same person back on the street. You gotta remember that no matter what you do – if we take somebody off the corner, if we make ten, fifteen, sweeps, it'll be deterrent maybe for a week or two. You go take the local guy off the corner, it's only a matter of seconds before somebody is on the corner taking his place.

I made a gesture of helplessness; this time he smiled at *my naïveté*. 'Look,' he said, 'we're getting homicides averaging one a night, maybe two. It's an instant addiction; once that's happened, they'll do anything for crack, *anything* – they'll rob, burglarise, commit violent assaults, murder. Then at the same time you have the major groups involved in all the drug wars, it's big money, very competitive, and it's a process of elimination – you're stealing my business, so hey, let me eliminate that problem – bang bang, he goes. It's not just here, it goes on constantly all around, it's everywhere you go.'

A familiar litany; when did you last pick up a Sunday supplement without a feature on drugs and crime? But as we drove back and forth across the beat (each car has its own patch to patrol), with these serious, practical men, it came alive in a way that no mere reading or watching television could do. I suppose that isn't surprising; when at any moment real, three-dimensional police may get out of their car with their guns in their hands, the reality of the drug war becomes as close as a bombing-raid on civilians who have until then known of war only by accounts from the far-off trenches.

May? The car radio came alive with rapid-fire directions, and the driver put his foot down and turned on the siren; we were looking for a tall black with gold chains round his neck, wearing a purple jacket with blue jeans, and the cops in another car had caught him in the act of selling heroin. We were reinforcements.

There was the man, the description exact; as we arrived, the other cops were handcuffing him. Ours searched him, and out came wads of dollars. 'Where did you get that?' 'My mother sends me money.' I was just thinking that I could improvise half a dozen better explanations in much less time, when Officer Krupke put his hand in the man's back pocket and pulled out a wad of high-denomination bills, neatly stacked, with a rubber band round them. He ruffled the wad like a poker-player shuffling the deck, and asked more heavily, 'Where'd you get *that*, then?' To my amazement, our singularly unimaginative dealer said only, 'Like I told you – my mother sends me money.'

The paddy-wagon drew up, and our friend was bundled in. I got close (too close, and saw one of the officers from the other car looking at me, fingering his club in a thoughtful fashion) and watched him carefully; he didn't seem afraid or even concerned. Yet he had been arrested *in flagrante* selling heroin; would he, too, soon emerge from the revolving door? I put the question to our cops as we got back into our car and resumed the patrol. 'Well, in the first place,' Krupke said, 'you were looking at a guy who had just swallowed three full packets of heroin, trying to get rid of the evidence.' I hadn't seen that, and raised an eyebrow, then said, 'Surely, he's going to be in a very dangerous condition, he's taken a massive overdose of heroin, after all.' With the first real feeling I had heard in any of the cops' voices, Krupke snarled, '*That's his problem*'. A moment later, his cool restored, he guessed that the tip-off had come from a rival dealer, not a concerned citizen.

Casually, one of the cops explained that although they could search anyone suspected of carrying a gun, the law forbade them to search even a known dealer for drugs; there was the same extraordinary lack of bitterness as his helplessness manifested itself. It all became even more casual; as we cruised, they would point out men standing on a corner as crack dealers, a group under the lee of an apartment block as waiting their turn to buy. 'Just watch,' our man said, 'when I turn my headlamps right on them, which ones walk away without looking round.' 'They're the dealers?' 'They're the dealers, and they know we can't touch them if we don't see it passed.'

After a few calls to the site of marital discord, and one to a madman who had started screaming of unintelligible terrors, we had the final bust of the shift, the one that did look like Starsky and Hutch. Suddenly, the cruising car swung into a housing precinct, where a knot of young people was gathered. The cops leaped out with the traditional cry, 'Okay, up against the wall, all of you.' Then the familiar soap-opera scene unfolded before me; everyone turned to the wall, all hands were high above heads, palms touching the wall, faces turned to it. Nobody tried to make a break for it, nobody cursed or swore; clearly, this was a ritual they had all gone through many times. Guns in hand, the cops went down the line, searching pockets and bags. Out of almost all, there came the 'pipes' in which crack is smoked; out of some, the stuff itself.

The cops threw it all to the ground, and stamped it into the earth. Then, just as I was assuming that they were about to radio for the paddy-wagon, they told the whole group to get the hell out, telling them, 'If we ever see any one of you again hanging out round here, you're going inside.' They vanished instantly. I asked why none had been arrested, and got a reassuring reply. 'They're only kids, they weren't dealers, just users. We don't want to make hardened criminals of them.'

I remembered something, and coughed discreetly. 'You were searching them for drugs,' I said, 'not guns. And you said you weren't allowed to. How come?' A weary look came over Krupke's face. 'Man,' he said, 'if we never did that, nobody would ever go inside.' All in all, New York's Finest had acquitted themselves well; if these cops were typical, I doubt if any Western force could do better.

I suppose I had better finish with my own story of How I Nearly Got Mugged. It was evening, a fine evening, and I was walking down Fifth on my way to my dinner. It was not dark, hardly dusk, yet not really light. I was walking along the side of the Park (something people are always counselled not to do), and I heard footsteps coming up behind me. Well, New York or no New York, I was not going to be alarmed just because somebody was going in the same direction as myself; that way, I thought, is the way to become a real New Yorker, too terrified to go about the streets at all.

The footsteps had almost caught me up; still I did not yield to New York panic, but kept my even pace. But now the footsteps had turned into feet, and they were seen to be carrying a young man, and he had fallen into step with me, and was matching me stride for stride; his right arm was a foot or two from my left, and I was between him and the Park. He turned his head and peered at me; well, maybe he thought *I* was going to mug *him*. We kept in step; he peered again, then again, then again; at last I began to feel afraid. Should I run? Should I stop? Should I turn round abruptly and start to walk the other way? Should I put my hand into my breast pocket to make him think I had a gun? Should I ask him what he wanted? Before I could sort through the possibilities and decide on one, he peered again, and spoke. 'Say,' he said, in cheerful, non-mugger, tones, 'that's a nice shirt

you've got on — where d'you get it?' 'London,' I said. 'London, eh?' he
said, in a tone of slight surprise; 'nice shirt.' And he quickened his step and
walked on ahead of me.

★   ★   ★

Early next day, a clear and sunny one, I went out for a walk, and immediately saw a sight that made me stop and goggle. On the eastern side of the
Avenue, opposite the Park, a woman was walking briskly along, holding
eleven — I counted them carefully — dog-leads, each of which had a dog on
the other end. The range of dog was very wide; I don't think there were
two of the same breed, and one or two of the bigger ones looked as though
they could make a reasonable breakfast out of some of the smaller. It was
noticeable that they all seemed well-behaved and presumably well-trained,
and their owner (keeper? buyer? seller?) was striding out with complete
confidence, in no way abashed or self-conscious; what is more, I realised
that I was the only person on the side-walk who was staring at this scene.

I soon discovered why. On the posts of a succession of traffic-lights, there
was a notice headed 'Dogwalking', which continued:

> Professional, Athletic, Affectionate and Responsible Dog Walking and
> Running at below competitive charges. References available. $10 an hour
> approximately. If interested, call . . .

A few enquiries elicited the information that dog-walking is big business
in New York. The busy two-job family, off to their respective offices first
thing in the morning, have no time to walk the dog, but they are reluctant
to leave the dog unwalked. In New York, at least, any perceived need will
be rapidly filled, at a suitable price. A need for dog-walkers arose, and lo!
dog-walkers materialised. The woman with the eleven dogs was one of
these, and the bill-sticker advertising his services on the traffic-lights was
another. Clearly, the woman with her herd was about to cross the road
(the scene took place at 76th Street) and enter the Park. Was the Park full,
I wondered, of scores of dog-walkers walking dogs? Every morning? Are
there baby-walkers, too, sisters of the baby-sitters?

I conceived a plan; I would join a dog-walker on his dog-walking rounds.
Perhaps I would lose my lifelong dislike and fear of dogs, in a kind of
saturation therapy, or at least have an opportunity to poison a few. A call
to Joe Buck, by common consent New York's leading dog-walker, led to
an invitation; I did not broach in advance my wish to take the leashes while

he supervised, and it was perhaps just as well that I didn't.

An early start: 7 a.m. at the corner of 72nd and Fifth were my instructions, and I was there at seven, where an amazing sight, almost uncanny, met my hardly-opened eyes. The entire pavement at the corner was carpeted in dogs; it took me a considerable time to count them, because they were not inclined to sit still while I did so, but the total was twenty-three, and they were all clearly wanting the action to begin. I inspected them fearfully, my first concern to assure myself that there were no Alsatians among them; there was none. I shook hands with Joe the dog-man, and saw that each dog had a very stout uniform canvas leash, attached by a very solid buckle to its collar. My aversion to the species has left me unable to name more than a few breeds, but I recognised retrievers, labradors, an airedale, a pekinese and a spaniel. (I glared at it with more than ordinary revulsion, for it was a spaniel which, by biting me badly when I was only seven years old, presumably set off my phobia, but it shamed me by its exceptionally friendly demeanour, and I found myself, to my astonishment, patting its head in reciprocal greeting.) There was also another, tiny, terrier-like beast, even more friendly, and I enquired its family name, to be told it was a Jack Russell. (Who *was* Jack Russell, and why is the dog named after him? And was he pleased when it was? I enquired of Joe; he said that Jack Russell was an English sporting parson, who bred dogs. Presumably, he *was* pleased.

Joe had two assistants: a pretty young girl who had had four dogs assigned to her, and a young man, of Cuban origin I guessed, who had all the very small ones. It was noticeable that even the tiniest had the same very stout leash.

Joe himself held a dozen; it was immediately clear that he was not going to hand the reins to me, and that I would be wise to decline the honour if he did. Some of them were big, tough animals, especially the retrievers, and they were literally living the cliché: they were indeed straining at the leash. I moved among them with circumspection, remembering not to put my hand out to pat them; I redoubled my caution when Joe pointed to the one nearest his left leg and said, 'Don't go near her – she's vicious and crazy.' A fine start, I felt, beginning to wish I had never had my bright idea.

It was time to set off; we were to enter the Park a little further down, then go through it, round the lake, and uptown, passing the Metropolitan Museum. Joe does not take his charges lower than 60th Street, where the Park ends and the pedestrian traffic would make the whole thing impossible; nor does he go higher than 96th Street. He reckons a normal morning walk should be about two hours, and he generally keeps to the same route, with diversions here and there.

The dogs lined up, or more precisely *were* lined up, by Joe; the dangerous one was still beside his left leg, with three beyond it; on his other side there were three reasonably genial ones in line abreast, and I was outside right marker. A second rank, five in number, lined up behind the forwards. It resembled the runners in an athletics tournament waiting for the gun; no, there was something else it reminded me of, and after a moment I found it. This looked like a chariot-race, and I examined the dogs to see if I could guess which one was Ben Hur.

We were off; I immediately discovered that the pace was so hot that I had to trot to keep up. I asked Joe if he might slow down the proceedings for a greenhorn, and he said he couldn't because the dogs just wouldn't go any more slowly: 'These fellers', he said, 'are kangaroos.'

I hit my stride, mindful that I was practically jogging, and puffed my questions to Joe as we sped along. How long had he been a dog-man? 'Thirty years,' he said, 'breeding them, training them, bringing them into the world, and letting them out of it.' 'You love them?' He became wary; I was shortly to learn the depth of the seriousness with which he took his work, and the respect he had for dogs, and he was not going to fall into any anthropomorphic trap this early.

Joe was a wiry, weather-beaten man, I guessed in his late sixties; he was plainly very strong, and even more plainly needed to be, because when six meaty dogs wanted to take to their heels, particularly since we were now in the Park, they took some stopping. Joe leaned back against the pull, like the anchor-man in a tug-o'war, and went on. What was his most used command? 'No.' And the second? 'Sit.'

The phalanx swept along; solo dog-walkers, presumably walking their own dogs, shrank back into the hedges, some of them prepared to die in defence of their own pet, and occasionally looking as though they might have to. But Joe had plainly met that situation a thousand times, and he steered the mob past swiftly and effectively.

The horde continued its advance. Can a dog, even with a walk in the park every morning, be happy in a city? 'It's the best environment a dog could have. There is no country any more, only suburbs, and the city is where they are happiest.' Obvious question: had he ever been bitten by his charges? 'There ain't a horse that ain't been rode, there ain't a cowboy that ain't been throwed. In other words – yes, hundreds of times – there ain't a dog-handler who hasn't.' How do you introduce a new dog, from a new client, into a pack that have grown to know one another? 'I interview the dog – and its owner.' Reject many? 'Sure.'

Do they fight among themselves? 'There are some bad-tempered ones, who'll start a fight if they can. That's where I get bitten most – breaking up a fight.' I had noticed that Joe had a newspaper sticking out of his back pocket; I assumed that it was today's paper and he hadn't finished reading it. But it was yesterday's, and he had. New York had recently passed a law ('A good law,' said Joe, 'it makes people think better of dogs'), which obliges any dog-owner to pick up the dog's droppings, on pain of a hefty fine. Colloquially known as 'The pooper-scooper law', it was being strictly enforced, and – remember America is the land of seized opportunities – there were already enterprising people selling mitten-shaped plastic bags for picking up dogs' waste product and depositing it in the nearest rubbish-basket. Rugged Joe scorned such niceness; he peeled off a page of the newspaper, scooped up the mess with a practised hand and tossed it, with the follow-through of the first action, into the basket. His one concession to coyness was to refer to the dog's action as 'going to the bathroom'.

Now Joe began to soften, to talk about the successive generations of dogs he had raised; at times, it was difficult to tell, amid the references to families and brothers, whether he was talking about the dogs or their owners. But when I suggested that some dog-owners used their pets as substitutes for children, he would have none of it. 'A dog is a dog and a human being is a human being.' And what about the dog-lover who leaves even the walking to a professional? Loyal Joe defended his clients as vigorously as his charges: 'Busy people can't spare a couple of hours a day to walk the dog.'

A rest on the march: carefully avoiding the crazy one, I moved among the pack, distributing a few wary pats. The throng of animals brought varying reactions from the passers-by, from amazement to indifference – presumably from those who had never seen such a sight before to those who walked the same route to work every day, and who therefore crossed the dogs' route. For their part, the dogs were blasé; few tugged at the leash in a desire to explore a stranger or two, fewer still seemed to want a mêlée, hardly any barked, though the old proverb 'A dog will not bark without an audience' suggested that they had missed a striking opportunity. Perhaps it was Joe's eye on them.

We had started early; when we finished the day had hardly started. What else had Fifth Avenue in store before nightfall? As it turned out, yet another surprise.

Americans do not do things by halves, and New York is foremost in sustaining the tendency to excess. But who would cavil at it when, on a beautifully sunny Sunday, Fifth Avenue from 48th Street up to 57th was closed to traffic all day for the annual Book Fair, in full 'The New York is Book Country Fair'? Right across the Avenue at each of the two streets which marked the limits of the Fair, a huge arch of yellow and green balloons had been erected early in the day (the Fair was open from 11 to 5), and every booth and stall flourished another bundle of them; from above – I went up to a balcony to see the whole Fair spread out before me – it made a brave show. All down the Avenue, too, the balloons were being pressed on the fairgoers; inspection revealed that they were all overprinted with the message 'I am a Bookworm in the Big Apple'.

This year's Fair was the tenth, and naturally the biggest. (As far as I know, nothing in the United States ever gets smaller.) There were 165 stands along the kerbs; not content with Fifth Avenue itself, these spilled into the side-streets at 52nd and 53rd. The *New York Times* had helpfully devoted a whole page to the Fair on the Friday before it, providing a map showing where every publisher or other vendor would be hanging out his shingle; Sunday or no Sunday, also, the six Fifth Avenue bookshops within the Fair's boundaries were open for business.

New York *en fête* is a splendid sight; the Avenue was crammed with huge throngs, many of them there to see the passing show rather than buy books, though many of the stalls were doing a very brisk business: indeed, at some of them there were long queues. And, like any fair, there were pushcarts at which the strollers could buy fruit and nuts and hot dogs and bagels and candy floss, promoters of every cause imaginable giving out leaflets, advertisers giving out plastic carrier-bags with appropriate texts printed on them, even a girl who was giving away *next* week's Sunday *New York Times* Book Section. There were also the eccentrics, drawn by the very idea of a book as repository of wisdom, preferably arcane, or as an icon to be venerated. I was stopped by a friendly man, elderly and cheerful, who wanted to know how he could get a wider publication for a book he had written and published himself; he showed me a copy, well bound but displaying inside all the *stigmata* of the amateur author. The book was a history of Scouting in the United States, with special reference to the Scout Troop he had led, and I had to tell him that I did not know, as indeed I did not, how he might persuade a professional publisher to take it on. He seemed not at all downcast, saying 'I got time – I'm retired, and the book took me three years to make.' There was a stall selling manuals of writing and allied disciplines, over which was the legend 'So You Want To Be An Author'; possibly he paused there to pick up some advice.

Street musicians are inevitable, I am happy to say, on occasions like these; at the exact point where the centre of Fifth Avenue is crossed by 52nd

Street a young man had set up a monster metal xylophone, which he proceeded to play with four drumsticks, a considerable feat for a man with only two hands. Further on, a couple were dressed in Shakespearean costume; the man played a guitar, the girl sang. At the Park end, a real old-fashioned busker had a cassette player, and as it blared out the *Radetzky March* or the Overture to *The Marriage of Figaro*, he played the first violin part, dancing most dexterously as he fiddled.

A beautiful maiden, decked out in lacy finery, pedalled a late nineteenth-century tricycle, lovingly restored to perfection; a man rode a genuine penny-farthing of the same era, and never fell off once, however slowly he had to go, to get through the crowds; and at the China Books stall, there was a camel. I thought at first that it must be a stuffed one, so still did it stand, but after a moment it curled its lip in the haughty camel way, and shook its head sadly at the absurdity of human beings, who have no humps. I wandered on, and came upon a policeman, dealing with the traffic at one of the intersections where cars could cross the Avenue; a woman burst out of the crowd and ran up to him, tugging him by the sleeve. I couldn't hear what she was saying, but he followed her back into the mêlée, and presently emerged, holding by the collar a little man who looked harmlessly crazy. The cop was clearly not minded to make much of a fuss, so he just shook his prey in a minatory manner, and sent him on his way. 'What was all that about?' I asked him. 'He was', said the cop, 'bothering the camel.' We stood and chatted. 'You from England?' 'Yes.' 'Where?' 'London.' Then 'Say – do you know Tooting Bec?' I admitted I did. 'I was there once – good old Tooting Bec.' As I strolled along, I thought if I could introduce the subject with sufficient care, I could win a lot of money inviting bets against the proposition that a policeman on Fifth Avenue would conclude a brief conversation with an encomium to Tooting Bec, immediately after warning a man that bothering camels was illegal.

By an enchanting coincidence, the ambit of the Book Fair fell just short of the most famous and delightful of all New York's bookshops, just off the Avenue at 47th. It was open all day, nonetheless, and a stream of visitors, sated by the wares on offer at the kerbs, wandered in and out. But wandering in and out is exactly what this particular bookstore is for.

'Wise men fish here'; they do indeed. The Gotham Book Mart, which has that rubric for its sign, must be – is – one of the most remarkable bookshops in the world. Roughly, the Gotham Book Mart did in Manhattan what Sylvia Beach, Harriet Weaver and *Shakespeare & Cie* did in Paris; that is, ran a bookshop the main purpose of which was not really to sell books, but to discover, assist and promote new good writers. It was founded by Frances Steloff, in 1919, when she was thirty-two; she lived to be one hundred and two, and although she retired from running the business when she turned eighty, she didn't retire very far; she lived above the shop, and was constantly to be found in it. When she wanted to buy the premises for a bookshop the owner of the building advised her not to; it was in the theatre district, and, he added, 'Actors don't read'.

A sweeping judgment; it is not for me to evaluate it. But she bought the place, stocked it, and flourished. Whether actors flocked to it history does not recall, though playwrights like O'Neill did, and the place caught on. Lawrence, Joyce, e. e. cummings, André Gide, Gertrude Stein, Ezra Pound – all these and many more her literary truffle-hound's nose sniffed out, and the post offices of New York and Paris grew rich on the traffic that passed between Steloff and Beach, the Gotham Book Mart and *Shakespeare & Cie.*

It is said that today there are more than 200,000 books on display (to say nothing of the famous basement, where Steloff used to store unsuccessful books like wine, until their writers grew famous and she uncorked the now precious vintage); it is also said that in all those 200,000 there is not one which will tell the buyer how to make a quiche, nor any which explains how to keep fit.

The shelves are explicit; here psychology, here art, here poetry. The signs, however, are more for decoration than guidance, and it is clear that all attempts to keep the sections from fraternising are in vain, largely because everyone engaged in running the shop thinks it would be cruel. But they are exhaustively assiduous at finding what the customer wants, even if it is medieval Latin lyrics which have absent-mindedly wandered into a section otherwise composed entirely of architecture. (Well, architecture and biography and law and travel and *other* Latin lyrics.) And if the staff cannot find it anywhere, however irrelevantly filed, so that they can only conclude that they don't have it in stock, they will ransack the shelves of other shops, and make publishers' lives a misery, until they can come up with the answer. And if the customer has gone cool on Latin lyrics meanwhile, or forgotten entirely about them, the Gotham's staff will shrug, and tuck the now superfluous book into philosophy, nuclear physics or Buddhism.

The Gotham exudes a warmth the moment you enter it; it is the warmth of books and those who love them, and indeed read them. It is said that visitors are free not only to browse to their content but to read, *gratis*, the literary magazines, of which there is a vast selection, though even such hospitality does not match that of a bookshop in Aspen, Colorado, with the memorably apt name of Explore, in which there is an alcove with comfortable chairs, the literary magazines on the table, and a regularly-replenished pot of coffee bubbling away. I suspect that the Gotham would do the same if it had the space. Indeed, I suspect that only the municipal zoning laws and such prevent the owners of the Gotham from installing a trout-stream on the premises, so that that sign – made in the handsomest wrought-iron, incidentally – can provide the wise men with the appropriate facilities.

I can't remember ever seeing fishing books in the Gotham, but they must surely be there, even if they are classified under mathematics, archaeology or Beethoven, for the real fisherman is as much a contemplative as the bookworm is, and if a reader can take a book to the water in case the fish aren't biting, why cannot a fisherman take a line to the bookshop while the staff search through French history, military tactics and calligraphy to find something on Mount Rushmore, farming or the proof that Bacon wrote Shakespeare?

★   ★   ★

Every year, for the St Patrick's Day Parade up Fifth Avenue, the white centre traffic-separation stripe which runs the entire length of the street is painted green. I didn't quite have the nerve to ask the Mayor, or anybody else for that matter, whether anyone had considered painting it black for the Martin Luther King Memorial Parade.

It would have been much more than a tribute to the martyred leader, for the MLK Parade did not start out that way, and its origins are much more interesting. The 369th Infantry Regiment of the 93rd Division of the United States Army was thus designated on 1 March 1918, and sailed for Europe immediately afterwards, the first Negro unit to see active service. (Mind you, it was shipwrecked three times on the way over.) It had an astonishing record in the few months more that the war had to run; the 369th provided the first American soldier in the war to be decorated with the Croix de Guerre, it was cited for bravery in battle eleven times, it served longer in action than any other American regiment, it never lost a man by capture and never retreated anywhere, it was the first regiment of all the allied armies to reach the Rhine, and finally it was collectively awarded the Croix de Guerre. And, incidentally, although the Selective Service Act had been passed into American law long before the regiment was raised, it was entirely volunteer, the only such American regiment that reached France. It was, inevitably, nicknamed 'Harlem's Own'. (What is more, and more curious, it is said that the 369th's regimental band brought the very first jazz to Europe.)

In 1959, by which time the regiment had been several times split up, re-assigned and re-designated, the veterans of the 369th instituted an annual parade in honour of those who had died in combat; when Martin Luther King was assassinated in 1968, the Veterans' Association decided to turn their annual parade into a memorial for the black martyr.

And so I found myself sitting in the saluting-base at Fifth Avenue and 69th Street, for the 21st annual Martin Luther King Memorial Parade.

Right across the street from the reviewing base there was a brass band, presumably one of the veterans' subsidiary bands, assuming that the main one was leading the parade. After the *Star Spangled Banner* went awry, when the soprano soloist lost her nerve, her head and – most noticeably – her entire sense of pitch, so that (since the band played on) the result was a series of harmonies that seemed to owe much to Schoenberg and more to Berio, things settled down. It was a perfect New York May day; a powerful sun in a cloudless sky, mitigated by a steady breeze, with not a trace of humidity; the days of rain which had preceded this were forgotten.

Onward, Christian Soldiers; *Lift Ev'ry Voice and Sing*; selections from familiar musicals; *We Shall Overcome*; on went the musical entertainment, and I assumed that they were filling in time until the parade arrived, when the ceremonies would begin, but apparently that's not the way it's done. Long before the parade could even be heard, far down Fifth Avenue, the tributes to King's memory had been given, the wreath laid, the prayers said, the Taps sounded.

And King's famous speech, 'I have a dream', recited. Hitherto, the performers (not just the skidding soprano) had been plainly amateurs, and none the worse for that; suddenly, it was plain that a professional was at the microphone. He was presumably a professional actor; at least, if he wasn't, he had a new career before him for the asking. There is said to be a recording of King giving the original speech, though I have never heard it, but if it had been delivered with the force, excitement, conviction and lung-power provided by Ron Dortch of the Manhattan District 369th Veterans' Association I wish I had been there. Mr Dortch even used that trick, fatal in an actor without complete confidence, the deliberate false stress which, handled perfectly, wakes up the line. 'Let freedom *ring*', he cried, as though he was declining an invitation to let freedom do something else altogether, and the prodigious number of variations he played on the phrase itself (it occurs at least a score of times in the speech) could surely not have been accomplished except by a man who knew exactly what he was doing. He got a huge round of applause, and well he might.

Mind you, the passion and rhetoric of the speech would have come through even if a much less skilful orator had been at the microphone. There are a number of versions of Martin Luther King's Sermon on the Mount which are promoted as the Ur-text, and collation of them for a definitive version is long overdue. But there are passages which proclaim themselves authentic by the sheer moral force of the words, and leave no doubt that they were spoken, in just that form, on that historic day.

In a sense we have come to our nation's Capital to cash a check. When the architects of our republic wrote the magnificent words of the Constitution and the Declaration of Independence, they were signing a promissory note to which every American was to fall heir. This note was a promise that all men would be guaranteed the unalienable rights of life, liberty, and the pursuit of happiness.

It is obvious today that America has defaulted on this promissory note insofar as her citizens of color are concerned. Instead of honoring this sacred obligation, America has given the Negro people a bad check; a check which has come back marked 'insufficient funds'. But we refuse to believe that the bank of justice is bankrupt ... So we have come to cash this check – a check that will give us upon demand the riches of freedom and the security of justice. We have also come to this hallowed spot to remind America of the fierce urgency of *now*. This is no time to engage in the luxury of cooling off or to take the tranquilizing drug of gradualism. *Now* is the time to make real the promises of Democracy. *Now* is the time to rise from the dark and desolate valley of segregation to the sunlit path of racial justice. *Now* is the time to open the doors of opportunity to all of God's children. *Now* is the time to lift our nation from the quicksands of racial injustice to the solid rock of brotherhood ...

There are those who are asking the devotees of civil rights, 'when will you be satisfied?' We can never be satisfied as long as the Negro is the victim of the unspeakable horrors of police brutality. We can never be satisfied as long as our bodies, heavy with the fatigue of travel, cannot gain lodging in the motels of the highways and the hotels of the cities. We cannot be satisfied as long as the Negro's basic mobility is from a smaller ghetto to a larger one. We can never be satisfied as long as a Negro in Mississippi cannot vote and a Negro in New York believes he has nothing to vote for ...

When we let freedom ring, when we let it ring from every village and every hamlet, from every state and every city, we will be able to speed up that day when all of God's children, black men and white men, Jews and Gentiles, Protestants and Catholics, will be able to join hands and sing in the words of

32 The shootist　33 Every dog has his day　34 The Avenue en fête　35 The crowd gathers　36 The cheerleaders

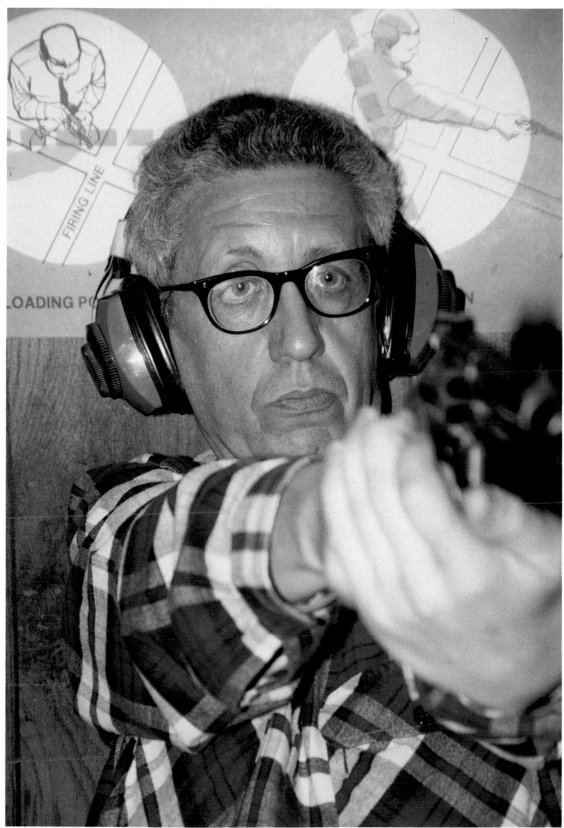

38

the old Negro spiritual, 'Free at last! Free at last! Thank God almighty, we are free at last!'

With a perfect understanding of the juxtapositions of drama, the organisers of the parade followed this demonstration of militant and muscular Christianity with an invitation to collective prayer: 'Stand up and take the hands of the people on either side of you', said the Master of Ceremonies, 'and tell each of them "God loves you, and so do I".' It was an extraordinarily moving moment, not least for me, since not only was I sitting between two very old veterans of the 369th, but the stand was sparsely populated at that point, so that all three of us had to stretch our arms to creaking point in order to hold hands. (Some will say that the prayer was sentimental, naïve, innocent. So it was, all three, and all the better for that.)

And then, from far down the Avenue, I heard the band. What I didn't know was that it was the first of *forty* bands. It began with a tribute to history; there were three men in meticulously authentic colonial costume, preceded by a lone flag-carrier – the flag, of course, was the original standard of rebellion. The three who marched abreast behind him constituted a drum-and-fife band, which I often think is the most grand and stirring military music in all history, far surpassing in its ability to make eyes water the biggest ceremonial bands, despite their massed ranks of tubas, trombones, cornets, flutes and the big bass drum. And when, as here, the trio were playing *Yankee Doodle Dandy*, it out-stirred not only the greatest regimental band and the Salvation Army at its best, but the Chicago Symphony Orchestra as well.

Behind the trio came a squadron of mounted police, smart and well-drilled, and behind them a huge open car in which there sat the Grand Marshal of the Parade, escorted by Brigadier General Samuel Phillips Jr. General Phillips may have been Jr, but his charge, sitting precariously on the back of the open tourer, was very Snr indeed; she was well over eighty, and plainly feeling overwhelmed. The designation of Grand Marshal is purely honorary; each year a distinguished black figure is chosen to head the Parade. I had been told that Mother Hale, this year's Grand Marshal, was a very remarkable lady, and that was a considerable understatement, as I discovered when I went up into Harlem to meet her;★ from her bearing, which I would call aristocratic if I dared, I sensed, even at that distance, a personality very much out of the ordinary. Later, she came and sat in front of me in the stand, and I had a chance to examine her close up; it only

★ See pp 240–3

37 New York's green peace   38 His Honour pauses in the Park

enhanced my feelings about her. In any case, she must have had a firm character to avoid wincing when the Master of Ceremonies announced the make of the car she was riding in, together with the name of the showroom at which it was bought, and the name of the sponsor who put up the money; but Mother Hale's dignity was equal to it all.

When the Grand Marshal was installed in the reviewing-stand, the fun began. It went on for more than two hours (possibly more, because I stole away after that length of time) and I began to be convinced that the armies of Ruritania had invaded and conquered the United States, so colourful and implausible were the uniforms worn by most of the contingents. I had, it is true, wondered how the 369th, however many bands it had, could sustain the entire parade, and the explanation was now close at hand.

A parade up Fifth Avenue gives the opportunity to an infinite number of institutions and organisations which have no connection at all to the subject of the parade, but are eager for a pleasant day out, especially if the weather is fine. This parade was no exception; indeed, it gave more such opportunities than most such parades, since the causes celebrated on St Patrick's Day and Israel Day and many of the other annual marches have sufficient followers to fill the Avenue from side to side and from end to end. (True, the definition of Irish for St Patrick's Day does tend to be stretched quite far – much further, indeed, than Mayor O'Koch, as he calls himself every March 17th, since he does make a joke of it, while many of those marchers who seriously claim Irish descent have no more right to it than is given by their descent to the floor in a Third Avenue bar after drinking too many doubles of Jameson's whiskey.)

The band of the 369th was followed by the bands of some of the other units into which sections of the much-merged regiment had been incorporated, and behind the music marched the men of the 369th itself, a huge phalanx that must have been fully a couple of blocks long; it was noticeable that the veterans marched as smartly and as sprightly as those currently serving. After the men of the 369th came their vehicles; well, they are a Transport Battalion now. The huge trucks, in impeccable line abreast, growled up the Avenue, and were followed by more military echelons (I believe I have used that much-abused word correctly – at any rate the OED defines echelons as 'Arrangement of troops in parallel groups each with its end clear of those ahead and behind') and more of their vehicles; no tanks, though, anywhere in the parade, presumably because the effect they would have on the already sufficiently pot-holed thorough-fare would give the city nightmares. Then there came the representatives of the American Legion and of the Red Cross. But civilian life was approaching, led by the New York Department of Police in a massive phalanx (yes – 'Set of persons etc., forming compact mass, or banded together for common purpose'), and it was clear that the police contingent had been deliberately drawn up to contain the maximum number of black officers.

On such a day, nobody could object to that, nor to the Boy Scouts and Girl Scouts, nor to the Fire Department, who came next, their warning lights on and their sirens sounding, nor the Jewish Veterans, nor – now we were completely in the piping times of peace – the Parks Department, who had also brought their vehicles, though these, presumably, had never contained anything more warlike than grass clippings to be disposed of or mowers to provide the clippings.

There was also Ronald McDonald; as befitted the most important person in the parade after the Grand Marshal, he was the only figure to have his own open limousine. Ronald McDonald is the symbolic embodiment, the Platonic ideal, of the McDonald hamburger. Not surprisingly, he was made up as one; his head, in clown make-up, stuck out of the monster bun, which was realistically daubed with tomato sauce *and* mustard (no point in offending half the customers, let alone all of them), and as he waved and smiled the cheers redoubled, echoing up and down the Avenue, acknowledging the true hero of our time.

The rise of the hamburger is an exceptionally interesting social phenomenon; I wouldn't be surprised if there weren't half a dozen PhD theses on the subject already extant. (That might be a joke, though then again it might not. I once came across a volume which was a register of all the PhD dissertations accepted in all recognised American universities for the previous year; presumably, it was an annual publication. Among the successful doctoral studies, in the field of Domestic Science, was one which was entitled 'Some factors influencing the palatability and slicing quality of corned beef'. I still treasure most the 'some'.) Hamburgers, of course, are much older than McDonald's; the original Wimpy Bars, after all, were based on the Popeye cartoon (Wimpy was the character who was always eating a hamburger), which certainly much antedated the Second World War. But only in the last thirty years or so has the hamburger risen to such gigantic culinary eminence. The very chains of hamburger restaurants are practically countless; and the number of outlets must be greater than the number of miles in a light-year,★ while as for the total quantity of hamburgers consumed world-wide in a day, a new kind of number system

★ 5,865,696,000,000 or 5,881,766,400,000, depending on whether or not it is a leap year.

would have to be invented to encompass the answer. Suspicions about the meat content have frequently been aroused; as far as I know no-one has tried to work out how many cows it would take to keep the world supplied with this ubiquitous product, but surely, however many it is, there aren't that number of cows anywhere?

But the greater mystery is why? Why has this form of convenience food caught on so completely throughout the world, outdistancing all its rivals, even the most popular (Kentucky Fried Chicken, for instance), to the extent that, not long ago, McDonald's signed an agreement with the Soviet Union to set up the first, though certainly not the last, of their restaurants in that country? Where Napoleon and Hitler failed, McDonald's has succeeded, and the invasion will soon take place. No wonder Ronald McDonald was felt to be an indispensable part of the parade, and no wonder that he was so vociferously cheered.

And then the victorious Ruritanians, striding haughtily as befits conquerors, and preceded in almost every case by bands of heralds, demanding tribute from the cowed and beaten Americans. In the city of New York, it seems that virtually every High School has its own band, and not only its own band but its own band uniform, and – inevitably – its marching equivalent of football-field cheer-leaders.

The uniforms were amazing; every colour in the spectrum that could justly be called garish was on parade, and the elaborate whorls and frogs and epaulettes and greaves and feathers and flowers would have been rejected as overdone by Busby Berkeley. It was noticeable that even the all-male schools had provided themselves with girl cheer-leaders, and these, always going ahead of the main body to sweep away the last resistance from the beaten enemy, showed what Ruritanian mettle really was. They swung their batons and their pom-poms and, in the case of the more adolescent ones, other things, and their skirts (though the skirts were so short that real swinging was mostly out of the question) with dash and vigour, keeping meticulous time with the inevitable band. One of the bands, as it approached, sounded very strange; it seemed to be accompanied by bells, and when it came abreast I saw that it was – the last two ranks of the band were playing glockenspiels, a charming miniature regiment of Papagenos. (Later on, somebody had got his signals mixed in a rather enchanting manner. A stirringly martial band swung into view, their insignia proclaiming them the New York City Transit Police Band of Irish Warpipes and Drums, and every drop of green blood in me stirred. But whether they knew it or not, they were playing *Scotland the Brave*.)

There were the city's Ambulance Services, there was the Transit Authority, there were the Building Services, there were even a couple of mighty trucks each sporting a huge crane. Nobody and nothing was left out; there was a contingent of children who were obviously in some way retarded – perhaps brain-damaged or suffering from cerebral palsy, many of them in wheelchairs or prams; some who were walking had to have a supportive arm as they shuffled along. The Master of Ceremonies abruptly changed the tone of his introductory patter; with great tact he introduced these children as 'special', an admirable word in the context. Our world is awash with demeaning euphemisms, and Americans are even worse than the British – they can't even bring themselves to call a lavatory a lavatory, but instead have devised an infinite number of more genteel words for it, the silliest of all (and the most frequently found) being 'rest-room'. But if Americans shrink from such naming of names, they are marginally less constricted than we are when it comes to any kind of physical or mental lack or loss. In Britain, even 'disabled' is frowned upon in some circles (I have even come across 'differently-abled'), though it is difficult to believe that those who suffer from such defects or damage are much cheered up by the use of weasel words to describe their condition.

But the strangest of these *délicatesses* is the treatment of the word 'Negro'. I, in common with most of my generation, was brought up to use that word, and to ensure, moreover, that it was spelt with a capital N; anything else, we were told, was rude and demeaning, and of course 'nigger' was a swearword that no decent person would use. When, after the Second World War, there began the great flood of immigration from the New Commonwealth (itself a wretched euphemism, designed precisely to avoid speaking of what it actually meant), we used for a time 'coloured', or 'coloured people'. That, as it happens, was what American Negroes called themselves; the principal organisation for them was The National Association for the Advancement of Coloured People. There was a brief attempt to sterilise into neutrality the word 'nigra' or 'niggra', which had previously been classified as no less offensive than 'nigger'; it was said that Clare Boothe Luce was involved in the promotion of the word, so that she could go on calling Negroes 'niggers' with impunity. (There was also an ancient story of the redneck Southerner who went to a reception in Washington, just before the First World War, where he met the famous freed slave, Booker T. Washington, a man who did much to advance the cause of his people. When he got home, he described the encounter, and in particular his dilemma as to what he should call Washington when he was introduced. 'I couldn't call him "nigger" ', he said, 'because he bore the name of the Father of the Republic. On the other hand, I couldn't call him "Mister" –

I never called a nigger Mister in my life.' 'Then what did you do?' asked somebody in the company. 'Why', he replied, 'I compromised – I called him Professor'.)

At some point, American Negroes began to reject the word altogether, though it has never been clear why; today, Negro is certainly considered archaic at the least, and, increasingly, offensive – so much so, that it can be dangerous to use the word, which has been replaced by 'black', used as a noun. But that brings me full circle, for if 'nigger' in my youth was strictly forbidden, 'black man' was considered hardly less derogatory, and therefore banned. In Britain, 'blacks' has been taken up enthusiastically by 'whites' of the left, and they have gone much further than the Americans who actually are black; today, in many parts of the country, 'blacks' is the only word permitted to describe Asians as well. What a high-caste Brahmin feels when he is called black hardly bears thinking about; the amount of racial hatred generated by such attempts to impose an artificial nomenclature must by now be immeasurable.

And now, even as I write, comes the news from the Reverend Jesse Jackson that the days of 'black' are numbered. The new buzzword is 'Afro-Americans', which is strictly speaking illogical, because although the ancestors of most blacks in the United States no doubt came from Africa, a good number came from the Caribbean. Presumably, Jackson is too young to know that the word Aframerican was coined and used, without giving racial offence, many years ago; H. L. Mencken used it frequently and naturally, suggesting that it was already familiar.

All of which makes matters more confused rather than less. The official account, in the parade programme, of the feats of arms that the 369th were responsible for, refers, without comment or self-consciousness, to the 'Negro Regiment of Infantry', though since that was the official designation in 1913 it may not be evidence, and certainly the document which lays down the composition, rules, etc., of the 369th Veterans Association refers to 'black and white former servicemen'. The Master of Ceremonies made only one allusion, in his running commentary, to the segregation in the United States Army right up to and into the Second World War; I think that, under pressure from Roosevelt, segregation was abolished, *de jure* at any rate, before the war ended. Certainly, the atmosphere in the reviewing stand, where there were both black and white senior officers, was so easy and natural that it was difficult to believe that any such discrimination had ever existed.

Yet two startling facts stand out. First, how recently it is that the legal framework of segregation and discrimination was dismantled. Second, how quickly it collapsed when it was given a shove by a determined man, Lyndon Johnson. Johnson's full term ran from 1964 to 1968; until then, there had been *no* serious or effective legislation passed in the United States designed to break the hold of the segregationists, since the rapid erosion of the laws passed in the wake of the Civil War. The key Supreme Court judgment, Brown v. The Board of Education of Alabama, in 1954, struck down the doctrine of 'separate but equal', the redoubt into which the South had withdrawn, seeing the battle ahead. But that was only a judgment; no legislation followed it. Martin Luther King was assassinated in 1968; that tragedy marked the beginning of the end. The Civil Rights legislation initiated by Johnson and steered through the Senate by his Vice-President, Humphrey ('Hold their feet to the fire, Hubert', LBJ would say, 'hold their feet to the fire'), took a long time to have its effect; obviously, there is still not full and genuine racial equality in America, and I vividly recall my visit to Miami for the 1972 Democratic Convention (which nominated the disastrous George McGovern), where George Wallace, still preaching segregation, did not seem at all like a prehistoric monster, but only a general who was slowly losing a battle.

And it was that recollection, and the recollection of what had since happened, that dominated my thoughts as I wandered away from the reviewing stand and up Fifth Avenue. Thinking of the speeches, from black and white, of the recitation of King's 'I have a dream', of white and black mingling in every section of the parade, of the variety and breadth of the participants, I felt strongly, and with admiration, the extraordinary unity that there really is at the bottom of this very diverse society, perhaps the most diverse society of any large and internationally significant state in the world. There are many nationalities in the Soviet Union, of course, but apart from the Baltic States, which have never accepted that they are part of the Soviet Empire, let alone of the Soviet State itself, and the Ukraine, where almost all the separation movements have come from, the effect of the diversity is much less than it is in the United States.*

Divided they stand; it would do the United States no harm to replace the *E pluribus unum* on the coinage by that apparently opposite motto. For it is *not* the opposite; it is an affirmation of the truly extraordinary fact that in the United States the diversity is fruitful and beneficial as well as a problem. The truth is that the least homogeneous nation in the world is the most united, and, in a curious way, this parade demonstrated the fact.

---

* How all occasions do inform against me! Between the ceremony of the parade and my writing this account of it – only a couple of months, after all – Soviet Armenia and Soviet Azerbaijan have come close to civil war.

Here were thousands of people who had come to pay homage to the murdered King, or at any rate who had come to spend a beautiful day marching up Fifth Avenue and singing or dancing or playing while doing so, or at the very least who had come to watch the parade go by. The vast variety of contingents somehow symbolised the vast variety of the country, though there had been no noticeable attempt to portray it, other than in mingling black with white, which – given the nature of most of the marching sections – would have been inevitable anyway.

It is not easy to trace the path that diversity takes on the way to unity. But there are clues; surely the United States has the most patriotic people on earth. Patriotism can take many forms; it can even be – and often has been in America – a force for intolerance. (There are few American institutions more repellent than the Daughters of the Revolution, who would have been, every blue-rinsed one of them, on the side of the British; it's a mercy they don't celebrate Benedict Arnold Day.) But for most Americans, their patriotism is simple and direct; when the National Anthem is played on any ceremonial occasion, Americans sing it *en masse*.

It is not in the least difficult for Americans of Polish or Russian or German or Chinese origins to be proud of both their old blood and their new-found land. The same, no doubt, can be said of Britain; but it is far easier in a country with Britain's immensely more compact size, and with Britain's immensely longer history. Across the American continent, and in places where the oldest building was put up less than a century ago, the depth of the roots is astonishing, indeed I believe unique.

And so I mused, as the parade went colourfully, cheerfully and musically by. But I had forgotten that it could not go by without one particular contribution; it is unlikely that Judgment Day could be allowed to go by without it. The ranking administrative figures of the city, sober-suited as befitted their offices, came in sight, line abreast. But one of them was not sober-suited, nor was he in line with his colleagues. He marched half a dozen paces ahead of them, and he wore a short-sleeved shirt and no jacket, and ever and anon he flung up his arms in a V-shape and marched a few steps before dropping them to his side. Mayor Koch was on parade, and the only surprise was that he hadn't painted himself black for the day. The Master of Ceremonies, wise bird that he was, announced that His Honour was approaching the podium, and then asked His Honour whether he would like to say a few words. To no-one's astonishment, least of all that of the Master of Ceremonies, Koch skipped nimbly out of the marching column, mounted the dais, and spoke. Ever the perfect politician, he spoke briefly, uncontentiously and warmly, and ended by wishing everyone a nice day. Then he skipped as nimbly back into line, and the parade continued.

In the evening, the Transport Company of the old 369th was holding a retirement dinner for two of its long-serving officers, and they invited me. They gave me an address in the Bronx, and I realised, with some alarm, that I had never set foot in the borough, and that it had a spectacularly dangerous reputation. Moreover, the Bronx is where the disaster happens to the hero of Tom Wolfe's *The Bonfire of the Vanities*, and the prolonged nightmare which follows takes place mainly there, too. I had instant visions of being mugged, murdered, robbed, arrested, sold dangerous drugs, set on fire or daubed with graffiti, and wondered if the 369th could lay their hands on an armoured car to take me there, or if there were firms in New York which rented them out. (I have no doubt that there is, and that a glance through the Yellow Pages would provide several names. What is more, they would quote me rates with and without fitted machine-guns.)

The pervasive terror of crime which infects even the most level-headed of New Yorkers I have already described; I have also claimed to be more or less immune to it myself. But the Bronx was something different; even if Wolfe's book was fiction, it was clearly based upon many thoroughly-explored layers of fact, and anyway I had seen television documentaries of its awfulness. (While I was in New York, which was after Wolfe had published his book, I encountered the Tawana Brawley case – which for all I know is going on still – in which the Reverend Al Sharpstone struts and frets his hour upon the stage, and demonstrates that it is possible to out-Wolfe Wolfe, or at any rate Wolfe's more egregiously implausible characters.)

Then I pulled myself together. The Bronx of dark fiction and darker fact is the South Bronx; I was bound for the North, and had no reason to believe that the Revd Sharpstone would leap out from behind a bush and finger me as a rapist. Nor did he; I travelled to the Bronx in a Manhattan yellow cab, and the indifference of the driver as we set off reassured me long before we crossed the Hudson Driveway Bridge.

The dinner was being held at a restaurant; as I got nearer, unmugged and unmurdered, I began to feel positively jaunty, and looked about as though I had known every stone of the Bronx all my life. So cocky did I become that when we passed through an area of modest prosperity and, very abruptly, entered on an obviously very poor slum quarter, I instantly deduced that the first neighbourhood had been white and the second black, and felt quite pleased with myself for my perception. But I was wrong; both areas were entirely black. So conditioned had I instinctively become (based, of course, on New York attitudes which I had unwittingly swallowed) that I had momentarily forgotten, despite all the pledges I had made to myself, that the blacks of New York are no less diverse than the whites; I had done no more than drive from an affluent black area to a poor black area. (I plead guilty, but ask for mitigating circumstances to be taken into account. Hitherto, when going out of an upmarket area into a downmarket one, the boundary *had* also marked the colour line. Perhaps warning signs would help: 'Proceed with caution – Steep fall in average income ahead'.)

The dinner was like all such dinners; charmingly maudlin speeches, lots of good old Benjy, records of long service and honourable conduct, do you remember when, a few manly tears, high good humour, and nobody at all the worse for liquor. (And, of course, yet again that amazing American hospitality: two dozen times someone came over to me to ask if I had everything I wanted, if everything was all right, if there was anything they could do.)

I got home as intact as I had gone there. And with a bonus. The Manhattan yellow cab had, naturally, a meter, which showed $17·80 for the journey. The Bronx cab had no meter; it was the equivalent of a London minicab. Here was the perfect scenario for an unscrupulous driver: an obvious limey who knows nothing about New York routes and even less about cab-rates in the Bronx – in a word, a sucker. And, as is well known, you never give a sucker an even break. Oh, well, I thought, it's been a very pleasant evening, what's another twenty dollars at the end of it? We arrived at my hotel: 'How much?' said I. The driver consulted a booklet; he took some time, from which I deduced that he was wondering just how far into the stratosphere he could take the fare without the greenhorn jibbing. He shut the book: 'Sixteen-seventy-five', he said, clearly one of those righteous men whom Abraham enlisted to placate God.

But as I went to bed I remembered the story of the Englishman arriving in Chicago by train (it is a very old story). He gets into a cab at the station rank and tells the driver to go to the Hotel Roosevelt. Now the Hotel Roosevelt in Chicago is right next to the railway station, and the cab-driver instantly realises that he has a monumental sucker in his grasp. So he carefully drives out of the station in the direction away from the hotel, and sets off on a monstrous tour of the city, taking care to arrive at the hotel, an hour later, from the side away from the station. 'How much?' asks the limey. 'Sixty-eight dollars', comes the straight-faced reply. 'Oh, no, you don't,' barks the Englishman; 'you think because I'm a foreigner you can fool me, but you can't. Last time it was only fifty-nine dollars, and you aren't getting a penny more.'

★   ★   ★

The Park at last, starting with Grand Union Plaza, just where it begins; here is a not very lively equestrian statue of General Sherman. Everybody – well, every American, anyway – knows that he was the general who went Marching Through Georgia, and also that, late in his life, addressing a class of schoolchildren, he begged them not to believe in the glamour of war, for 'War is Hell'. But there is a third clue to Sherman, and it is the most significant of the three. For many generals have made stirring advances, and all generals know, even if they do not proclaim it, that war is hell; but not all generals, and practically no politicians, are capable of making their position as clear as Sherman did when, before the 1868 Presidential race began, there was a movement to have him seek the Republican nomination. Sherman made clear that he was not interested, but his supporters continued with their efforts, until Sherman brought the campaign to an end with these magnificent words: 'If nominated I will not accept, if drafted I will not run, if elected I will not serve'. That, you might say, told 'em; but the point of the story is the contrast with most democratic politicians the world over, who calculate to the last convention vote how much of an advantage they will gain by saying at first that they don't want the nomination, then gradually build up the pressure with the aid of their campaign managers, and then, with a touching show of reluctance and grief, throw their hat in the ring, and thereafter fight hell for leather to gain the prize they had yearned for from the outset. (Mind you, in this instance, the result was that the American people got General Grant instead. Maybe one last effort should have been made to change Sherman's mind.)

There is a man who eats Central Park; not eats *in* Central Park, but eats it. And he does it for a living. We may as well start exploring the Park with him.

His name is Steven Brill, and he carefully dresses to look like a lunatic, with an untidy beard at the bottom of his face and a pith helmet, of all things, at the top. He is an eco-freak with a sense of humour, a rare combination, and he believes – oh, *how* he believes – in natural foods. He was, of course (well, one look at him makes it of course), a student in the late Sixties, but he retained a good many of the beliefs, attitudes and ideals of that fateful decade; his interest in natural eating and cooking gradually led him to botanical studies and the vegetarian and herbal press. (You didn't know there was a vegetarian and herbal press in New York? Neither did I, but it seems that there are many magazines in the field, including *The Sproutletter* and *Vegetable Voice*.)

In the late Seventies, he inevitably began to explore the plant life in Central Park; by then, he was sufficiently expert to know a poisonous mushroom from a harmless one. The vegetable riches growing wild in the Park led him to organise groups to study the edible flora under his direction, and to learn what to cook and how to cook it. (Also, presumably, why.)

His fees were moderate, and the enterprise thrived, until one day he was arrested; it seems that there were by-laws prohibiting the picking and eating of the Park vegetation. ('It's like', said the prosecutor, 'going to the zoo and eating the animals.') In the end, sense prevailed; the charges were dropped (in any case Mr Brill had wisely eaten the evidence), and he was hired by the Park authorities to conduct his tours with official approval. He has been doing so ever since.

I loped along with him, gingerly nibbling when he told us to; a surprising number of his finds were praised for their medicinal properties, but his patter, obviously polished over many such communal visits, was stimulating and engaging. ('Has anyone ever disobeyed you, eaten something poisonous, and been ill?' 'No, some people have picked the poisonous things, but only to serve to their in-laws.') He was obsessed by the life, but not a fanatic; the distinction is crucial. (He was at pains to stress that although he would point out rare species, they were not to be plucked, let alone eaten.)

My townee nature resisted the experience; inevitably, all the specimens looked alike to me, and certainly tasted so. But his crazy, hilarious enthusiasm was infectious; people in the group were stuffing plastic bags full of leaves and flowers, and their creased brows showed that they were trying to memorise the recommended method of cooking. I *think* I have got right the method he recommended for his special pancake:

> Make a pancake batter, put the leaves into it, pull off the flowers and add them, and the pancake comes out as a fritter; instead of an apple fritter, you've got a Black Locust fritter.

I forbore to say that I would much prefer the apple fritter.

That was, you might say, only a taste of Central Park, Manhattan's lung, recreation ground, free entertainment, public garden, sauntering-space and jogger's and mugger's paradise. Fifty-one streets long and four Avenues wide, it can be seen clearly from an aeroplane at its cruising height five miles up; its length is fully one-fifth of the entire island, and New York could never have survived without it, at any rate after the motor car had been invented.

For all its perfectly rectangular shape, Central Park is gloriously untidy, the paths wandering aimlessly, the contours haphazard, all symmetry avoided; in fact, as the map shows, there isn't a straight line anywhere inside the four ruthlessly straight lines that enclose it. (It isn't even flat; there are miniature hills in it.)

It was a derelict land when the idea of a park was born; derelict in two senses, because the boulder-strewn wilderness supported homeless squatters living in tents. They were unceremoniously bundled off it, as were the boulders, then the whole construction took some twenty years (including the Civil War). It has lakes and skating-rinks, a theatre, more than a thousand species of tree, tennis-courts and playing fields, a mighty reservoir and playgrounds, a tiny zoo embedded in one corner and the mighty Metropolitan Museum of Art in another, and when the sun shines on it, especially at an hour when the joggers are not abroad, cluttering the paths, it is a magical place, where all ages and tastes are carefully thought out and catered for. You can get married in Central Park (for that matter you can get married in Grand Central Station, and somebody did while I was in New York); there was a wedding party going on there when I was strolling through it, and a very old-fashioned wedding, too, with a bride in full fig, and toppers galore.

And of course, a horse-drawn carriage for the first part of the journey to the honeymoon. But the horse-drawn carriages of Central Park are in trouble. One of the horses had recently dropped dead in the shafts, just like Black Beauty's poor friend Ginger, worked to death by a cruel master. There was no suggestion that the Central Park beast had been ill-treated, but you can guess what is coming: an agitation, with placards, demonstrations and letters to the press denouncing the whole idea of the carriages as unfair to the animals.

Now there is a case for abolishing the trade altogether, though it has nothing to do with the condition of the horses, and everything to do with the rapacity of the coachmen. It has occurred to me that the carriages are the exact equivalent of the Venetian gondolas. Once upon a time, they were the principal means of getting about in Venice and New York respectively, but when the automobile had established itself in the latter, and the *vaporetto* in the former, they became anachronisms, and were relegated to the status of quaint tourist attractions; their numbers declined and are still declining, and they will never rise, because nobody will take either as a serious means of transport.

But that does not exhaust the similarities. What is the universal mark of any tourist attraction everywhere in the world? Overcharging. Every guidebook to Venice, when it gets to the gondola-ride, coughs discreetly behind its hand and suggests that the visitor engaging one (and it is indeed still a lovely experience) should make quite sure to agree the price before the journey starts. So, *mutatis mutandis*, does every guidebook to New York. After all, there are no meters in either, and there is no lack of plausibility in the patter of your average *gondoliere* and hackney-driver, as he demands from the unwary a sum that would suffice to fill in every pot-hole in the city with solid silver, or to build the long-promised barrage that is to stop Venice sinking, its piles similarly adorned with precious metal.

Anyway, mindful of my environmental duties, I inspected each horse as the carriages trotted by. Possibly, I had picked an unrepresentative sample, but there was not one that looked overworked. It is true that I would be hard put to it to list the tell-tale signs from which experts could deduce that the animal was suffering, but I decided that I would look out for those with their ribs showing clearly (ill-fed), those visibly panting (exhausted), and those which seemed to shrink from their driver (beaten). To my unequine eye, they all looked sleek and moved without apparent effort, and I deduced that my ancient and persisting enemies, the Single Issue Fanatics, were once more up to their tricks. Besides, the Central Park horses not only don't gallop, they don't even trot except on rare occasions; the normal gait is a steady walking-pace. For that matter, to judge by the long line of hopeful drivers lined up at the corner of the park, and the scarcity of willing passengers, the horses are much more likely to die of boredom than ill-treatment, so rarely must the turn of any one of them come round.

Beneath a tree, an improvised jam session was going on; it was plainly not a professional performance, but a bunch of friends playing for the sake of it. They were bass, trumpet, trombone, bassoon, drums and guitar. A good sign; the guitar was not electric. (You may say that it wouldn't have been much use in the circumstances if it had been, unless the oak behind them was equipped with a socket. But I have heard the welkin deafened from battery-operated ones in my time.) I wandered over and sat on the grass; I was the group's only audience, but they didn't seem to mind, not even when, in a break, they asked me where I came from (do all the peoples of the world have a built-in instinct that tells them when a stranger is in their midst?), and in the ensuing conversation I admitted that theirs was not my kind of music.

It was a good scene, for a good reason. These young men were making music to please themselves, the birds, the fluttering leaves and any strolling passers-by who felt like stopping to listen. They sought neither fee nor fame, nor even an audience, apart from the categories listed. Their music, and their mutual pleasure in making it, was the only end in view; if a talent scout from a recording studio had passed by and been impressed (I had no means of telling how good they were), they would presumably have opened negotiations (or possibly they wouldn't). But they were not on the look-out for such good fortune; their good fortune was their music, their friendship and the sun that shone on them, and it was enough.

I bade them farewell, and their music followed me as I strolled over to the model-boats pond. This being the United States, the model boats were five feet long, meticulous replicas of full-size vessels, and radio-controlled. O for the simple joys of a more simple childhood; I have in my time made wooden scooters, and can remember to this day how it is done. (Two planks, two ball-bearing wheels, a block, three eyelets, a bolt, a piece of stout dowelling for the handlebars; if feeling fancy, a bit of linoleum on the middle of the base, and an Oxo tin at the back for anything from a spare wheel to a bar of chocolate. Do children now make *anything*?)

There are a lot of picnics today, drawn in by the sunshine. One of them is amazingly elaborate, with tables and chairs and champagne; such gatherings always draw itinerant performers to them, and this is no exception. From nowhere, a musician materialises, a violinist, and the very one who entertained at the Book Fair; once more, he is playing along with his cassette-player; up comes *Eine Kleine Nachtmusik*, and here is our wandering musician leading them with his fiddle. More my kind of music, so when he took a break I asked him if he had thought up the idea of the invisible accompanist. 'Oh, no,' he said (after the regulation 'Where you from?'), 'it's been going for years – before cassettes were invented.' He explained that for budding musicians, the record companies used to put out discs with everything but the solo part on them, and presumably the cassette idea had followed.

On I went, this time pursued by Monte's *Czardas*, another reminder of my youth (there was a busker at the Prom queue who used to play it on a saxophone, of all things), and found myself at the roller-skating rink.

Safety wheels were obligatory (though I dare say the American passion for litigation and listening to hungry lawyers must have led, over the years, to many a claim for $5,000,000-worth of compensation for a grazed knee), but they certainly didn't cramp the skaters' style; for a time I thought that I was watching a skating contest or even a professional demonstration of the art, so skilled and apparently effortless were the performers, so intricate their arabesques. But what was, to an English eye, extraordinary was the wide age-spread of the skaters. Surely at a rink in Britain almost all the participants would be at most in their twenties, yet here there were middle-aged men and women, and some much older than that; I watched, entranced, a grey-haired old lady, who couldn't have been less than seventy, turning the most elaborate figures, even including that most alarming of techniques, the backwards figure-of-eight.

Central Park boasts that its visitors cannot get lost in it, but it reckons without me; I have never even been able to cross it by the shortest route. But that is what is so nice about it from the point of view of a visitor; if you can't wander aimlessly in a park, where can you wander aimlessly? And if you don't want to wander aimlessly, what are you doing in a park? One of the pleasures of getting repeatedly lost in Central Park is meeting the statues. I was delighted to discover that the subject of statuary in New York is as controversial and heated as it is elsewhere, and the heat has been warming the Park practically since it opened. At any rate, Calvert Vaux, one of the two joint designers of the Park, denounced the statuary that was springing up everywhere, saying that the park was for pleasure and recreation, 'not for sepulchral memorials'.

I know what he meant; Max Beerbohm suggested that in future, when it was desired to commemorate some great man lately dead, it should be done not by unveiling a new statue, but by veiling an existing one. The eyesores of public statuary in London, even when they were not designed by the late Oscar Nemon, have excited varying degrees of disapprobation for very many years, but the characters chosen by New York to be memorialised in stone, marble or bronze are a crew even more haphazard than those of London. Though 'chosen by New York' is unfair; it seems that until comparatively recently donors willing to meet the cost of erecting a statue in Central Park could do so with impunity and no doubt satisfaction. Nothing else could explain some of the choices.

Alice in Wonderland and Hans Christian Andersen need no explanation. (New York being what it is, the Park authorities hire a story-teller in the summer to read to children at the base of those much-loved figures.) Other childhood favourites are Mother Goose and Walter Scott. Robert Burns causes little surprise, and Shakespeare less. Figures from American folklore such as the Indian Hunter and Balto (he was the leader of the dog-team which managed to get through to Nome, in the frozen far north of Alaska, with the life-saving drugs needed to stem the city's uncontrollable diphtheria epidemic in 1925) also explain their places. Eagles and Prey, Tigress and Cubs, Dancing Bear and Dancing Goat likewise justify themselves. But then it becomes odder. Why Daniel Webster alone of American statesmen? Beethoven, to be sure, but why Schiller? If Victor Herbert, why no other composer of popular music? (Hush, children; one careless word and we may have Andrew Lloyd Webber.) Who was Sophie Loeb that she, and

39 You can even get married there ...

she alone, shall have a fountain – no, a Fountain? Who was A. H. Green that he should have a memorial bench? Who was Fitz-Greene Halleck, and why is he here, rubbing shoulders with the mighty dead?* Why, of all the units which fought bravely in the Civil War, is the only one to be provided with its monument in Central Park the Seventh Maine Regiment?

Other problems are more easily solved. American philanthropists are more generous than any others in the world; but they have never taken Shakespeare's advice to do good by stealth, and blush to find it fame. The most striking example of the desire of wealthy donors to have their names immortalised with their gifts is to be found in the Metropolitan Museum, which I shall come to shortly, but Central Park has its Delacorte Theater, its Wollman Memorial Rink (where I saw the skating granny), its Lasker Pool, its Alice H. and Edward A. Kerbs Memorial Boathouse and its Abraham and Joseph Spector Playground. (There are even Goldman Band Concerts; possibly these are concerts by the Goldman Band, but I doubt it.)

Central Park is nothing if not catholic in the tastes it caters for; apart from the boating, tennis and skating (ice in winter, of course), together with the weddings and the picnics, it offers football (both American and soccer), baseball, basketball, squash, fishing, horse-shoe throwing, ping-pong, concerts, square dancing, handball, rented bicycles and rented horses, marionettes, bowls, bird-watching and any amount of eating and drinking. And jogging, of course; and Steven Brill and his plant-eating expeditions. And, for heaven's sake, Cleopatra's *Other* Needle, twin sister to the one on the Embankment in London; I had a terrible fright when I came upon it quite unawares.

And an annual Festival called You Gotta Have Park, where the whole town turns out with its You Gotta Have Park badges, and raises immense funds for their beloved green rectangle.

And a tiny zoo, beautifully laid out, where one end of the Polar Bears' pool finishes in a huge glass plate, so that you can go round and watch them hurl themselves in sport or frustration (who can say which?) at the spectators, and where I had an enchanting experience: there was a woman with a small boy who insisted on being lifted up against the glass so that he could get as close as possible to an embrace with the nice cuddly white animal. But the mother had one arm in a sling, heavily plastered; she turned helplessly to me, and I knew my cue. I picked junior up and held him above my head, flat against the glass. The bear in turn obliged, rubbing

---

* Later: a bad poet. The mystery deepens.

himself against the glass, while junior kicked it in a transport of joy. I began to wonder just how thick the glass was, just what was the weight of water and bear combined, what junior's shoes were made of, but Bruin soon tired of the sport; he splashed off up to the other end of his pool, and I landed junior safely.

The zoo has a Lucy G. Moses Temperate Territory. Tell that to Moses, who lived in a singularly intemperate one. But it packs a great variety into its pocket-handkerchief size. There is a very handsome pool for the seals; I cannot persuade myself that the seal is not perfectly conscious of his role as the clown of the beasts, nor that he doesn't love playing it. I don't know what a seal's wink would look like, but surely they must be employing it when they rise from the water, do a double back-somersault and land on the surface with a mighty splash, designed to wet any spectators who have failed to back off when they saw what was coming. Dolphins play, for certain; but their play is like adult human diversion; there is a time for seriousness and a break for relaxation. In other words, the dolphin is a serious beast capable of merry-making; the seal is a comic character all through. We must avoid the anthropomorphic fallacy if we can; but with the seals we can't. They were born to figure in cartoons about circuses; indeed, they were born to figure in the circuses themselves.

A patch of tangled undergrowth and bracken sheltered some tiny deer; a pool was studded with stone islands, on which monkeys basked (I didn't know monkeys went with water); another, much smaller, pool proclaimed itself the otter's patch, but peer as I might, I could see none. I peered more intently, and still saw no otter, but I did see three gleaming, knobbly black heads with bulging eyes: alligators. But surely otters and alligators cannot cohabit? The otters would go down in a single bite, would they not? (Perhaps they have done, which is why I can't see any. I can see a lot of tortoises, though, which even alligators presumably find a hard nut to crack. Or possibly New York's zoo is the one place in the world where nature is *not* red in tooth and claw.)

Except, perhaps, where humans are concerned. That polar bear, for instance: everywhere else, even at the alligator pool, there are low ledges for visitors to lean or even sit on as they watch the animals. Not here, though: the barrier goes all the way up, eight or nine feet high. Any lower, and with one swipe from one of those mighty front paws the bear would have been served his dinner. It's a pity, I thought, that an animal so beautiful and majestic, yet playful in his divings and splashings, which make him also truly endearing (else why are there so many stuffed toys in the polar bear's shape and colour?), should be so very dangerous to human beings.

But then I collected myself; why shouldn't it be? Human beings, after all, didn't invent it, and what are the lords of creation on one side of the barrier are no more than a tasty snack on the other. There may be two kinds of anthropomorphism, not one.

The Central Park zoo is charming, not least because of the Delacorte Clock, round which, as the hour strikes, a set of bronze animals revolves gravely, the elephant playing the concertina, the goat naturally a set of pan-pipes, the hippopotamus a violin, the bear a tambourine, the kangaroo a cornet, and the penguin a drum. Charming, yes; but should a zoo be charming? Especially, perhaps, this kind, where the animals are kept in conditions as close as possible to their natural ones (the arctic zone includes a huge showcase which is plainly kept below freezing point, where the ducks waddle about in their natural icy habitat); a charming zoo is a tame zoo, and no zoo should be tame. Presumably the absence of any of the big cats is based on the impossibility of offering them anything like their original surroundings, and the unwillingness to put them in cages, even a spacious one. Even so, I think something is lost.

But at the far end of the park, something is found. Wildness, merry-making, informality step back; a perfect formal garden astonishingly closes this astonishing greensward. A huge, lovely lawn, meticulously cut, is surrounded by thick, handsome bushes; at one end another series of bushes has been topiarised into the spectacle of a green staircase; behind that is a handsome old wall, softened by creeper. On each side of the lawn, with hedges for dividers, is another garden, strewn with perfectly regular and symmetrical flower-beds, one with a miniature pool and statuary at the end, the other with a beautiful fountain amid bronze figures. A comparison leaps inevitably to mind: Glyndebourne. It has the same beauty, the same variety of colour, the same blazing green (they must practically empty the Park's huge reservoir to keep the grass so rich and ripe beneath the New York sun), the same air of peace and tranquillity. I had it for half an hour entirely to myself, and its beauty and harmony were such that it became almost impossible to believe that just a few feet away was the blaring, racing, sweating, raging traffic of Fifth Avenue.

I forgot to mention that the You Gotta Have Park festival includes as a sub-division a project called Walk with your Doc. (I read it first as Walk with your Dog. Who wouldn't?) It was part of an enterprise called Feeling Fine Systems Inc., and its directors were taking no chances: those who wished to Walk with their Doc had to sign a release waiving all rights and claims to damages 'arising as a result of my participation, including but not limited to any injuries I might suffer ...' The Mayor, of course, led off, pausing only to recommend everyone to take an aspirin every day; the sun was in my eyes as he gave this strikingly injudicious advice (I could hardly have been the only aspirin-allergic person in the crowd, and some might not yet have discovered their condition), so I couldn't see if the doctors were going pale, but I dare say they were. Nothing abashed, the Mayor strode off with a wave. But he relented later, and I sat beside him on the rim of the fountain, where he told me about the pot-holes in his city, and especially the ones in Fifth Avenue; he made them sound useful, charming and scientifically interesting. A moment later, he insisted that Central Park was 'very safe'. Shortly after that, he repeated, to everyone within earshot, his advice to eat an aspirin every day, this time graciously allowing an exception for women not yet past the menopause, in order to avoid heart disease.

An interesting man, then, this Koch. All these claims were put forward in perfect seriousness ('. . . that pot-hole can stay filled from six months to six years, depending on the depth of the street . . .'); he clearly sees his task as portraying New York in the very brightest of colours. I suspect that if I had asked him about all those murders in his bailiwick, he would have improvised a rationale for this remarkable tally, possibly based on the praiseworthy diligence of the New York Police Department in managing to find the bodies.

Koch is a genial-looking man; genial-looking and genial-sounding. Still, I wouldn't go for a nocturnal walk with him in the very safe Central Park if I were in the course of thwarting one of his dearly-nurtured plans for the city. By all accounts, even those of his enemies, Koch is financially honest; by all accounts, even those of his friends, he has made up for his own honesty by appointing some of the most lurid crooks the city has ever had in its administration. It took me some time, accompanying him on his rounds, to notice the two men who looked not at him but at the crowd, and some further time to realise why each of them had a T-shirt loosely wrapped about his right hand; this is, shall we say, a controversial Mayor. Though he won't even let anyone pay for a lunch *à deux*, that baby's-bottom countenance should not fool anyone; as Jerome Charyn says in his book *Metropolis*,★ the Mayor's motto ('He conjures up indignities like a vengeful toad') is 'Mess with me and you'll get hurt'. And Koch does not forget. When Mario Cuomo beat him handsomely for the Governorship of New York, Cuomo made an enemy for life; if Koch ran for President, *and won*, he would not abate the smallest part of his hostility. They have long memories in these parts.

★ Avon

There is no British equivalent for the Mayor of a large and powerful American city. We have mayors, of course, though they are almost entirely ceremonial, and we have leaders of our municipal councils, who do have some real powers, but the bruising fights for American mayoralties are unknown. Nor is the American system a ladder on which a Mayor is likely to climb to supreme office; the Governor's mansion is the highest goal reasonably available, and in a city like New York the Mayor has more power than the Governor anyway. Koch had been in Congress before running for Mayor, but a Congressman from a New York district has still less power and influence. (The only New York Mayor with an eye on the White House was the absurd Lindsay, who sowed the seeds of New York's financial ruin, and announced, when he left the job, that he would rather like to be President, the only doubt in his mind being under which party banner he should run. He chose the Republicans, entered a few primaries, got derisory votes, pulled out and has never been heard of again, thank God.)

There is also no equivalent in Britain for the corruption in a large American city. As I write, the number of New York officials under indictment runs into scores, and any hope that the suicide of Donald Manes might provide a respite (by blaming the dead man for his own share and the share of all the others) has long since gone. Is America's financial corruption another facet of her violent crime? Have we been treating the violence as something without progeny or parents, self-contained and having no connection with anything else? Is America – or at least are her big cities – endemically criminal rather than endemically only murderous?

Any Mayor of New York who wants to stay Mayor must form his own coalition, and ideally it must include the blacks, Jews, Hispanics, Italians, Irish and the labour unions. Koch is remarkable for antagonising three of the ingredients: the blacks, the Hispanics and the unions. But he did not do so simply by failing to guard his tongue; he did it deliberately, feeling that the political composition of the city had changed, and was still changing, in a direction that demanded a new disposition of forces. His violent attack on Jesse Jackson was believed to have been an explosion of pent-up anger; it was more likely a signal that he would no longer court the blacks, since he had sources of votes which would be more favourably disposed to him if he showed that he was no admirer of black influence, let alone achievement, and the same applied to Puerto Ricans. (The politics of New York are labyrinthine; but the ethnics of New York are much more so.) Mayor Koch knows which groups are falling behind and which are advancing; at the time of my sojourn in New York, he had made no speech lauding the enterprise of the Koreans of the city, but if he hasn't made one yet, he soon will.

Koch could, and would, talk in glowing, enthusiastic terms about the delights of the South Bronx, Bedford-Stuyvesant and the most crack-infested corners of Harlem; he would praise Hell as a very desirable area if it was in New York. It was not surprising, then, that his eyes lit up when I mentioned Fifth Avenue. 'This Avenue', he said, 'is like the Champs Elysées for Paris, and we have to be very protective of it, especially about the number of parades – we now have a moratorium on any new ones.' I said it seemed as though there was one a day, and he said no, about twenty a year. Then the politician peeked out from beneath the enthusiasm:

> We have all the major ethnic parades like the St Patrick's Day Parade and the Israeli Day Parade, and the Ukrainian Day Parade and the Polish Day Parade and they are wonderful and I go to every one of them and I love them all.

Undoubtedly; if alligators had votes, he would go to the Alligator Day Parade, and love that too. But there was no mistaking his affection for New York's noblest thoroughfare:

> It has six of the really wonderful museums in this city, what we call Museum Mile, and just taking a walk on Fifth Avenue you see the great Public Library with the two lions in front of it, and it's recently been restored under a marvellous head of the library system, Vartan Gregorian, and oh! people love Fifth Avenue. We have a lot of nice streets, you know, Madison and Park are streets that are known all over the world, but I would say the street that runs all the way from Greenwich Village, starting at Washington Square and running all the way up through to Harlem, that's the street that people here love. You know, in earlier days, before 1960, Robert Moses wanted to turn the street known as West Broadway into Fifth Avenue South. But that would have been a phoney; West Broadway is West Broadway, and Fifth Avenue is Fifth Avenue, and I love it. This is a wonderful town, a wonderful town!

The politician had got back under the enthusiasm; this Mayor would not stop loving Fifth Avenue if he lost his office, and he would go on thinking New York a wonderful town, though a very ungrateful one. He rejoices in the 'Landmark legislation' which belatedly forbade the owners of historic or specially beautifully buildings to demolish them or sell them for demolition; belatedly, because by the time the legislation was through New York had been comprehensively denuded of some of its finest and most graceful architecture. 'But we still save a lot', cried Koch, 'and you can't tear them down any more, they are landmarks. And we love it!'

Oh, we do. And what do we think is so special about Central Park?

Well, Central Park is known throughout the world as one of the world's great parks, if not the greatest park. This is genius, this park; it's eight hundred and forty acres, and it's entirely artificial, the trees weren't here, the hills weren't here, it was just a slum shanty town. Many people have wanted to build in it and the people have stood up on their hind legs and said no, because if you had let all the people build all the things they've wanted to build since the park was created, it would be just a park of cement. Instead it's eight hundred and forty acres of lush flora and fauna.

Fauna? I had visions of dappled deer, of foxes and badgers, of beavers damming the lake, of a leopard or two and a bear with a Koch button pinned to its chest.

Well, maybe not too much fauna, but squirrels – we've got squirrels. You seen the squirrels?

I had seen the squirrels. They undoubtedly voted for Koch. Sensible squirrels.

Now if you didn't know who this man was (though you would, because he would make haste to tell you), what would you take him for? An extrovert, to be sure; vain, certainly, hugely supplied with energy. But what would you think he did for a living? The curious fact is that the most political figure in New York would not be taken for a politician, let alone a brutally realistic, vindictive, cunning, ambitious, skilled and successful one. The innocence of his appearance, the freshness and fluency of his discourse, his light-hearted demeanour, his genuine informality, his no less genuine demotic attitudes – these would deceive even the sharpest and most cynical eye. It is quite possible that he hasn't read a book for a dozen years or more, and he seems none the worse for such abstention; it is just as likely that he hasn't had a long conversation about something other than politics for at least as long, again with no apparent ill results. On his foray into the Park, he had to listen to not one, but *two*, immensely bad and boring speeches by the Parks Commissioner before he could clear his own throat, but there was no sign of impatience, no visible flagging of attention or interest; this is a consummate politician. I recall an item from a news-film of Harry Truman, at the Convention which nominated him as Roosevelt's

Vice-President in 1944. Truman, on the platform, had fallen asleep, pre-sumably because of the oratory he had just been compelled to listen to, when one of the speakers mentioned him in favourable terms; there was a round of applause, which woke Truman up, and he automatically began to clap. You could define Koch as a man who, while he might fall asleep during the speech of a comrade, if only in self-defence, would be in complete command of himself the moment he woke up, no matter what or who had woken him.

Surely the clue to Ed Koch is that he enjoys the job. On that point, there can be no doubt; as I sat beside him while we talked, and as I trotted obediently along while he toured the Park, the relish and zest in his voice and face were unmistakable. Nor were they to be confused with the enthusiasm, slightly touched with surprise, that is the mark of one who has gained a much sought-after position but who cannot quite believe his luck. Koch manifestly believes that the voters got it right when they elected him Mayor (and, *a fortiori*, that they were wrong when they didn't make him Governor), and his enjoyment of his office, which with other Mayors has often been a crown of thorns, is deep and crisp and even.

But he is not entirely invulnerable and, more surprising, he does make bad mistakes. In July, 1988, he visited Northern Ireland. The province has long been a necessary stop-over for American politicians courting the Irish vote, and although the proportion of Irish-descendant New Yorkers is smaller than their Bostonian cousins, it is still very substantial, so Koch, sooner or later, had to make the pilgrimage. He followed hard on the heels of one of the Kennedy scions, a nasty little man who came ignorant and left quarrelsome *and* ignorant; Koch must have smiled as he prepared, thoroughly briefed, for his own visit. Head high, he marched towards the banana skin.

Guided by the Minister for Northern Ireland, Tom King, Koch toured the province. He returned to New York as though he had been to Damascus rather than Belfast; he denounced the IRA, he praised the British garrison as guardians of the peace, he spoke to British journalists in terms amazing by any American standards, and more amazing still by the standards of a Mayor of New York:

> I don't regret for one moment what I said about the British in Northern Ireland. Tell Mrs Thatcher and your brave soldiers that not only myself but the majority of Americans think they are doing a good job. The British are not an occupying force but safeguarding the peace. The IRA are a disgusting organisation that has to be stamped out. And if I discovered any of my democratic political

colleagues or supporters backed them in any way I would spit in their faces.

Then the storm broke, *and the Mayor ran for cover*. The Irish–Americans whom he had denounced for supplying support and weapons for murder called him to heel, and to heel he obediently came. Had he said that the British in Northern Ireland 'are playing a positive role'? He had; but now, 'I foolishly used an expression which caused great pain to many Americans. I regret this deeply.' Had he said 'the British are not an occupying army'? He had; but now he explained that they are, and indeed had been for 800 years. Had he said that 'British troops should be in Northern Ireland until a political solution has been worked out, otherwise the blind among us can see there would be a bloody civil war'? He had; but now 'the British troops have been transformed from a protector of civilians to an instrument for assuring British domination.'

Now when Ed Koch wedges his foot that deep in his mouth, the whole town sits up and gasps. It is easy to see what possessed him when he was in Northern Ireland; even with Cardinal O'Connor, quite useless with hatred, at Koch's elbow ('He has his constituents, too', said the Mayor), he saw reality for himself, and having seen it, called it by its name. For some hours after the name-calling started, he sat tight; but when he counted the New York-Irish, and measured the intensity of his wish for another term as Mayor, his nerve broke.

The eagerness and satisfaction with which people thousands of miles away from the scene contemplate murder has often been remarked upon, especially by those who are running the risk of being murdered. But I know of no more extreme form of this vicarious advocacy than the American-Irish thirst for English blood. Of course, many of them are descended from Irish immigrants who had fled their native country pursued by starvation or persecution; but that is true of very many American immigrants and their descendants, and the lust for other people to be killed (and to do the killing) is unique to the American-Irish. Heywood Broun, as liberal and tolerant an American as any man who ever wrote in the American Press, called the Irish 'the cry-babies of the world', and it is an excellent phrase, bitterly full of meaning. Think of the Indians, the Cypriots, the Kenyans, the Malaysians – of all the subject peoples of the British Empire – who struggled in their different ways (sometimes through massive violence and counter-violence) to be free to govern themselves, however badly. Yet the most striking phenomenon of the ending of the empire was the speed and completeness with which such newly-enfranchised nations made friends with the mother country, all passion spent. They might put up memorials to those whom the British executed or jailed as rebels, but the hatred – often more apparent than real, and in any case inspired solely in the cause of independence – disappeared with astonishing speed once independence was gained.

With the single exception of the Irish; the cry-babies have still not mopped their tears, and continue to blame others for all their ills. Mayor Koch, well-briefed though he was, probably does not realise how little interest the Irish who actually live in the Republic take in the cause of their brothers in the North, and their indifference is significant; they are the nearest to the struggle, and have a sensibly pragmatic attitude to the violence, which consists of a fervent hope that it won't start to happen in the Republic. But beyond that, very few would lift a hand to unite Ireland.

Why, then, are so many American Irish willing to lift a voice in the pleasant cause of murdering Englishmen at a distance? And their attitude is by no means only an attitude; many of them actually give *money*, of all things, to the cause, not all of them in the nightly shakedowns in Third Avenue bars, where common prudence dictates a contribution for the rattling box. (Noraid, incidentally, the organisation set up to raise funds for the IRA gunmen, is frequently denounced by the British government, and was – courageously – by President Reagan, but neither should worry too much, since most of the money contributed is stolen long before it can embark for Ireland, and most of what does get there is stolen by the recipients; I doubt if Noraid have succeeded in having the legs of more than half a dozen Irish children blown off by gelignite paid for by the organisation, which surely indicates a disproportionate effort.)

We are not supposed to say such things today, but the truth about the Irish in Ireland is that their country, delightful though it is to visit, should really be classified as part of the Third World, and although they have, most enviably, found a way of life that offers a higher level of serenity than in any other impoverished nation except India, they limp tragically behind most of the world in terms of initiative, energy, enterprise and success. From afar, the mess looks romantic; but then, in the Celtic Twilight *everything* looks romantic, which is why the Celtic Twilight was invented. And – we are certainly not supposed to say *this* – the Irish contribution to the United States has been strikingly meagre. It has given the country, or at least the eastern part of it, many politicians and policemen, and a few crooked but successful nineteenth-century industrialists; but a comparison with the success of the Jews and the blacks (these two very different from each other but each much more different from the Irish), and for that matter the Poles, and now the Chinese, leaves the Irish far behind.

A far cry from Mayor Koch? Not really. He spoke out bravely and truthfully about the situation in Northern Ireland; he called the IRA by their right name; he saw, and stated, the necessity of a continuing British presence in the province; he damned the claim that a British withdrawal would not lead to a bloodbath, even while his travelling companion, the Cardinal, was continuing to make it; and then he went home and faced his own political necessity. To that necessity he bowed, leaving the Irish suspicious of him and the realists contemptuous; the day will go down in New York as The Day Mayor Koch Forgot to Duck. If he is defeated in his struggle for re-election, his successor may institute it as an annual celebration.

He is a strange man. At least, I think he is. Consider: he came into the mayoral office just after New York had been saved from bankruptcy, but when it was by no means clear that it *had* been saved. (Felix Rohatyn, who organised and led the rescue, said 'Saving New York is like making love with a gorilla – you don't stop when you're tired, you stop when the gorilla's tired.') The famous *Daily News* headline that had followed President Ford's refusal to use any Federal funds to help New York – FORD TO CITY: DROP DEAD – was in fact a fake; Ford had indeed insisted that he would not bail New York out, but the 'Drop dead' was a paraphrase, to put it mildly. But Koch had lowered himself into the cauldron, without knowing whether he was going to be cooked, and naturally, when he found he wasn't, he moved rapidly to claim some of the credit. Well, we can agree that he is out for Koch: 'Mess with me and you'll get hurt.' We can agree that when he has served himself he will loyally serve the city. But in a situation which does not permit him to serve both, not even consecutively – which is what the fiscal crisis was – which would have come first?

I had read about him, talked about him, heard much about him; now I was talking *with* him, at no more than an arm's length. From this position, and to my own surprise, I found he passed the test. No politician in his office can be entirely honest politically, and very few indeed have even been honest in any way at all. But Koch struck me as a man who, when the very last chip was down (and not one moment, or one chip, before), would put himself second to the city. You don't have to take my word for it; William Buckley, doyen of the American political right, has no reason to love Koch's politics, and as a matter of fact doesn't. But he knows Koch, and this is his conclusion:

It seemed for a while as though everyone who surrounded Ed Koch was on the take – even as the objectives he sought to serve were atrophying. The schools were rotten, crime increased, people who could were leaving the city – It is saddening, and reminds us that maybe Theodore H. White was correct when he said thirteen years ago ... that New York is, in fact, ungovernable. But even if that becomes history's verdict, I for one shan't escape the memory of the shrewd, thoughtful bachelor congressman setting out to help other people's children, and the riotously enthusiastic municipal mayor who thought for a while that he was grooving with destiny and who, right through the thicket of angry charges, denunciations, dismissals, innuendos, left some of us with the feeling, back there, that here was a good man.

Who am I to disagree? But I shall add one more straw to Buckley's pile. Ed Koch is a middle-aged bachelor, who for a time squired – most implausibly – a former Miss America, and whose name has not been linked with that of any other woman at all, let alone plausibly. But nobody in New York – a town well supplied with malice and with ample reasons to deploy it – has suggested that he is a homosexual.

Dwelling too much on Ed Koch is dangerous; it can lead to hallucinations, if not worse. One day I came out into Fifth Avenue opposite Tiffany's, around which there had gathered an enormous crowd. Since it was a Sunday, the crowd could not have implied a sale or a celebrity customer, but it was difficult to get near enough to discover what was going on. Then I saw a banner, strung across the top of Tiffany's doorway, though I couldn't see, through the throng, what message it bore. As I wormed into the crowd, I saw a platform built in front of the door, below the banner, and at once I knew what had happened. The Revolution had begun, and where more appropriately than with Tiffany's, hated centre of the hated rich, whose doom was now sealed? With any luck, I reckoned, I shall see the first batch of *aristos* arrive in their tumbril for execution.

I was now in the thick of the fray, and caught a clearer glimpse of the platform; the only figure on it I could see, however, was an enormous gorilla, which hardly advanced my understanding, particularly because it was very obviously not a real gorilla but a man in a gorilla skin. What would a gorilla be doing in a revolution? Was he the executioner? If so, what is the symbolism behind the curious form of an executioner-gorilla?

Before I could think of any answers to these questions, sanity went through another ordeal, this one threatening to take me up a creek from which no traveller returns, for it seemed that the Revolution was taking place to music; I could glimpse figures other than the gorilla on the platform, and heard a pleasant light tenor voice singing, to the accompaniment of a small orchestra, a song – the words were perfectly clear – which had for a refrain the line 'That is why I'm proud to be, The mayor of your town'.

It was at once apparent that the Revolution had not, after all, broken out. But instead, it seemed, Ed Koch had gone to the almost incredible lengths of hiring an orchestra, a platform, a banner *and a gorilla*, solely to get himself once more into the public eye.

Then the crowd swayed enough for me to get to the front, and all was plain – disappointing, but plain. The singer was *not* His Honour, but an ordinary professional musician; the Revolution was far away as ever; and the banner over Tiffany's door read 'Love your landmarks'. The whole thing, including the song (which presumably dated back to the era of Mayor Wagner or even Gentleman Jimmy Walker) was to raise interest in New York's 'listed buildings'. There were stalls along the Avenue, where interested passers-by could join the various historical, architectural and preservation societies; landmark-lovers wandered about giving out leaflets; the singer on the platform struck up 'New York, New York, it's a helluva town'; and gradually the crowd began to disperse. I never did discover what a gorilla had to do with New York's landmark buildings.

★   ★   ★

It started with a bag-lady. She was sitting on a bench in the sunshine, all her belongings, in a couple of plastic bags, beside her. It was a sunny day. She was on Fifth Avenue opposite Temple Emanu-El, the biggest synagogue in all New York (of the Reform persuasion), with probably – no, certainly – the wealthiest congregation of any synagogue in the world. Perhaps – a strange thought – of any place of worship, no matter what religion. It was time to think about Jews, and New York.

Everybody knows that New York City has the greatest concentration of Jews in the world – two million of them – outdoing any city in Israel, and constituting by far the largest ethnic group in the city. The most interesting thing about this rubric is that it isn't true. It hasn't been true for some years, and it is getting less true all the time. The largest ethnic groups in New York are the Hispanics and the blacks; both now comfortably outnumber the Jews, and there certainly are not as many as two million Jews in the city any more. The demographic truth is that the Jews of America are not reproducing themselves in sufficient numbers to stop their population falling, and the social truth is that many Jews have moved out of New York City. Some say that there are only a million left, with another million in the outer suburbs. It seems unlikely; even biology and a distaste for the city combined cannot have reduced the numbers so sharply.

Never mind; the bag-lady is certainly not counting, and I doubt if the Hispanics or the blacks are. And it is the bag-lady who, at the moment, interests me. Across the road, snaking down the street at the side of the synagogue, is a long line of men and women who are going to be fed by the charity of Temple Emanu-El because they have not got the price of their own meal. I take it that when the line begins to move into the building, the bag-lady will join the line. Meanwhile, she is sensibly resting her feet and sunning herself at the same time.

Inside, it might be a cathedral, probably Romanesque (it has a pitched roof); it is certainly dark enough. As my eyes became accustomed to the twilight, the vastness of it was apparent. Like everywhere else in New York they scatter facts like seeds. It will hold 2500 worshippers, it is 200 feet long, it is 100 feet wide, it is 103 feet high; it is paved with Travertine marble, the Sanctuary is 30 feet deep and 40 broad; there are 55 rows of pews, the pitched roof is of walnut; the doors of the Ark are of bronze, the organ has 7681 pipes, 116 stops and 32 bell chimes, the rose window is Gothic in design and was made in England; it is the third Temple Emanu-El in New York, the first one having been built in 1845 in a much less fashionable area, the second in 1868 and sited on Fifth Avenue though at 43rd Street, and the present one at Fifth and 65th, in 1929, replacing (doubtless with a frisson of satisfaction) Vincent Astor's purpose-built mansion. I was assured that his ghost has never been seen.

The Jews may be declining (though they still have one hundred synagogues in Manhattan alone), but you wouldn't know it in Temple Emanu-El, particularly when talking to its Rabbi. Now the Rabbi of a place like this would have to be a formidable man, but I was so unprepared for the smart, suave, clean-shaven figure who greeted me that I had to tell him first that when I was a boy the Rabbi didn't look a bit like him. (A few years before, I had told Rabbi Julia Neuberger the same thing, but it didn't mean quite the same, and anyway *she* blushed.)

Dr Ronald Sobel did not; he acknowledged my point and suggested that he looked more like an investment banker. But he talked like a very modern man of God. He immediately launched into a discussion of the problem all Jews face, and secular ones like me most of all (I had introduced the topic). 'What are we?' he said: 'Are we a religion, are we a people, are we a civilisation, are we a culture?' I forbore to give him my own answer, which has long been 'I'm damned if I know', but he went on to point out that the increasing secularisation of the western world is not a recent growth:

This is not just a phenomenon of post World War Two, or the twentieth century or the nineteenth, or post the Enlightenment or post Emancipation; it goes all the way back to the Renaissance, which began the secular tide.

And now? There are more young people today at Temple Emanu-El. Are the numbers huge and dramatic? No, but there are certainly more.

It occurred to me that the two huge modern incoming waves of religious revival – resurgent Islam and fundamentalist television Christianity – are not exactly propitious indicators for a renaissance in Judaism, but it then occurred to me that apart from the tiny zealot sects in Israel, whose members stone motor cars seen driving on the Sabbath, there hasn't been a fanatic movement in Jewry for many centuries. (I suppose anti-semitic fanaticism is quite enough for Jews to cope with.)

Now just down the Avenue, at the Tiffany Ball, I had noticed – I could hardly have failed to – that there was an enormous proportion of Jews among the names of the sponsors and donors and advertisers. The phil-anthropic enterprises of Jews, and in particular American Jews, and especially in New York, are on a scale so gigantic that they have bred psychological theories in explanation. One of these is the guilt theory: Jews have been persecuted so long, so often and so variously that they have come to believe, unconsciously, that they deserve it. Presumably this is reinforced, and was perhaps originated, by the deicide accusations of Christianity down the ages – indeed, until as recently as the Second Vatican Council. (I dare say Archbishop Lefebvre believes in it still.) I was once told by a Jewish taxi-driver in London that the two groups of passengers who most con-sistently over-tipped were Jews and prostitutes.

Dr Sobel preferred a more scriptural explanation – well, he is a Rabbi – and argued it with considerable eloquence, drawn from what was plainly a sharp and well-filled mind.

Jews are generous because they are responding to an ethical imperative that is deeply embedded in both Rabbinic and Biblical Judaism. One reads the pages of the Hebrew Bible, and on virtually every page one is confronted with a demand, a divine demand, a God-centred demand, to care for the orphan, to care for the widow, to care for the deprived. It all begins really in the very first pages of Genesis. There is the first moment of fratricide, of murder, and God asks the question 'Where is thy brother?', and the response is, 'Am I my brother's keeper?' And indeed then the rest of the Hebrew Bible and the totality of Judaism that emerges thereafter is a resounding affirmative: Yes, I am my brother's keeper.

Well, the queue was now stretching right down the block, and the soup-kitchen would shortly be in action. Only, said the Rabbi gently, they did not call it a soup-kitchen, and his mien suggested that he would prefer it if I didn't, either. So what is it? 'It is our lunch programme.' I indicated that a lunch programme by any other name . . . but no: 'These people are our *guests*; there is music, there are flowers on the tables.' And – more gently still – no, I could not watch them at their meal.

I was warming to this wise and businesslike man, and tossed him another fire-cracker: just opposite, across the most opulent street in the world, the bag-lady would be sleeping tonight. For that matter, she would probably be sleeping there in January, too. So?

So,

I believe that America is the greatest democracy the world has ever known and I would want to live here at this time more than any other place at this time or any time past. But right here in the chateaux of this great wealth, of Fifth Avenue, within the chateaux and the great wealth there is profound, profound poverty. And this contradiction between great wealth and abject poverty is a profound indictment of our country at this time. That while we are the wealthiest nation today that the world has ever known, as well as the most democratic and liberal, we should have so much poverty and so much hunger and so much homelessness is a terrible indictment.

And so?

At the end of December last we opened up, in addition to our Sunday lunch programme, where we have fed thirty thousand human beings, we have opened up a shelter for men. We did it in conjunction with the Marble Collegiate Church, which is Protestant, and with a Catholic Church, the Church of St Francis de Sales. So here we have an example of real interfaith enterprise. But we are doing more than simply providing shelter; we deal with the stupendous bureaucracy of our city, we are providing health services, job training, legal advocacy, drug abuse rehabilitation. And we are doing all of this at a cost per person per day of less than one half of what it costs the City of New York to warehouse five hundred human beings where all they are doing is providing a cot and a place to sleep. And we are grateful – grateful, not proud – that we can do it. But beyond our gratitude is our hope that we won't have to do it much longer.

I went out through the Synagogue (we had been talking in the Rabbi's study) into sunshine so fierce after the darkness that my eyes began to water; perhaps the guests of the Sunday lunch programme, who were just filing in (in, that is, to the Isaac Mayer Wise Memorial Hall) may have thought I was weeping at their plight.

I wasn't; but I was thinking about it. Is poverty in wealthy countries the tail without which the dog could not wag? If people are free to become millionaires – billionaires – multi-billionaires – must other people be free to fail, to slip through the cracks into the dungeons of abominable poverty? Cannot a free economic system work unless the race is always to the swift?

I think not. But in that case, what do we do about those who fail completely, who do not become billionaires or millionaires or even people with a modest but reasonable competence? What do we do about the bag-lady and the Sunday lunch guests? It is no use telling ourselves – though we do – that the bag-lady has at least got *some* possessions in her bags, and the lunch guests are at least guaranteed *one* meal a week, and the homeless man has got *somewhere* to sleep. It is true, but it is a truth which leads nowhere. The 'trickle-down' effect is another truth in a cul-de-sac, even if it is true at all, which I begin to doubt. I believe, as fervently as any member of the Institute of Economic Affairs, that minimum-wage laws, rent-control, high marginal tax-rates, flat-rate state benefits, can only *increase* unemployment, homelessness, national decline and poverty; very well, but while their abolition is *reducing* these stains, but has not yet brought about their complete extinction, what do we do about the unemployed, the homeless and the very poor?

Give them soup-kitch – that is, Sunday lunch? Let them sleep in inter-denominational shelters at half the cost of what the city pays to provide a quarter of the godmen's facilities? Raise money at the Tiffany Ball to help them to a job? But the Sunday lunch programme cannot feed all the hungry, the ecumenical shelter cannot sleep all the homeless, Just a Break cannot place all the unemployed. Where does the State come in? More pertinently, *how*? What can, and should, nations do, as nations, to relieve real distress?

Jews have no more responsibility to answer such questions than other people; no more, but no less. There is a Federation of Jewish Philanthropies in New York, which provides support to 130 organisations who need it. Up towards the top of the Park, the Mount Sinai Hospital, which goes on for block after block, is made colourful by the signs bearing the names of the benefactors – Guggenheim, Annenberg, Klingenstein – their alms-giving is on a stupendous scale; surely they are practising what Rabbi Sobel preaches, the Jewish *duty* to those less fortunate.

I don't know. But I had one more question to ask Rabbi Sobel, and I went back into Temple Emanu-El. I sat for a while in the little ante-chapel of the Synagogue (84 feet long, 50 feet wide, 45 feet high, seats 350 people), and gave up thinking about poverty and affluence. I thought instead, for the thousandth time, about what I mean when I say I am a Jew: what *I* mean. I don't practise the religion, and I wasn't brought up in it. I don't take part in any specially Jewish activities, and I like my bacon crisp. I have never suffered from anti-semitism, but you don't have to be a Jew to deplore prejudice. On the other hand, my name is Levin, and you can't get a name much more Jewish than that. Am I a Jew at all? I can say only this: I *feel* myself part of an ancient and unbroken tradition of Jewish culture, the twin towers of which are a veneration for learning and a sense of duty to seek the answer to the ultimate questions 'Why am I here?' and 'What am I supposed to do about it?' I feel very powerfully some of the great Jewish symbols like the Passover dinner, though I haven't attended a *seder* for very many years, and for that matter, I hadn't been in a synagogue, except for weddings and funerals, for even longer. And although I now find myself more at home with Christ than Jehovah, something tugs me from an ancient past.

How ancient? Certainly, on my two brief visits to Israel, I felt nothing that could be described as homecoming, nothing to identify with, nothing to make me feel, even slightly, a stranger in my native Britain. And yet there is a tiny clue, which takes an odd form. Whenever I hear or read about a Jew who has done something shameful, or committed a crime, I feel uneasy. Not for social reasons, not for anything as rational as fear that it may increase anti-semitism, but because in some curious way, which I cannot define, the miscreant has touched, has *stained*, me, and not only me, but what I cannot help but think is my people.

I got up and went to ask the Rabbi the last question. No, the food at the Sunday lunch programme is not kosher.

★   ★   ★

There is no music on Fifth Avenue, and no theatre. But the arts are by no means neglected; indeed, no other street in the city, and probably none anywhere in the world, can boast an array of public art galleries to touch the Museum Mile (the very traffic-light poles bear the name). There are nine in the stretch, and three of them can hold their own against all comers: the Frick, the Guggenheim and the mighty Met.

Was it planned, this procession of buildings crammed with art lovingly displayed? No, of course not; but the effect, as of choice pearls on a necklace, is such that it might well have been, and my march up Fifth Avenue was slowed down in the most delightful manner by my need to explore the walls of these treasure-houses. Mind you, though it is possible to see every item in the Frick in a day, even with a good deal of lingering over old favourites, and to do much the same at the Guggenheim, particularly if the current exhibition merits no more than a glance, thus leaving time for the Guggenheim's permanent collection, the Met, on the other side of the road, defies total comprehension, let alone total inspection. A visitor can drown five fathoms deep in the statistics before looking at a single picture, and anyone who enters the Met in a state of bravado, confident that since he has seen the Uffizi, the Hermitage and the Louvre, the Met's profusion holds no terrors for him, is in for a powerful shock. Of *course* it is the biggest museum in the world; I have calculated that to walk briskly round every room, without slackening pace and without looking at a single exhibit, would take upwards of two-and-a-half hours.

We had better get going.

The Frick Collection was compiled by Henry Clay Frick. Indeed, it *was* his collection, and the beautiful mansion that holds it was his town house. Now Frick was a brutal, dishonest scoundrel, and a tightwad to boot; where now is the sanctifying purity of truth and beauty? 'There's no art to find the mind's construction in the face', said Shakespeare, and no-one has the right to say that Frick didn't enjoy his pictures as much as any visitor to the house with the three dollars' entrance fee and a few hours to spare rejoicing in genius. And it would be a singularly high-minded visitor who felt guilty about enjoying such ill-gotten gains. Nobody seems to know whether the pictures (and furniture, of which there is a good deal, mostly as choice as the pictures) are in the same positions as they were when Frick dined at home, but Frick was not a man too shy to display his wealth and what he could buy with it; he would not have had his treasures stored away. One of the few attractive qualities of the American robber barons of the late nineteenth century and early twentieth is that, although it was likely that they had little or no artistic taste, they had enough sense to find men who had plenty, and to take their advice. This, of course, is where Duveen came in, as the greatest dealer and vicarious collector of his era, perhaps of any era. As it happens, Duveen was as crooked as most of those whom he served, and possibly more so; but the combination of men of stupendous wealth but no knowledge, with a man of great knowledge and stupendous greed, must have been one of the most fruitful and lasting partnerships in all art history. And Frick was one of Duveen's best customers.

The house itself, inside, is a beautiful, airy creation (the architects were the ones who built the New York Public Library), with a lovely oasis in the form of a glass-enclosed vestibule with an oval pool and a gently plashing fountain; I wonder that all New York doesn't crowd into it in a heatwave. But the walls are adorned (the pictures are lavishly spread, too, not crammed) with one of the world's most astonishing arrays of master-pieces. As important art galleries or museums go, the Frick Collection is very small; only ten blocks north, the Met probably has more acres of floor-space than the Frick has pictures on display. But Frick's collection is, in the full meaning of the word, choice. It is unlikely that any private collection that size, and very few much bigger ones, can or could dem-onstrate such majestic and unerring eclectism. Possibly even the Thyssen collection has a less broad range than this one, and Thyssen's is far larger. Frick has at least one picture or sculpture by (and from their best work) Renoir, Vermeer, Boucher, Hogarth, Gainsborough, Reynolds, Fragonard, Houdon, Giovanni Bellini, Titian, El Greco, Rembrandt, Van Dyck, Hals, Velazquez, Bronzino, Veronese, Goya, Holbein, Pollaiuolo, Constable, Lawrence, Romney, Turner, Piero della Francesca, Duccio, Van Eyck, Whistler, Claude Lorraine, Degas, David, Hobbema, Georges de La Tour and Chardin.

But between the catalogue and the pictures falls the shadow. Henry Clay Frick was a monster, a criminal, even an accessory to murder. To be sure, he was a man of his time (1849–1919); moreover, though it is difficult to believe, he was by no means the worst. He started his appalling career as a purveyor and operator of coking-ovens, and speedily found himself holding two-thirds of the trade in his domain; they might as well have called Pittsburgh Frickville. Eventually, he joined forces with Carnegie, who was an even bigger crook than he was, though a startlingly philanthropic one; it was Carnegie who coined the magnificent slogan, 'A man who dies rich dies disgraced'. (Curiously for so determined and unsentimental a man, Carnegie was a lifelong pacifist, and came close to trouble in the First World War for maintaining his views and giving public expression to them.) Mind you, despite the famous slogan, his net fortune when he died was more than 23 million dollars – and that was in 1919. We shall come to his house, which is now also a museum, further up the Avenue.

Frick's finest hour was in 1892, after he had got together with Carnegie. The scene was the Homestead Mill (steel mill, that was – these people ground faces not bread), and the occasion was a strike and 'sit-in' by the workers, who had been told that their wages were to be cut. Frick, as Carnegie's gofer, was in charge of the eviction, and he engaged a massive army of Pinkerton men, taking no chances (in a steel mill, after all, there are plenty of materials for making barricades, and perhaps even more for making weapons). The ensuing battle was one of the bloodiest in America's industrial history; it lasted nearly a week, and left a dozen or more corpses in its wake.

They were amazing creatures, these rogues. Their equivalents today are sanitised and essentially respectable, for all the corners they cut; few of them would bug a telephone, let alone hire a hit-man to knock off a troublesome competitor or an employee who knew too much. But *their* lust for money was of an entirely different order from today's multi-millionaires; ours are fascinated by the complexity of their financial operations, and enjoy riding the whirlwind and being deposited gently to earth with not a hair out of place and another billion in the kitty. They also pride themselves on their skill in prediction and in seizing the opportunity their rivals have missed; a harmless form of vanity. Deep psychological motives are attributed to them, but I have never seen the need to explain in those terms what drives the engine; it is true that today's mega-rich are in one respect like yesterday's, in that few of them can stop amassing money long after they have enough to buy anything at all on earth that is for sale. I can understand that, too; if they were the sort of men who would stop when they had enough, they would never have got where they were in the first place. And yet, when all the points of similarity have been listed, they are *not* the same as the original Fricks and Carnegies and Rockefellers and Morgans and Vanderbilts and Goulds and Hearsts and Mellons.

That hugely entertaining book, *History of the Great American Fortunes*, may be forgotten now, though it shouldn't be. Gustavus Myers was an economic historian, in no way singular, and would be wholly unknown if it had not been for that book. It was published in 1909, to very little acclaim and much nervous denunciation, but it gradually made its way into the world, and into history; Myers kept it up to date, and so scrupulous and thorough was his research that its findings, though rejected, could not be faulted as to the facts. His touch is light, though he was entirely serious, but I challenge any reader today (I wouldn't be surprised to learn that it is still in print) to read it right through without being seized by a wild and uncontrollable laughter. The laughter is not from disbelief, though incredulity is never far away; it is the same laughter that is generated by the sight of a hippopotamus or a wart-hog, and it is based on the undoubted but inexplicable fact that such creatures cannot be truly comprehended in their full grotesque nature, so that we fall back, in defence, on laughter. As the parade of gigantic wickednesses goes by, with the floats consisting of treachery, blackmail, violence, forgery, theft, ruin, broken promises, hatred, madness and very occasionally imprisonment, the scale on which they practised their villainies so dwarfs anything we can rationally imagine that we let our reason go: let it go, and laugh. Logan Pearsall Smith (one of those American writers who settled in Britain) has a happy conceit which sums up these Great Beasts: 'my memory echoed the names of people who had been famous for their enormous pleasures; who had made loud their palaces with guilty revels; and with Pyramids, Obelisks, and half-acre Tombs, had soothed their Pride. My Soul kindled at the thought of these Audacities.'

Some of them must have been afraid of hell-fire (the mystery is that some plainly weren't); Carnegie was surely one, considering his benefactions, and indeed his retirement long before his death. There was something of the miser in many of them, even the big-time spenders; Frick was no miser, but he gave nothing away, though he willed his house and collection to the City of New York, to be inherited after the death of his widow. I doubt if one visitor to the Frick in a hundred knows or cares who he was, still less what he did, yet those who do know have a bonus as they go round his glorious walls. There is another passage of Logan Pearsall Smith, irresistibly reminiscent of these monsters, and I murmur it to myself (it would hardly do for me to declaim it aloud, for more than one reason) whenever I visit the museum:

> I love to lie in bed and read the lives of the Popes of Rome. I think I could read for ever the biographies of those Pontiffs. For while I am absorbed in the doings of one Innocent or Pius, the Pope before him fades away; the earlier Vicars of Christ have all vanished from my failing memory; I am ready to read anew, with ever-renewed amazement, the outrageous goings-on of those holy and obstinate old men.

Assuredly, Frick and his like had much in common with some of the Borgia Popes, and indeed could have taken lessons in treachery, profanity, robbery, murder, promiscuity, simony and many another form of wickedness from Alexander VI. But it is time to go and look at Frick's pictures.

We make first – we must – for St Thomas More by Holbein. The fashion today is to diminish More; true, he took no bribes, but he had no objection to burning heretics, and his attitude to the Jews was by no means *comme il faut*. And his opposition to Henry VIII's marital and theological plans was really very legalistic; give us Luther every time, banging nails into the door of Wittemberg Cathedral, rather than this over-subtle psychologist, resplitting hairs already thoroughly split. The argument over men's actions in their historical time will never end; how many allowances are to be made for great rulers or religious leaders who did things that in our day would be far outside any definition of civilised behaviour? Toleration, after all, is an upstart youth as the history of the world goes; what do we think now of men who were so consumed with saving souls from eternal damnation that they cast bodies into fire at the stake? Well, we think they were wrong; but if they were right, they are still right – can you *prove* that there isn't a hell for heretics? We cannot expect men in bygone ages to lift themselves by their own bootstraps onto a plane that was to them invisible; yet we cannot simply resign our own principles and accept that morality is an eternally movable feast.

So we go and look at him, and such dilemmas fade in the brightness of his character. Holbein caught him 'twixt wind and water; the mouth is set in a straight line, and the eyes are piercing, steady and ready for pain, yet it would not take much to make him laugh (perhaps Holbein did tell him a joke, then had to persuade him to re-adopt his serious mien), and indeed it is not difficult to conjure up More laughing, which you certainly cannot do with his great brother in the struggle, John Fisher. (In the film of Robert Bolt's *A Man for All Seasons*, there is a most moving glimpse of Fisher, who went to the scaffold shortly before More did; as I recall, More is looking out of the window of the room to which he has been confined, and sees Fisher below in the courtyard – I cannot remember whether he is on his way to his death. Fisher does not look up, so no last greeting is possible; they had not been allowed to communicate in their respective prisons. The wrench we feel is assuredly of our time; More and Fisher, trusting in God's mercy, fully expected to meet after death. Can you *prove* that they didn't?)

As More twitches his luscious robe, a last thought occurs: were men really prepared to die for their belief that Henry VIII could not marry Ann Boleyn because he was still married, in the eyes of the Church, to Katharine of Aragon? Look at that face again, ignoring the chain of office, and even the gently interlaced hands; look at that mouth, which may indeed break into a smile, but is capable of setting as hard as a rock, and in the end did so: Thou art Peter ...

It is time to leave the Drawing Room, and visit the West Gallery, though not before pausing before Titian's portrait of Aretino. Aretino was an amazing rogue, undoubtedly touched by genius. Frick himself would have revelled in his company, but there is a greater avatar: François Villon. With no more than 3000 lines, Villon has assured his place in eternity as one of the world's half-dozen supreme poets; five-and-a-half centuries after his birth (I have to put it like that because in 1463 he vanished utterly from history into a darkness that no scholar or searcher in archives has ever been able to illuminate) the iron clang of his verse, like some ancient gate shutting, is as clear and piercing as the day it was written. But Villon spent most of the years we do know about drinking, brawling, thieving, stabbing (he killed a priest) – and repenting; no doubt he dashed off his verse between hangovers, and we know that he wrote one of his greatest masterpieces – *The Ballade of the Hanged* – while awaiting (not for the first time) his own execution. Somebody – a painter in the Villon drinking-circle, perhaps – must have at least sketched him. In the 1489 edition of his poetry there is what purports to be a woodcut of him, but it has no provenance, and even if it is genuine, it is too bare and rigid to tell us anything about him. Certainly, if there had been a painting of him, Frick would have bought it; as it is, he had the second best in Titian's Aretino, who is said to have died laughing at a rude joke. I dare say Villon did the same.

We have lingered too long at Titian, but here is the West Gallery, and Rembrandt's Problem Picture. To be sure, that does not refer to the self-portrait; in all art in all history there is nothing that speaks so plainly across the centuries as Rembrandt's studies of himself. But in the same room is the mysterious Polish Rider. Nobody knows why the picture was given that title; it shows a young man on horseback, but scholars have studied even the bit, the reins and the saddle, to say nothing of the rider's clothes and the scenery, without finding anything that can be confidently labelled Polish. Like virtually every Rembrandt at one time or another, it has been pronounced false (it used to be said that Rembrandt painted in all 317 pictures, 425 of which are in the United States), but scholars are notorious for getting so close to pictures that their noses are in danger of poking through the canvas, the very worst standpoint for judging genius and its validity. Step back three paces from the Polish Rider; he will still be mysterious, slightly startled, and gracelessly seated (on a horse which is steadfastly ignoring him), but he is as authentic a Rembrandt as the self-portrait.

And that self-portrait – ah! It was painted at the nadir of his fortunes: bankruptcy, widowerhood and the death of his only son had followed rapidly one after the other, and even Rembrandt must have shuddered at what new blows Vulcan's hammer had in store for him. But when he took his palette in hand, and propped the canvas at the correct angle to the mirror, the blood of genius caught fire in his veins, and this stupendous masterpiece repeats, as do all the late self-portraits, the only truth that men cannot deny: that man, son of woman, is born to trouble as the sparks fly upwards. Rembrandt no more knew why his fate was what it was than where he got his genius from. But he knew, as well as he knew that he held a brush in his hand, that it was his duty to use the latter to try to discover the truth about the former. Look at the eyes: they are brimming with pain and loss, but they are not defeated, and they neither blink nor waver: the Lord giveth, and the Lord taketh away; blessed be the name of the Lord.

Now to the South Hall, for Vermeer, pausing first at a painter who cannot be listed in quite the front rank of genius, but whose claim to immortality does not rest entirely on his painting. Meindert Hobbema reversed the traditional pattern of the painter who discovers his genius and abandons his job, and frequently his family also, to follow his muse; Gauguin is the most notable, romantic and spectacular in this genre, though we must not forget Gerard Dou, one of the very few truly amateur painters of genius – perhaps the only one. (He was a very wealthy man, and did not need to paint for a living, which would usually be thought to inevitably vitiate however great a talent. But in his case it didn't. There is no point in speculating on what greater heights he might have scaled if he *had* had to buy his bread with what he earned at his easel.)

Now we all know that Henri Rousseau was a customs officer; indeed, we could hardly not know, since the contemptuous epithet attached to his name – 'Douanier Rousseau' – has stuck so firmly that many people are under the impression that Douanier was his Christian name. Well, Hobbema went in the other direction; he gave up painting to become a customs officer, and his decision was not based on an inability to sell his pictures. It occurs to me that the world would be a pleasanter place if some of the most notable contemporary painters would withdraw gracefully from the *salons* and start life anew asking passengers at London Airport whether they have anything to declare.

Vermeer at last, in the South Hall. He is the runner-up in the championship contest for the smallest number of pictures sufficient to establish the artist as one of the greatest geniuses in history. The undoubted champion is Giorgione, who seems to have painted well under twenty, and possibly fewer than fifteen. But Vermeer's total is almost certainly below forty.

Never mind the width, feel the quality. What is the first, deepest and most steadfast of Vermeer's principles? The truth: if his life depended on it – if his *salvation* depended on it – he would reply, quietly but without any doubt at all, that that was what he painted because that is what he saw. There is nothing strengthened in Vermeer, nothing exaggerated, nothing sweetened, nothing highlighted, nothing arranged, nothing emphasised. A woman, a bit of bread, an archway, a tiled floor, a bowl of milk, a lovers' meeting, a lute, a soldier's plume, a piece of paper – what came to hand he painted, and he painted with such unobtrusive but world-shaking power that the world is still shaking with it. Standing in front of any one of the Frick's three Vermeers (do you realise that this one museum, founded by such a brute, owns nearly ten per cent of the world's entire extant stock of Vermeers?), you feel that anything can happen; you may experience levitation, perhaps, or choking in the grip of the authenticity you are looking at, or hallucinations, which would surely take the form of seeing the figures in the picture move, and having moved, speak. (I suppose I ought to learn Dutch, in case it happens to me one day.) *The Officer and the Girl*: how many thousands of variations on that theme has art played over the years! Yet they all vanish, consumed in the fire of Vermeer's passion for God's truth. You can weep real tears when you realise that the two figures (legend has it that the girl is Vermeer's daughter) have been dust for more than three hundred years, so alive are they in their frame, so longing for more life in their open prison of paint, so real to us as they were to themselves and the man who immortalised them, and died poor – so poor that his widow had to sell two paintings immediately to feed the family.

Next stop, El Greco. What *am* I going to do about El Greco? Why, it may be asked, do I feel I need to do anything about him? Because I find his work largely detestable and am convinced that he was colour-blind. There is indeed only one word for his palette: hideous. But why does not the world use the term? Because, as I have to admit, he was also a very great genius. The Frick's *Christ Driving the Money-Changers from the Temple* demonstrates the genius and, to me, the reason why I would normally hurry past. El Greco is plainly inspired by his theme; it is, indeed, one of the most vivid and paintable scenes in the Gospels, and there are hundreds of versions of it, perhaps thousands. Even I cannot deny the *vigour* of El Greco, here matched perfectly to the theme of Christ's assault on the profanation of the holy place. Has anyone ever discovered how and why the money-changers set up their stalls in the Temple? They clearly did not care about committing sacrilege, but presumably others than Christ did, and there must have been plenty of other places for their business. But that mystery fades away in contemplation of a much greater theme: this was the only violent act Christ ever committed. Most pictures of it, including this one, show him with a whip in his hand, not only scattering the polluters but physically chastising them for the pollution they had introduced. It matches, I suppose, Christ's last act of gentleness, as also his last miracle, in replacing the centurion's severed ear, struck off in the mêlée of his arrest. It must be significant, though I am not sure of what, that the earlier scene has been painted – demonstrating its greater hold on the world in general and its artists in particular – a hundred times for every version of the later one.

Gainsborough is out of fashion; so much the worse for fashion. Of course, he was fashion*able*, and he took care not to offend his vain, aristocratic and rich patrons, for which he has been much censured by later and more severe ages. I can't see why; he was a portrait painter of genius (and a landscape artist second in England only to Constable, as the Frick's twin Constables demonstrate in the Dining Room), and only Rembrandt *really* painted his subjects warts and all. Gainsborough's biographers insist that he despised his patrons, for their frivolity and shallowness, but either the biographers are wrong, or Gainsborough rose above his feelings, for there is not the slightest visible hint of contempt, even when the sitter's vanity would have been bound to miss it. Sargent, who stood in the first line of descent from Gainsborough, had some of Gainsborough's putative scorn for his clients, though at the height of his fame and success he was as fashionable as they were; it is said, though I have never been able to see it, that he did insert in his portraits, subtly, a tiny worm of truth and impurity, and let it eat away at his sitters and their pretentions. But Gainsborough played fair; his patrons commissioned him for a certain view of themselves, and whatever he thought about them, he gave them what they had paid for. As it happens, the Frick's Gainsborough is one in which his genius soared over the heads of the fashionable folk; literally so, for the top two-thirds of *The Mall in St James' Park* are pure landscape, and the figures who throng the scene are confined, mere extras put in to get the balance right, to the bottom of the frame. Gainsborough's last words were 'We are all going to Heaven, and Van Dyck is of the company'. It is a beautiful farewell, not least because Van Dyck was yet another painter who took care not to offend the hand that fed him.

Boucher was another, but the absurdity of Boucher is so great and so charming that it is impossible to rebuke him for anything. Unlike Fragonard, who yearned to be serious, Boucher knew exactly what to do and how to do it; it was to give his aristocratic sitters whatever they wanted, and a bit more, as the Frick itself demonstrates eight times over; the series of panels in the West Vestibule were painted for La Pompadour herself, and reflected the world she inhabited, even if it didn't exist. Boucher may have been lucky to die well before the Revolution; else he would surely have perished on the guillotine as a 'collaborator' of the aristos. History is full of court painters nimbly switching their allegiance to a new master when the old had been overthrown, but I cannot see Robespierre or St Just sitting for Boucher (Danton might have done), and the old dog could never have learned enough new tricks. Fragonard survived the Revolution; he lived to 1806. He may have been lucky; indeed, he *was* lucky, for David befriended and helped him, and eventually got him an administrative post in the new Louvre. But in any case, his style went out of fashion when his clients went out of the country (or to the scaffold), and nobody seemed to want to pursue him. (The Frick has a David, too; is there *any* artist not represented in this amazing place? It certainly has both a Greuze and an Ingres. An echo sounds: Bernard Berenson, deploring Picasso's retirement from realism, said it was a waste because 'he could draw like Ingres'.)

The Frick also has a Georges de La Tour, one of the most mysterious painters ever born; even Giorgione's *La Tempesta* is less haunting, and two qualities make him unique. First, he paints human flesh as no artist until the twentieth century did (he was born almost exactly at the beginning of the seventeenth and died almost exactly half-way through it); some find his tones macabre, and it is indeed easy to see all his figures as corpses. But look more closely; the flesh is alive, but so strikingly *simplified* that its real nature can be missed. The truth is that de La Tour's people, however grand, are all homely, domestic portraits – as indeed can be seen clearly in his Frick master-piece, *The Education of the Virgin*; he was lucky not to be burnt at the stake for the blasphemy of making the Virgin this modest, cosy, simple housewife.

But it is de La Tour's other property that makes him so mysterious; his extraordinary obsession with lighted candles. A candle, lit, is a beautiful thing; it is not surprising that many of the world's great religions incorporate them into their deepest rituals, nor that even in the age of modern electricity, many a dining-table is adorned with candles, even though there is no question of them being needed to shed light. Yet the artist's passion for lighting his pictures in this fashion seems to have no symbolic meaning, and hardly any iconographic purpose either. Nor, obviously, is it something like an extra signature or trade mark. I don't know how many of his works incorporate a lighted candle, indeed I don't know how many pictures by him exist. But that circle of light created by the trembling flame (he has clearly studied very closely just how the light of a candle is thrown) suffices to announce him even if the picture is on the other side of a gallery. I suppose someone has devised a theory to account for his strange addiction.

I left the Frick joyful and refreshed, as I always do; I know of no gallery in the world (well, perhaps the Schiavoni in Venice, with its nine

Carpaccios and nothing else) that offers so choice, so well-balanced, so beautifully-housed a collection, and one small enough to be inspected at leisure in its entirety without exhaustion, physical, psychological or artistic, setting in.

The sun was out. I crossed the road, and it abruptly went in. Just opposite the Frick there is a tasteful little monument to one Richard Morris Hunt, built in a graceful semi-circle of steps, with a bust of Mr Hunt in the middle and a tablet recording that the structure was erected to recognise his services to art in America. But that, irrespective of the fact that I had never heard of Mr Hunt, was not the point, nor the reason I shivered in the noonday warmth. In the middle of the steps someone had painted on the stone in large capital letters, 'I have AIDS. I am 22. Help me. You speak. Help for AIDS'. The message concluded with a painted heart and a dollar sign. There was nobody there; presumably whoever inscribed the message on the memorial had been sitting on the platform of it with some kind of receptacle for money beside him. Then I began to wonder whether he had taken up his pitch here day after day, collecting enough to keep him going, until he was too weak to get there, perhaps just strong enough to get there but not to mount the steps. Boucher and Fragonard, and even Gainsborough, suddenly seemed not only frivolous, but empty.

Walking up the Avenue on the park side, I saw a bench, empty except for a newspaper, neatly folded, on which rested a book, no less neatly aligned. I could see at once that it was a hardback, and therefore not likely to have been abandoned (in any case there was a capacious street rubbish-bin only a few feet away on the kerb), but where was the owner? My own curiosity tends to work *a posteriori*; there is an old after-dinner question that asks what you do if a window is suddenly shattered by a missile flung into the room, a stone with a piece of paper, evidently written on, wrapped round it; do you first rush to the window to see who did it, or do you first pick up the stone to read the message? For me, it is the message, which means that I did not spend much time looking for the owner of the book, but went over to the bench to see what it was. It was *Beyond Belief*, the account by Emlyn Williams of the Moors Murders; the newspaper it rested on was *New York Newsday*.

I like such tiny, insoluble mysteries. What New Yorker (a British visitor would be unlikely to buy *Newsday*) was so interested in the Brady-Hindley case that he or she would buy the actor-playwright's account of it (long out of print), and then leave it on a park bench? I checked the date of the newspaper, in case it would deepen the mystery by being years old (there is a Charles Addams cartoon of a man strolling along a beach and coming upon a man in swimming-trunks asleep, with a newspaper over his face, on which the headline is 'Archduke Ferdinand assassinated at Sarajevo'), but it disappointed me; it was that very day's issue. I waited a few moments to see whether an absent-minded student of English crime would hurry back to rescue his forgotten book, but no-one appeared, and I walked on, leaving the riddle to the next passer-by, or, more likely, to the next homeless bag-lady who could sell it to a second-hand bookstore for a few cents.

Very well, very well, the Metropolitan Museum of Art is the biggest gallery in the world. Yes, it is bigger by far than Britain's National Gallery, than France's Louvre, than Russia's Hermitage, than Italy's Uffizi. Possibly it is bigger than all those put together; I think I heard someone in a position to know say that it covers sixteen acres. Or was it sixty? Or six thousand? Its handsome flight of massive steps declares without a word spoken that there is nothing in the world to match it, and when the visitor has climbed the steps and entered the building he will soon be obliged to agree.

Not only would it be impossible for anyone to walk round every item in a day; I don't believe it could be done on a bicycle. It has rooms the size of football stadiums devoted to the art of one African tribe, of one brief period in European painting, of one single exhibit. (This is the hall that accommodates the Egyptian Temple of Dendur, and it isn't a replica of the Temple of Dendur, it *is* the Temple of Dendur, dismantled stone by stone by a grateful Egyptian government, and reassembled stone by stone in the Met. But the great advantage of this gargantuan collection is that it can concentrate its fire at the point where it is most needed. A single example will show what I mean: the Met has nineteen Rembrandts, the centrepiece of the collection *Aristotle contemplating the bust of Homer*. But so vast an array gives a visitor much more than the joy of looking at such pictures; it offers a survey of the work of Rembrandt that makes us far more aware of the meaning of Rembrandt to art and the world which no single item, however glorious, can provide. The lavishness of this collection (it is impossible to fight off the statistics for ever, and the Met claims to have 3·3 million works of art) is such that it can be truly eclectic and comprehensive, and, above all, intelligible, for the space available makes sure that everything on display can be seen without crowding or confusion, the greatest boon any art gallery can offer its patrons.

Of course (but why should it be of course?) the Met, like almost all leading art galleries in the world, holds special exhibitions of one artist or school or theme, and – because it is the Met – these have to be the world's biggest. There was a Fragonard show when I was there, and there were 300 items in the exhibition; the catalogue weighed $7\frac{1}{2}$ lbs. As it happens, the show convinced me of something I had long suspected, which is that I don't care for Fragonard at all. His technical mastery is of the very highest order, especially in the red chalk drawings, but compared to, say, Chardin or Boucher, he is empty, mechanical and false. But I could never have come to that conclusion, not even, I think, in the Louvre, had not the Met scoured the world for Fragonards, and put them on its walls in such reckless profusion that I could no longer deny the evidence of my eyes and feelings.

That, I suppose, is something of a left-handed compliment for the Met, but it is also an indication of the significance of having art in such quantities in one place, for the permanent collections of the Met (which is still busy acquiring even more) have much the same effect as the special exhibitions. It would be possible for someone wholly ignorant of art to become a true expert simply by spending enough time in the Met, without any guidance or even a catalogue; such a tyro would begin to see affinities, chronologies, styles and methods, cross-references, recurring themes and influences, and the more he gazed, silent and unaccompanied, the more he would understand – not just know, but understand. The previous director of the Met was a great one for stunts, though he eventually went a lot too far, and his last years there were replete with altercations and scandal; the present one, Philippe de Montebello, is more cautiously flamboyant, but the test would be a respectable one, and if it worked, a most memorable: hail, then, the man or woman who walked into the Met knowing nothing of art, and emerged a year later as one of the world's leading experts and connoisseurs. (Make that five years.)

But no visitor, learned or naïve, could fail to notice one of the most ubiquitous, and touching, of all the Met's wonders. It is the culmination here of the American philanthropists' desire to let the world know of their benefactions; on a good, healthy hike through the Met the sharp-eyed hiker will come upon the Robert Lehman Collection, the Lawrence A. and Barbara Fleischman Gallery, the Richard and Gloria Manney Rooms, the Sackler Wing, the James and Margaret Carter Federal Gallery, the Charles Engelhard Court, the Berggruen Klee Collection, the Israel Sack Galleries, the Blumenthal Patio, the Josephine Bay Paul Gallery, the Nathan Cummings Collection of Precolumbian Art, the George M. and Linda H. Kaufman Galleries, the Lester Wunderman Collection of Dogon Art, the Erving and Joyce Wolf Gallery, the Thomas J. Watson Library including the Jane Watson Irwin Center for Higher Education and Arthur K. Watson Reference Room, the Josephine Mercy Heathcote Gallery, the Robert Goldwater Library, the Irene Lewisohn Costume Reference Library, the Helen and Milton A. Kimmelman Gallery for Special Exhibitions, the

Bashford Dean Gallery, the Grace Rainey Rogers Auditorium, the Wrightsman Galleries, the Astor Court, the Gioconda and Joseph King Gallery, the Lila Acheson Wallace Wing, the Marietta Lutze Sackler Gallery, the Esther Annenberg Simon Galleries, the Ruth and Harold D. Uris Center for Education, the Sharp Gallery, the Joan Whitney Payson Galleries, the Raymond and Beverly Sackler Gallery for Assyrian Art, the Douglas Dillon Galleries, the Benjamin Altman Galleries, the Charles Z. Offin Gallery, the Harry Payne Bingham Galleries, the Stephen C. Clark Galleries, the R. H. Macy Gallery, the André Meyer Galleries, the C. Michael Paul Gallery, the Dr Mortimer D. Sackler and Theresa Sackler gallery, the Hagop Kevorkian Fund Special Exhibitions Gallery, the André Mertens Galleries for Musical Instruments, and the Robert Wood Johnson Jr Recent Acquisitions Gallery.

Now although that catalogue (I certainly must have missed a few) betokens a certain *naïveté*, and induces a certain smile, it testifies once again to the stupendous generosity of the American rich. Some of these collections, of course, are the collections the donors made in their own lifetime and left to the Met on their death; others are given when the collector stops collecting or runs out of wall space; but many are simply endowments: ah, says the patron, you need a new room, and I shall pay for it to be built and equipped, my price (a modest one) being to have my name attached to it in perpetuity.

It *is* a modest price, and the almost unimaginable and quite immeasurable riches of the Met would not exist if that price had not been paid. And take the measure of the few that *can* be measured: the Lila Acheson Wallace Galleries of Egyptian Art comprise something like forty rooms, and she wasn't finished even then; upstairs, she endowed an entire wing to house modern art, and although there is a good deal of junk in it, there is also a good deal of fine work, and in any case we are not here evaluating the quality of the art, but the generosity of the endowment. (Lila Acheson Wallace, to be sure, was unlikely to beggar herself, however big her donations; she was, after all, the daughter of the man who founded *Readers' Digest*. Still, she gave the money.)

Our hiker – thoroughly exhausted by now – must pause a while at the Robert Lehman Collection. The Lehman Wing, which is indeed an entire wing of the building, is filled with the works of art collected first by his parents and then by him; he simply gave the entire treasure to the Met. But the point is the quality of the collection, which includes, among *hundreds* of other things, some of the greatest works of Botticelli, Giovanni Bellini, Memling, David, Holbein, El Greco, Goya, Ter Borch, Rembrandt, Ingres, Corot, Monet, Renoir, Cézanne, Degas, Derain, Bonnard and Balthus. The

42

43

45

4

47

49

50

Lehman collection would be a very important art gallery if it was self-contained and somewhere else, as the Lila Acheson Wallace Egyptian Galleries would in most places in the world be *the* museum. But here they are both, and many more such garnerings, swallowed up in the vast spaces of the Met. Who now will smile at Robert Lehman and Lila Wallace? Besides, we British can hardly sneer; only two men have had colleges named after them at both Oxford and Cambridge: Jesus Christ and Isaac Wolfson.

I went out into the sunshine and Fifth Avenue, though not before visiting Vermeer's *Girl with a Jug*, who reminds me of my beloved *Servant Pouring Milk*. I wondered again at the fortunes of the American rich, with their tens and hundreds and thousand of millions, the richest nation the world has ever seen or ever will see. Most countries have national art collections, which are bought and housed at public expense. Only the United States rejects this principle, with the result that the Met must fare for itself. Well, and hasn't it? Is there another gallery in the world, public or private, which can touch the mass *and* quality of the Met's holdings? It is possible to be surfeited by such glory in such richness; but it is also possible to come back another day – scores or hundreds of other days – to gorge on the feast without getting indigestion. If my ignoramus-to-scholar experiment is too fanciful to be realised, something like it is happening every day the Met is open, as New Yorkers and visitors soak up the liquid gold of art that lies in pools throughout the mighty museum, and come back for more. To provide so much for all who enter the Met's portals, does it really matter if within the portals there is a Jack and Bell Linsky Gallery, a Martha and Rebecca Fleischmann Pre-Civil War Decorative Arts Gallery and an Iris and B. Gerald Cantor Roof Garden?

Particularly, I may say, when such benefactions free the Met's funds to stage an exhibition like the Degas show that was to be seen in its galleries from October 1988 to just a little way into the new year.

'That was to be seen . . .'. But it very nearly wasn't. New York, and other American cities with art galleries showing popular exhibitions, have devised a bizarre practice of rationing visitors. Sometimes they do it by controlling the queues of visitors so that the line moves with discouraging slowness, but more often they sell tickets in advance to the exhibition, for all the world as though they were dealing with theatre-goers, tickets which, strictly limited in number, give access to the treasures *at a specific time*, before which no amount of pleading will get past the custodians.

For many years, I believed that this system was devised to ensure that there would never be a crowd before the pictures, so that the visitor could

48 Lashing out   49 Mother Hale's serenity   50 Mother Hale's charges   51 Mother Hale's successes   52 As the sun sinks slowly in the west

enjoy them in peace and comfort, or alternatively that it was to spare the visitor from waiting hours in line. Both theories were comforting, testifying as they did to the thoughtfulness of American museum curators; only now, when at the last minute I had managed to secure a ticket to a show that had been comprehensively sold out months before, did I discover the extraordinary truth.

It all goes back to the Coconut Grove. The Coconut Grove was a Boston nightclub in the 1920s, very popular with the young people of the Jazz age. One night, when the place was more crowded than usual (a fiercely-fought college football game had taken place in the afternoon, and the supporters of the winning side had crammed the place for their celebrations), it caught fire, and the death-roll was in hundreds. It was the biggest such disaster in American history, and it led to the rigid, and stringently-enforced, fire regulations that the United States have ever since had. Anyone who has ever been into any public building in the United States, from a cinema to a shop, knows that there are signs prominently displayed throughout the place, specifying exactly the maximum number of people who may be on the premises at any one time. I have never seen a fire inspector counting the people in an American restaurant or public library, though no doubt spot checks are made from time to time; anyway, the mystery of the ticket-only system for art galleries was solved by the man who obtained my ticket for me. Conscious of my virtue, I presented my ticket at the time specified, and was waved in.

Into magic. Degas is too readily classified as an Impressionist; he was a bridge to and from Impressionism, but was truly *sui generis*, going his own way, making his own experiments, concentrating on his own themes.

Concentrating! There were nearly 300 items in the Met's exhibition (it had started in Paris and was going on to Ottawa, and each of the three venues had a different selection), and its scope and size made it possible for groups of pictures with the same inspiration to be hung together. Thus, there were walls full of ballet-dancers and scenes from their world; another stretch of baths; another of nudes; another of self-portraits; another of family groups. Genius – this kind, anyway – needs space, for such comparisons; at first glance, a whole wall of ballet-dancers in the wings looks repetitious, even monotonous, but linger (once inside the exhibition there is no ejection-time) among them, and they will all come individually alive. So they should, of course; after all, Degas' fascination for the subject lay precisely in the infinite number of variations he could make from the theme, and the musical term is indeed the appropriate one. Take the Goldberg Variations, or the Diabelli: the theme is transmogrified so greatly and so many times that it all but vanishes, yet 'all but' never means entirely. Degas' variations do not permit him to dissolve the theme so completely; the girls and their tutus are still girls and tutus. But the genius of Degas, with the shifting of a foot here, the slightly higher tilt of a chin there, achieves the same essence that the piano, with its greater freedom from naturalism, can do so much more easily. (Why, Degas would have asked – probably did ask – should art, or anything else for that matter, be easy?)

Or take the nudes. There are two groups: the earlier ones are almost Renoir-like – luscious, at ease, infinitely human. The later ones are almost grim, which instantly rules out the comparison with Renoir; these women may not have suffered, but they have seen suffering, and understood it. Their innocence has gone, but their reality is now deeper. I went back and forth between the two sets, again and again, and wondered at a man who could encompass with such apparent ease two such astounding forms, so different from each other yet so equally filled with meaning.

And the portraits? The *self*-portraits? The racing scenes, in which the contestants do anything but race? The landscapes? The millinery? Has there ever been a painter with so voracious an eye, so instant a seizure of what he saw? (No wonder he was fascinated by the infant art of photography.)

There is a story of a group of Degas' admirers, deciding after lunch to visit the great man. He came to the door, palette in hand. The leader of the group bowed low, and said 'Est-ce-que nous vous dérangons, cher Maître?' 'Beaucoup', said Degas, and slammed the door. Well, all great artists are single-minded; that is one of the clues that lead to the realisation that they are great artists. Degas, however, was practically a recluse; for most of his career, certainly long after he had been acclaimed as a genius, he preferred to exhibit his pictures in mixed shows, allowing them to mingle with those of others. (Allowing? It was much more insisting.)

The great museums and galleries of the world are caught in a perpetual trap. In today's conditions, only they can mount these huge, all-embracing shows; only they have the money, the security, the 'pull'. So they spend several years putting together the definitive statement about Degas, Gauguin, Cranach, Constable, Botticelli, Dürer, Velazquez, Titian, Cézanne (thank God no definitive statement can be made about Turner), whereupon they are criticised for tearing the pictures up by their roots, to display for the uncomprehending queues on Bank Holidays, instead of leaving such artists mingling on their own walls, where their time and manner can be judged in context.

Yet how else, now the Grand Tour has been replaced by the Package Tour, are such geniuses to have their full effect, if not by assembling hundreds of their works in one place? Far better, surely, to risk surfeit by looking at two or three hundred works of Degas in one place at one time, than to see them one by one, or dozen by dozen, and never fully experience the giant tidal wave of his genius, which is what every visitor to the Met, clutching his time-stamped ticket, was offered.

It was still a sunny day; but when I emerged the very sky looked pallid and without joy beside the glory inside.

The Guggenheim poses a problem. Well, it posed enough in the sixteen years of its building (neither Solomon Guggenheim, who commissioned it, nor Frank Lloyd Wright, who built it, lived to see it open), but the difficulties it encountered, from the nervousness of the planning authorities to the mechanics of putting it up, were the Museum's problems; I am talking about the visitor's problem, indeed the passer-by's. The question that should have been settled many years ago, but simply won't lie down, is: is the Guggenheim a joke?

Many terms have been used to describe it, none really fits; I think of it as either a turban or a soufflé. Hampered by its constricted setting (it should have been put in the Park, like the Met), it is difficult to take in properly, but from no angle can it be described as beautiful. Amazing, different, startling, forceful, bold, hypnotic, unique – all these adjectives and more can be used to describe it, but beautiful it isn't.

That, however, doesn't make it a joke; if we laughed at every unbeautiful building, or even limited ourselves to positively ugly ones, we would be in stitches throughout all the hours of daylight. The evidence is in two parts, one inferential, the other tangible. Wright was a genius, without doubt; Brendan Gill's searching, comprehensive, clear-eyed biography of him, *Many Masks*, nothing extenuates nor sets down aught in malice, and Wright emerges from it as the towering figure he insisted that the world should accept. It is true that Wright had a singularly harum-scarum private life (his own autobiography, it is now clear, is not to be trusted on this or any other subject) and an even more harum-scarum attitude to other people's money, but no-one can deny him genius; he was flawed in his character, and certainly the designer of some colossal mistakes, yet with only a handful of true peers in his chosen art and profession.

Yes, but he was also a wag, a prankster, a man fond of laughter and of inspiring it. The Guggenheim Museum was one of the last commissions he received; certainly the last principal one. It was not a house, after all; he would not jest, in his building, with a private client's home or office. But the temptation to fool all of the people all of the time with a huge public structure designed to hold a collection of non-representational art (that, incidentally, was one of the stipulations that Guggenheim made) must have been very powerful, possibly irresistible. He knew that by now his reputation was such that he could be sure that anything he produced would be hailed by the arbiters of public taste, and he would certainly have shared the attitude to the art world which Picasso expressed in his remark, 'If I spit, they will take the spit and frame it'. One last, lasting, superb joke, then, in the middle of the most sedate part of Fifth Avenue, with the certainty that no-one would dare to say that the Emperor had no clothes? Surely his hand must have trembled, as he began to draw the Guggenheim Museum?

That is the circumstantial evidence; his known witty character, his life-long addiction to the game of *épater les bourgeois*, a sensation in the middle of New York, a position so impregnable that no voice would be raised against it without at once being drowned in the chorus of approbation, however uneasy. If you were Frank Lloyd Wright, could *you* resist?

As for the physical evidence, which the jury can see and touch, *si monumentum requiris, circumspice.*

Andy Warhol turned the Guggenheim into an icon, with scores of photographic reproductions in psychedelic colours; the technique has – in a rare instance of the copy being more famous than the original – burned the Guggenheim's appearance into minds that would have been resolutely closed to the reality. Warhol certainly thought the building was a joke, and made no bones about it; what is more, his treatment of it must have made thousands, perhaps millions, of the same mind, though as far as I know no art or architectural critic or expert has admitted it publicly. I shall no doubt, be rebuked, or more probably ignored, for even opening the possibility. Yet look at the thing: it is absurd.

That it is one of the most amazing buildings in the world cannot be denied; but neither can anyone *truthfully* deny that it is largely hideous and almost entirely useless. Its proportions are ludicrous outside, and its function as an art-exhibiting space almost impossible to realise inside. Is this not one of the finest jokes of the twentieth century? Not convinced? But the final proof is to come. The Guggenheim is the most enormous *fun*. Going up or down the mad ramp that is all the place consists of gives the visitor with any imagination an overwhelming desire to get hold of a doormat and slide, at a constantly increasing speed, down the finest (and certainly most expensive) helter-skelter in the world. I could find nobody to tell me what the angle of incline is, or indeed whether it is constant throughout (there is a cross-section drawing of the interior in the guide to the Museum, but it is too small to be of much use); I would guess it is about nine degrees, so it would need a good shove in the back if the mat and its passenger were to get off. But once moving, they would have a wonderful ride down the six turns of the spiral; the helter-skelter even has, as fairground ones do, a level stretch right at the end, to slow the participants down. Is it possible that the Guggenheim is an even bigger joke than the joke on the art establishment? That he actually meant it as a helter-skelter? (Certainly, I was very powerfully tempted to go out and bring back a ball, and set it rolling from the top.)

It is wonderfully light and airy – well, so it should be, for there is nothing at all inside the shell, not so much as a chandelier. Inside, the sheer beastliness of the exterior cannot be guessed at (joker or no joker, Wright *was* a genius), and looking up from the floor or down from the highest stretch of the ramp, the sight of the walkway with people dotted at random all the way along (the wall that runs down all the way along the ramp is about three feet high, so they are always visible) is charming.

But even the Guggenheim's genuine admirers cannot get round their treasure's ineradicable fault, to which I was alluding when I said that the function of the place was impossible to realise. Early on in the Guggenheim's building the people in charge delicately pointed out to Wright that there was a fallacy built into the design (they got short shrift from the architect), which is of course still there. When the exhibition is of normally-shaped 'easel paintings', how do you hang them? That is, do you hang them sloping to the same extent as the floor does, or do you hang them parallel to the sidewalk outside? In either case, the eye of the beholder feels uneasy; the rigidity of the square or rectangle that is the picture collapses when it is disoriented because of the slope. I would not go so far as to say that you can get sea-sick at the Guggenheim, but you can certainly get dizzy.

Mind you, Wright (or somebody at the Museum after his death) cheated; on three of the 'floors' there are rooms off the ramp, where the Guggenheim's own permanent collection of pictures and sculptures are housed. It is, of course, based on Solomon Guggenheim's collection; this started out, when Guggenheim made his fortune, as Old Masters, but when he fell under the sway of a crazy – well, fairly crazy – Baroness called Hilla Rebay, she persuaded him not only to collect modern art instead, but to limit his collecting to strictly non-representational art. Meekly, he complied, and his accessions are what we see in the three huge bays, though after his death (and her ejection from the post of Director, which she held from the opening of the Museum), the policy changed; modern art was still acquired, and boldly, too, but some of the most adventurous and experimental artists of our time have painted recognisable figures or objects, and the

Guggenheim has risked the Baroness's posthumous wrath by buying such breaches of her adamant principle.

Art ran in the family. Solomon's niece was Peggy Guggenheim, whose Palazzo di Leone on the Grand Canal became a museum in her lifetime, and remains one, given in perpetuity to Venice. She must have had the finest eye of all; like Sylvia Beach in Paris and Frances Steloff in New York, with their encouragement and patronage of writers, Peggy Guggenheim encouraged and bought the paintings of artists whose fame was to grow great. She made the garden of her house a sculpture-court; I always wish that the *vaporetto* will slow down as it passes the Leone, so we can have a good look (obviously you cannot get a comprehensive view of the garden while you are in it), but it never does. The Leone is the least tall palace on the entire canal; it is indeed only one storey (I can hardly call it a bungalow, though strictly speaking it is). J. G. Links, whose word on Venice is to me as Holy Writ, says that when it was built, in the sixteenth century, the powerful figure who lived next door, and had therefore had an empty space beside his own house, was so enraged by the thought of a neighbour that he pulled strings till the upstart was obliged to promise that his palace would be no more than one storey high; nor is it, to this day.

The Guggenheim is made of concrete; painted off-white. The paint is peeling and cracking now; close up, it looks dilapidated. Yet, joke though it may be, it cannot be ignored, nor should it be. If it *isn't* a joke, it is still a considered statement by America's greatest architect. It is badly sited, but that is not Wright's fault. It is like nothing else anywhere, and has led nowhere; woe betide any lesser architect who felt inspired by it. Whatever it is, not even its most passionate admirers could call it – not just the shape, but the whole ambience as well – lovable. Down the street, the Frick most certainly is; it is the most lovable gallery I know. Its proportions are human – well, it was built as a house, after all – and the arrangement of the furniture and carpets, together with the hanging of the pictures, has been done with the greatest sympathy and taste. No wall is overloaded with art, the eye is not assaulted by demands shouted from the walls; on the contrary, the visitor makes his way round a room slowly, absorbing the beauty. A visit to the Frick is a joyful experience; not so the Guggenheim. At any rate not until it really is transformed into a helter-skelter, and we can toboggan down the ramp, laughing all the way.

In the entrance hall, there is a handsome bronze plaque let into the floor; it gives the details of Wright's creation, and round the rim is this rubric: Let each man exercise the art he knows. Impeccable sentiments; only later, if at all, do we realise that the statement is meaningless.

Of the great Rogues' Gallery, the most fascinating of them all was Andrew Carnegie. Rockefeller was boring, Frick was a gangster, Ford was a man of one ruthlessly pursued idea (two, actually – the assembly-line and anti-semitism), Hearst was mad, Morgan and Mellon had the sense to keep out of the limelight, something that in any case was easier to do in banking than in manufacture. But Carnegie was surely the most complex character of them all. I have never come across a really good biography of him, at least if a good biography is one which enables the reader to fully understand the subject. Yet the paradox of his life suggests that it would be a compelling study.

Start with his house, which is now the Cooper-Hewitt Museum (part of the Smithsonian – its official title is the National Museum of Design). When he built it, at what is now 91st Street, the area was open country; Fifth Avenue had petered out much lower down. It was his decision to build so far north (actually, Manhattan does not lie on the North-South axis, but a good dozen degrees off it) that encouraged others to push the street further uptown.

He proclaimed that he was going to build 'the most modest, plainest and roomiest house in New York'. His idea of modest was striking; the house had sixty-four rooms, and there were nineteen live-in servants. (Nor was the house unbearably plain; the elaborately carved wooden ceiling in the main hall is not exactly King's College chapel, but it isn't exactly an igloo, either.) That contrast between word and deed is characteristic of Carnegie, of whom it may be said that he amassed the most stupendous fortune of even those days, when the competition, after all, was fierce, with no apparent aim, beside living comfortably, *other than giving the money away*. And although it is impossible to estimate his fortune with any exactitude, it is not unlikely that at its height it topped what in today's money would be around ten billion dollars.

He defined the wealthy man's obligations in these remarkable terms:

To provide moderately for the wants of those dependent upon him; and after doing so to consider all surplus funds which come to him simply as trust funds, which he is called upon to administer. The man of wealth thus becomes the mere trustee and agent for his poorer brethren.

And he went even further:

Poor and restricted are our opportunities in this life, narrow our horizons, our best work most imperfect; but still men should be thankful for one inestimable boon. They have it in their power during their lives to busy themselves in organising benefactions from which the masses of their fellows will derive lasting advantage, and thus dignify their lives.

His particular passion, probably derived from his Scottish origins, was for education; he knew that then, as now, it was the key without which the door to success would rarely open, and he set himself, in the most practical way, to offer hope through learning to those who most needed it. The 'Carnegie Libraries' he founded made no charge for admission or borrowing, and the tally of them was an almost unbelievable three thousand.

The libraries were typical of his hard-headed attitude to philanthropy, which has endured to this day; he would have been delighted (if so dour a Scot could ever admit to experiencing delight) by the famous Oxfam poster-slogan: 'If you give a man a fishing-rod he can feed his family; if you give him a net he can feed the village'. There is, incidentally, no evidence of an abrupt conversion, an instant spiritual illumination, in Carnegie's life, though it is tempting to think of him as the sinner who suddenly sees the light on the road to Damascus and changes his life forthwith. Carnegie really does seem to have held his philanthropic views all his life, and to have started giving them tangible expression as soon as he had the money to do it with.

In the Cooper-Hewitt Museum the ghosts do not walk; the nineteen servants are not clattering transparently up and down the stairs, nor does the stern shadow of the great benefactor look over a visitor. On the other hand, most of the exhibitions are feeble and badly arranged, the only exception being an enchanting group under the title, 'What might have been: Unbuilt architecture of the eighties'. It was a series of projects, drawings, models and the like, of building plans that never came to fruition. Some failed because the money could not be raised, some because the builders could not get round the planning laws, but some, which constitute the most charming part of the exhibition, were purely fantasies, never intended to be put up. There are massive skyscrapers, clearly inspired by Frank Lloyd Wright's unrealised dream of a mile-high tower ('There's nothing so timid', said Wright, 'as a million dollars'), villages planned to the very last brick, buildings in weird or comical shapes like children's toys infinitely multiplied, and finally, the most endearing of all, a see-saw which was to be the length and width of a street, with real houses on each side. Carnegie would no doubt have thought it frivolous.

★   ★   ★

A private garden on Fifth Avenue? A private *garden*? On *Fifth* Avenue? You don't mean Central Park, do you? Or the Rockefeller Plaza? Or one of the florists? Come; I have now walked the entire length of Fifth Avenue, several times, up and down, on both sides, from its beginnings at Washington Square to its end at 141st Street. *Where is the garden?*

Don't do as the New Yorkers do; follow the tourists. New Yorkers walk with their eyes looking straight ahead or down; the visitors, stunned by the skyline, look heavenwards. Where do you find a garden on Fifth Avenue? Why, on a roof, of course.

To be precise, on the roof of a sixteen-storey apartment building at 98th, where Steven and Kappy Mott have created not one garden, but two; the tiny space, which has a kind of corridor running round two sides, is half filled with vegetables, while the corridor and the space on the other side is crammed with flowers. The whole layout is, among other things, a triumph of human intelligence over geometry; given only the measurements, most people would swear that it couldn't be done, that a few pots for flowers and a patch for herbs could be accommodated, but nothing more. Hardly believing what I could see, I started on the edible side, and asked Mr Mott how many separate items he grew in it. His reply rendered me speechless for some time: 'Well,' he said, 'when I last counted them up, there were about two hundred, including ten different varieties of tomato.' There were aubergines, courgettes, cucumbers, squash, cabbages, lettuces, corn, peppers, broccoli (ugh), red chillies, spinach, chives, parsley, tarragon, dill, thyme, coriander, mint, basil and – before my very eyes – the ten varieties of tomato (the peppers come in equally numerous strains); the only vegetable they have failed with is the globe artichoke; shucks. But I was not surprised when Mr Mott said, 'With a little deliberate care and preparation in planning, we could spend the entire summer here, my wife and myself, and have our entire diet made up of what we grow here on the terrace.' (Later, at our alfresco lunch, I asked if everything before us, bar the pepper, salt, bread and cheese, had been grown where we sat, and he inspected the table and said, 'Yes.' Then he explained – or do I mean admitted? – that his neighbours had vetoed his desire to keep a cow up there for fresh milk; there was no hint of reproach when he added that at the Motts' previous apartment on Park Avenue at 74th, they had kept six chickens. Well, I suppose the eggs were fresh, anyway.)

I took him for a New York businessman, and so he is, but he was a farm boy bred, and in his early life was surrounded by cows and pigs and chickens and home-made butter; clearly he brought his roots, literally as well as metaphorically, to the city. I am no gardener; for me, vegetables come from greengrocers and flowers from florists, but I think I understand, and I am sure I admire, those whose passion it is to grow living plants, whether vegetable or flower (and even I know that many edible plants are preceded by very beautiful flowers, starting with cherry-blossom.)

There is an obvious satisfaction in contemplating a vase of flowers that you have grown yourself, and a kitchen table laden with the vegetables you have picked from your own-sown land. But it is more than that. It is, after all, the oldest preoccupation of mankind; to plant a seed and tend it, watch it grow, cull it and eat it. It is a mysterious and profound process; it is almost creating life, not just nurturing it. The human race would not have survived if it had not speedily acquired the knowledge and understanding of growing things to eat; but the combination of usefulness and beauty is fused in the act of faith implied by putting something into the earth and then waiting patiently (for nature cannot be hurried) for it to rise from the dead, utterly changed. It is no wonder that through history, including pre-history, so many rituals are based on the most elemental aspects of agriculture, from the rites of the corn-goddess to the Harvest Festivals of England, the altars laden with sheaves of corn and the loaves made therewith. Even hunting, which is presumably almost as old as agriculture, has nothing to compare with the elaborately solemn celebrations which attend the knowledge that all is safely gathered in. The advice with which Voltaire ends his great satire on certainty can sum up: Leave all this philosophising and let us cultivate our gardens.

With which reflection my host and I went round the corner to the flowers. I am a very unobservant man, but even I noticed that the flowers, which seemed to burst from their earth with joy, must have been planned to a thought-out colour scheme, and a colour scheme, moreover, devised by someone who had more than a superficial understanding of colour and what it can do. For the moment, I held my peace and admired.

When we sat down to lunch, it was at once apparent that the table was also planned to a pattern – not a pattern in the formal sense, that is, the repetition of a motif, but a pattern in the sense that a painting has one. In other words, harmony. There was a bowl of fruit, another of vegetables, the gleaming purple of the aubergines striking fire from the yellow peppers; it continued with the dark bread, the pale soup sprinkled with nasturtium petals, the sharply contrasting colours of the two cheeses, the whole picture bound by a vivid orange cloth, flung with artful haphazardness diagonally across the table. At last, with the flower-beds still ringing in my eyes, the obvious solution was before me. 'Wait a minute,' I said, 'wait a minute, There's an artist in this house – who is it?' Steven blushed with pride:

'That's my wife,' he said; 'she's a sculptor, actually – all those carvings you saw' (I had indeed seen them, but carelessly deduced that they were a collection rather than a creation) 'are hers.' Sculptor or no sculptor, Kappy Mott had an eye for colour that Matisse and Cézanne would have commended; when we went back into the apartment I looked more closely at her work, and suddenly saw one carving that I had missed before, when Isaac Stern leaped at me, perfectly caught in his combination of intensity and geniality.

The clue to Isaac is his voracious zest for life, and it occurred to me, looking at him, that the Motts exhibited – not only in her art but in the attitude of both of them – something of the same enjoyment, curiosity and eagerness for experience that he has. Pat on cue, Steven proved me right, when he said 'My notion is that the entire city should be made into a floating garden. The most wasted real estate in any city is the roof-tops – to make it green, to provide just one more contribution to beauty and clean air, is the duty of every landlord and every tenant.' I was not in the least surprised when, as I was leaving, he revealed yet another agricultural ambition – to keep bees. There are wild bees in New York, and Steven drew my attention to some of them browsing among the mint-flowers, saying 'As long as we're providing the bees with their food why not get the bees to provide us with honey?'

Why not, indeed? 'It takes a certain amount of learning', he said, but as I said farewell I had no doubt that he would sooner or later have his own hives and his own honey therefrom. It also occurred to me that his dream of a cow on the roof was not quite as fanciful as I had imagined.

★   ★   ★

Among the countless guidebooks to New York, there is one, by Michael Gitter, called *Gitter's 24 Hour New York*. It crams a very great deal, in an abbreviated style, into a very small space. In particular, the author lists the addresses and phone-numbers of a large number of facilities that visitors to New York (or, I should imagine, many residents) might want to know. They include restaurants, bank-machines, hotels, gas-stations, news-stands, parking-lots, garages, pharmacies, supermarkets, grocery stores, even swimming-pools. He lists them by areas, and since with New York's grid it makes sense to use the numbers of the cross-streets as the boundaries of the section he is dealing with, the pattern will be something like 14th to

32nd, 33rd to 49th, 50th to 72nd, etc. But close inspection of the book reveals an interesting phenomenon. Almost all the listings of places, services and needs catered for, peter out in the high nineties. Now obviously Mr Gitter does not wash his hands of the inhabitants of New York merely because they live north of the Park; he would list whatever there was to list up there. The truth is that there is very little to list.

Take a single example: bank cash-dispensing machines. He lists twenty-three on Fifth Avenue – Chase Manhattan, Chemical, Bowery Savings, NatWest, Manufacturers Hanover, Bank of New York and others. Not one is higher than 60th Street. Well, since the Eastern side of Fifth Avenue is entirely residential for the whole length of the Park, it is not surprising that there are no banks or bank-machines listed between 59th and 110th. But Fifth Avenue goes on for another thirty-one blocks; for that matter some of the Avenues west of the Harlem River (where Fifth ends) go a great deal further – Eighth gets to 160th, and Amsterdam to 193rd, while Broadway is last seen passing 240th, apparently heading for Montreal. What plague, what weird mutation of the Neutron Bomb, has apparently wiped out every bank in the top two-fifths of Manhattan?

Such was my introduction to Harlem. For Fifth Avenue, in addition to its raffish downtown, its busy commercial midtown, its elegant hometown, has an uptown, where de dark folks live; and some of them might as well live on the far side of the moon when it comes to sharing in the general affluence of the United States, and more particularly New York City, and more particularly still Fifth Avenue.

Fifth Avenue ends at 141st Street, where it meets the Harlem River; well, no sense in getting your feet wet. From Frawley Circle, at the northern end of the Park, Fifth is black, and it gets steadily blacker as it goes on. There is one very significant symbol on its way north; between 120th and 124th – you have to go round it, east or west – stands the Marcus Garvey Memorial Park. It used to be called the Mount Morris Park, but was re-named in 1973; note the date, it is important in this story.

Marcus Garvey was a Jamaican con-man with an eloquent tongue; he came to the United States in 1914. He claimed that he had come to lead the black people of America back to Africa, where they, or their forebears, came from. This ingenious idea, turning Moses on his head, rapidly gained a huge following; Garvey's vanity and roguery were huge and brazen – he gave himself fancy titles like 'Provisional President of Africa' (later 'Emperor') and presented his leading followers with titles and decorations even gaudier. Yet the numbers in his organisation swelled to millions, and these were almost certainly genuine millions, not figures of his fantasy. Other black leaders saw through him, but had to tread warily in their attempts to curb him; in the end, the law curbed him – he was convicted and imprisoned for a share-swindle involving a shipping-line he had created, with which he had promised to sail home to Africa one day with all his followers aboard. When he came out of jail he was deported, and his organisation rapidly collapsed.

Such figures have been thrown up again and again; Father Divine was believed by many to be just that; Malcolm X was taken seriously for years (he has a street to himself in Harlem); Congressman Adam Clayton Powell could and did get away with the most flagitious behaviour by insisting at the top of his voice that any criticism of him, let alone prosecution, was racist; a lesser but more criminal figure in the same mould was 'Michael X', who tried to be a big shot in London, but was eventually hanged for murder in his native Jamaica.

America survived the noisy but ultimately insubstantial 'Black Power' movement and black politics is represented now by figures such as the eloquent Julian Bond. These know that black advancement must be gained through the normal, white-dominated political road; by their lights, Jesse Jackson is a survival from an earlier era, whose style and message, strongly attractive to many though they are, will ultimately die out.

And yet, in 1973, Mount Morris Park changed its name to that of a crazy crook with the gift of the gab, and Fifth Avenue must tip-toe round it, trying not to smile, if it wants to carry on northwards, while on that northwards journey there isn't a standard bank, operating nation-wide, with a cash-dispensing machine available.

Fifth Avenue, as I said, ends at 141st Street. What with the freeway that runs along the river, and what with an abandoned bridge over the speeding cars, it is not easy to decide which is the very last building that can claim to be on Fifth. The choice seemed to be either a large laundry, or The Armoury, which is a regimental headquarters for the New York National Guard. But just as I was thinking I might as well toss a coin, three young blacks came across the road and vanished into – literally – a hole in the wall. The hole was let into the end wall of a curious brick structure, and was no more than two feet square, it was four feet or so off the ground, thus making it a matter of skilled acrobatics to get through it at all, yet there was no other way into the structure, which was itself a mystery. It looked as if it might have been used to house electricity generating machinery or the like, though that could not explain the absence of any door. It sloped into the ground at one end; all in all, it was perhaps ten feet wide and fifteen long, and seven high.

This is where the last men on Fifth Avenue dwell. I explained what I was here for, and made an appointment for a few days' time, with the youngest of the three, called Eddie. I promised to pay him for an interview; I couldn't stay to do it then and there. Next day, I picked up the paper and read that a man living right up at 141st and Fifth had been murdered. That seemed to me too much of a coincidence, but as I read on I realised that one of the three men I had seen was the victim. It turned out that there were two of these brick structures, identical in character and both lived in. The dead man could not have been Eddie, as the newspaper account said that the victim had been elderly; apparently he lived in the other brick-house, and a gang had burnt him out, then chased and beaten him. Trying to get away from them, he had run into the freeway and been killed by a car that did not stop. (To be fair to the hit-and-run driver, I must say that it would be quite impossible for any car to stop on the freeways of New York, as the rushing stream of nose-to-tail metal offers no opportunity to slow down, let alone come to a halt.)

I went back to The Last Home on Fifth Avenue. I first inspected the premises of the dead man; they stank of fire. Then I went over to Eddie's; his companion, the third of the group, was not there. Eddie invited me in; it was a struggle (I am no acrobat) but finally I was there.

There was no light at all, other than the feeble patch entering from outside the hole. There was no heat, no water, no amenities of any kind. The place was almost entirely filled with rubbish – not his, clearly, but what was left when the place was abandoned. Bricks, bottles, wood, tin, cardboard, paper, every kind of filth; it had an earth floor, which made it even filthier. Eddie had no furniture at all, other than the bits of a ruined beach-chair and a dirty, dilapidated and torn mattress. And that is where, and how, the last inhabitant of Fifth Avenue lives.

Eddie, it was plain, was frightened; at our earlier meeting, he had been light-hearted, though monosyllabic. Meanwhile, however, there had been a murder a few yards from his home. Eddie was streetwise; a twenty-three-year-old black living in those conditions would have to be. No, he hadn't been there when it happened, indeed didn't know that anything *had* happened. No, he didn't know that man, if there was a man. No, he hadn't seen anything, heard anything. No, he had no idea why they had done it, particularly because he didn't know anything about any 'they' or any 'it'. Yes, the police had asked him questions, and he couldn't tell them anything.

I abandoned my interrogation; if the cops hadn't pulled him in, it must have been because they realised it would be a waste of time asking Eddie questions to which the answer would invariably be No, Nothing and

Never. About his life, however, Eddie was, if not exactly forthcoming, willing to speak. Just.

Where was he born? 'The Bronx.' How long had he lived here? 'A year.' What is this place? 'Dunno.' Do you live here on your own? 'No.' Who shares it with you? 'A guy.' A friend? 'Yeah.' What do you do for a living? 'Clean cars.' For a company, or on your own? 'My own job.' Do you get welfare? 'No.' Why not? 'Dunno.' Have you got anywhere to go? 'One day.' You haven't any water – how do you keep clean? 'The hydrants.' You haven't got any kind of lavatory – how do you manage? 'Use the Armoury.' You don't live very well, do you? 'I'm happy.' You're happy? 'Only way to survive.' Are you afraid, living here? 'No, nobody bothers me.' They bothered the man who got killed, didn't they? 'I don't know anything about that.' Can you fight? 'Course I can fight.' You may have to – have you had fights? 'Plenty.' Do you have a weapon? 'I'd find one.' I live in a house which has got light, heating, windows, TV, a sink, a toilet – wouldn't you like these things? 'Of course.' In winter, it must be freezing here, surely? 'Yeah, kind of.' You got any furniture? 'No.' There must be roaches here, I guess? 'Yeah, I guess.' Might even be rats? 'I never saw one here.' You must be very tough to live in such conditions and keep going? 'That's right.' Who would you like to change places with most if you had another life? 'Can't really say.' Do you envy the rich people down on Fifth? 'Dunno.' What would you like to do, to change it? 'Just wanna be alone.' You don't need any help? 'I can take care of myself.'

I paid Eddie, as promised, and walked away thoughtfully; I had taken the precaution of asking my cab-driver to wait, however long I might be. The paradox was vivid; Eddie kept himself clean in impossible conditions, so he hadn't given up. But he had told me at our first meeting that he made $200–$300 a week washing cars. Now in New York two or three hundred a week is no fortune; still, he could get something better than this hideous hole in the ground – maybe only a one-room apartment in a tenement, but *anything* would be better than this. Why doesn't he mind more – enough to break out of the hole?

As he would say: dunno. I took the cab back to Marcus Garvey Park, and joined the chess-players whiling away the afternoon in the friendly sun. An elderly man, neatly, even smartly, dressed, motioned me to a game of chequers. 'I'm the Lizard,' he said, 'nobody beats me.' (Well, *I* didn't, anyway.) As we played, we talked; he turned out to be a thoughtful man, who had clearly lived in the vicinity for very many years, and watched it go up and down, up and down, yet all the while the mean line through the vicissitudes went on relentlessly down. Is it worse now, for blacks? Yes, he said, economically. Housing, for one thing: 'Yeah, we have a hell of a housing problem.' In what way, particularly? 'We never had living quarters like this before – the places used to be nice and clean, all of them.' I wondered if I should introduce him to Eddie, but he startled me by saying that Koch has helped the blacks; indeed, 'If we didn't have Koch for mayor I don't know what it might be like.'

He talked on, this resigned but not pessimistic elder, while beating me at chequers every time. I asked him, if he wanted to change things, what he would start with. 'With myself', he said: 'you can't do as good for me as I can do for myself, in any given society.' All of a sudden the view from Britain shrank; if we are struggling with the 'dependence culture', and finding that it is more tenacious than we supposed, where did the Lizard get his own self-sufficiency? The answer is as obvious as the question: nowhere but within himself. But the more interesting question is: do we all have the capacity for that kind of self-sufficiency (which need have nothing to do with material wants at all)? Or do some lack the quality that alone can lead them to any kind of fulfilment? My answer is quite unequivocal: we *do* all have that coiled spring in us, ready to push us on. The old Lizard (he's just huffed me again) knew about that spring and what it is for, whence his upright bearing, his clean, pressed clothes, his relaxed conversation. Eddie was in a hole metaphorically as well as literally; he washed himself, but went no further in self-reliance. Yet he made money – little enough, but who said my wise old friend made any more? Of one thing I was certain as I took my leave: that his apartment, however small and poor in facilities, would be meticulously clean. But Eddie, when he hears a rustle in his squalor, and thinks it might be a rat, just shrugs.

Leaving Eddie, I had seen a printed notice wrapped round a post; it turned out to be a police notice, asking for anyone who saw the man who was killed on the freeway to come forward. I knew they would get no help from Eddie; I guessed they would get no help from anybody. Apart from a natural and general desire to keep out of such things, as far up as 141st Street anyone who had information about a killing would be very unlikely indeed give it to the police. Yet how will the crime rate come down if all the witnesses to all the crimes are struck deaf, dumb and blind immediately afterwards? The gang who burnt out Eddie's invisible friend and chased him to his death in the traffic were not out for money; men who live in holes like animals are not targets for robbery. The gang must have been simply out for sport; brutal, murderous sport. The thought of truly wanton murder, with no gain involved, is one of the most chilling thoughts the violence in this violent city can provoke. But I was now on a less grim errand. This was a visit to a rap club; naturally, I had first to discover what a rap club is, and how it is different from, say, the Athenaeum.

It is very different from the Athenaeum. A rap club is a club for dancing and all that goes with it, but with a difference. Its entertainment, though it includes singers and comedians, is based mainly on rap. The man who ran it was called Chris, and he sat me down and explained patiently, as to a child learning that twice two make four, that rap music is music with a very strong and repetitive beat (I was to find out later that he had not exaggerated either the strength or the repetitiveness), to which a rapper improvises or memorises a monologue – spoken, not sung – to the music, or rather *over* the music, for there is little rhythmic or verbal connection between the two.

The words, as I learned later in the evening when the floor was cleared and the rappers came out, are not just jabber or nonsense; the whole thing is worked out with great care and meaning. The rappers I heard had rehearsed their performances, because this was a talent-spotting night and they were taking no chances, so they had fully memorised their raps. The rap was delivered at astonishing speed, and since some of them went on for a quarter of an hour or more, without the slightest pause, even for breath, the number of words in a full-length rap must be the equivalent of a leading actor's part in a substantial play.

Yet not even that exhausts the surprises of rap for one who had never so much as heard of the art until now. The rap rhymes in a wide variety of forms – couplets, triplets, even something like a sonnet sequence, and the whole has a strong though rough metre. It was enormously impressive; the words themselves were delivered with obviously studied care, and if you filmed a rapper, then slowed down the playback, you would find he was exaggerating his lip movements for clarity.

Before the rappers started, the club members danced; there was a tiny floor, with the traditional spotlights, and since it was in a cellar, it resembled nothing so much as a Paris *boîte*, except for the fact that the entire clientèle was black. It seems that the *boîtes* of Harlem like their music loud; the music was amplified to a level at which I became genuinely scared that it would cause me real bodily harm. I remember reading that at open-air pop-concerts, with tens of thousands of people in attendance, when the music has to be greatly amplified, since some of the audience may be a hundred yards away or more, warnings are given against going near the loudspeakers, as it is dangerous. I could well believe the danger; in the anyway confined space of the rap-club cellar the noise was almost beyond bearing, and I could *feel* the pounding beat inside my head.

That was plainly a minority view. The crowd, all young (few over twenty, I guessed), were hurling themselves about in a frenzy of enjoyment, their energy suggesting that apart from the danger of brain-damage from the music, there would be a good many broken bones before the evening was out.

Of course, nothing like that happened; they all seemed to be equipped with bat's radar, for although the dance-floor was packed there were no collisions. What is more, they were not simply wriggling their bodies and throwing their arms about (they all danced alone, making for themselves a kind of space, though there wasn't any), they were doing it in perfect time to the music.

They were all very happy. I moved in and out among the hurtling bodies, nearly getting knocked over a dozen times, and collared an engaging young man – sixteen, perhaps – called, or rather shouted, Joe. He was engagingly articulate, answering my idiotic questions ('What do you get out of it?' – 'A great charge') while continuing to gyrate. 'How long can you keep this up?' I bellowed. 'Oh,' he yelled, 'I can go on all night.' I could well believe it.

The music never stopped, though the rhythm changed from time to time, and nobody showed any sign of wanting a breather. Eventually, however, the floor was cleared for the performances. There were straight-forward singers, duos (including one which – if we are keeping the Parisian club *argot* – was something of an apache dance) and comedians. I can't say that I felt that they were the funniest men in history, but the audience certainly did; again and again they would *literally* fall off their chairs and roll helplessly on the floor.

It was a heartening experience; everybody was happy, nobody was drunk, nobody was aggressive, nobody as far as I could tell, had drugs. They were all perfectly respectable young people, enjoying themselves noisily, and doing no-one any harm. But just as I was about to leave, it curdled. I could not discover what had happened, but some kind of fracas had started. Some people came down the stairs, others went up, there was a good deal of pushing and swearing. Outside, a girl was screaming abuse at a man; it seemed that someone was trying to get out and others were trying to keep him in, and there was a group on the sidewalk, silent but looking as though they would be willing, even keen, to join it. Partly because I didn't want the evening to turn sour, and partly because I was getting scared, I thought it best to go home, fairly swiftly, and did.

★   ★   ★

'Hope beyond the dope'; a catchy phrase, not easily forgotten, and well worth putting on posters in an anti-drugs campaign. It came from Elder Samuel L. Williams of the Baptist House of Prayer, at 126th Street, just round the corner from Fifth Avenue. 'Elder' is, I take it, a position in the Baptist Church; I also assume that he is an ordained Minister, though for the occasion on which I met him he was billed as the Emcee.

Not inappropriately, for what we were about to receive. For this was an invitation to attend 'An evening of great Gospel music', in the heart of black Harlem, and I was assured that it was going to be the real thing. The leaflet advertising the event promised the Golden Sons of Brooklyn, the Sunset Jubilaires, the Wearyland Singers, the Gospel Seekers, the New York Specials and the Sweet Tones of Israel. A full bill, then; no wonder the invitation said 'Doors Open 6 pm; Program 7 pm Sharp'. The audience, however, must have been regulars, for the first of them began to trickle in at around 7.30, and the performance began well after 8 p.m. So I had plenty of time to wander about, and found a table with a vast variety of leaflets advertising the same kind of evening as I was about to have. The LeGree Baptist Church (the name must be either an appalling coincidence or a very good joke) offered, among others, the Pentecostal Heavenly Jubilees and the Soul Converters of the Bronx; the Salem United Methodist Church had signed the Gospel Ambassadors and the Reflections of Faith; the Childs Memorial Church presented the Wandering Souls, the Travelling Sons and the Swanee Quartet; the Mount Moriah Baptist Church led with the Martin Luther King Fellowship Choir in An Evening of Joyful Praises in Song; and the Metropolitan Church brought up the rear with the Soulenaires, the Gospel Crowns and the Mighty Clouds of Joy. It seemed that all over Harlem, every night, the joint was jumping with Gospel music; indeed, I had had a clue to its widespread attraction, for I had lost my way getting to the church, and found myself at another hall about to present a similar programme. They provided directions, and added that if I couldn't find the place, I would be welcome to come back and share their own evening.

Emcee Elder Williams was a grave and very human figure, with a gentle and attractive character. He began the proceedings with a brief service; simple prayers and a psalm. Nothing out of the ordinary there, but he then proceeded to work himself up into a great shouting performance with triumphant cries of 'Praise the Lord!' I had a powerful feeling that that was not his natural style, but adopted because it was what his congregation, particularly on such an evening, would wish.

The audience was interesting, for a good many reasons. It was not surprising that they were almost all black, nor that they were tidily and respectfully dressed. But this was, after all, a performance they were at, for all that it was a very special kind; I had expected clean clothes but informal ones. Not a bit; all the members of the audience had donned their very best attire. There was not a man without a tie, not a woman without her finery. Clearly, they take their Gospel singing seriously up at 126th and Fifth.

They do indeed. The church was tiny; simple bench pews, a dais, a lectern, no decorations. The Gospel Seekers took the stage – more exactly, they lined up at the front of the audience. There was a man whom I took to be the lead, with another four or five singers and three musicians – two on guitars and one drummer. They all had trail-mikes on stands; the lead took his and strolled up the aisle, singing a gentle, mild song; no histrionics, no great fervour, just pleasant crooning, while the backing sang along behind him.

I thought to myself: is that all? Where is the excitement that such events are supposed to provide? The lead singer, a middle-aged man, moved quietly back down the aisle, and handed over to one of the other singers, much younger and looking much less sedate. Suddenly, the place caught fire. The singer, solely by his performance, whipped up a frenzy – no lesser word would describe it – of such extraordinary force that he had the entire audience quite literally dancing in the aisles, clapping, shouting in rhythm, waving their hands above their heads. The amplification in the rap club had been almost unbearable; to my incredulous and terrified ears this was very considerably louder. I remembered that at the shooting range participants had to wear ear-muffs or plugs against ear-drum damage from the noise; well, every thud of the drums was far louder than any shot. And then, with the noise rising to a level at which I was experiencing physical pain, I looked at the drummer himself, and realised that he was perched right beneath the speaker, where the danger must be at its highest.

He didn't look in the least uncomfortable, however, so I decided that he must be either used to it or deaf, and began to concentrate on the singing. And what I had to keep reminding myself about was that these pop groups – for that is exactly what they were – were singing, with colossal, passionate, utterly abandoned force and conviction not about lost loves or sexual thrills or Lucy in the sky with diamonds, but solely and directly about Jesus Christ and the Lord, and what Jesus and the Lord will do for us if we will only allow them to, and how we should love them and praise them and worship them. Every one of their songs consisted of these same exhortations (well, the ordinary pop groups have a pretty narrow range of themes), and it seemed that there was an infinite number of variations to be brought into play.

The singing itself, forgetting its content (but who, listening, could forget it?), was of the very highest professional standard; these men were highly skilled musicians, though using their talents for a purpose very different from that pursued by the secular pop groups. (There are, of course, God-inspired pop singers – Cliff Richard for one – and recently some pop groups have appeared with religious and quasi-religious attitudes in their songs; moreover, Bob Dylan's 'A Hard Rain's a-Gonna Fall' which was written in the Sixties, is not only based on religious feeling, but in an apocalyptic religious feeling. But all these put together still make only a tiny minority.)

The singer acting as lead (they passed it from one to another) would break off and give a kind of exhortation, or describe his own conversion experience, while the band vamped behind him and his fellow-singers simply crooned wordlessly; then, at a signal like the trill at the end of the cadenza in a concerto which signals to the orchestra that they must be ready to take up where they left off, they all burst again into song.

Each group had its own smart uniform, spotlessly clean, though as the sweat poured off them in the intensity of their music their clothes began to wilt. Each group had one man whose specialty – plainly regular in this kind of singing – was to break into a hugely powerful falsetto, which made him clearly audible above even the loudest musical din. Of course, there was rhythmic clapping, led each time by the Emcee Elder, who would exhort us (despite the fact that no exhortation was necessary) to clap; the phrase was always 'Put your hands together', which did not mean in prayer but in rhythm. The strong beats made it easy.

The words were not easy to follow; of course, the entire audience knew all the songs well, and frequently sang along with the musicians; one which made itself clear above the music was called 'Jesus is knocking on the door of your heart, Why don't you let him in?' There could have been no disposition on the part of even the most patronising spectator of such a scene to think of these people as simple, innocent darkies, toiling in de cotton-fields and praisin' de Lawd; Uncle Tom's Cabin has many mansions, but none big enough to hold performances of such power, sophistication and conviction. Yet the gulf between the *basis* of their work and that of the Mick Jaggers is huge and unbridgeable, despite the fact the *technique* is so similar. As the musicians hurled themselves into their singing and playing it was deeply affecting to hold simultaneously in mind and feelings both the musical and religious nature of the experience. Though I have used the word frenzy, there was nothing hysterical about these scenes, nothing to suggest that the performers were high on anything other than their Christian beliefs; and when, in a break, it was possible to talk to Elder Samuel Williams, he made the point explicit:

There is an entertainment factor or feature involved in that you stand before an audience and you give them something and you feed off their energy which they give back to you. But basically most of the artistes that you have seen perform here tonight have had a religious experience – they've had a personal experience with Christ. They can empathise with the artiste because they have also had that same kind of experience; knowing that God has done something in their life and so therefore they just feed off of what they're saying. They can testify, for example, that when your friends turn their back on you that the Lord will give you new friends. They can adjust and appreciate that and show their enthusiasm – you see them standing up clapping their hands, they're just honouring what has been said by the artiste. The frenzy comes from the spirit. That's the religious side of it, it comes from the spirit of God. Unless you've really experienced that you can't understand it. It's not really a figment of one's imagination but it comes from outside and it touches something on the inside, which allows you to be. There's a difference in having hysteria just for hysteria's sake and being excited about what's going on in your life, what God has done for you and that's what you saw exhibited here. And the Gospel – which is the good news of Jesus Christ – extends a hope beyond the dope. I cannot get away from that because no matter what church you go in the gospel is being preached. Here tonight people came out to the service to get a little closer to God, to feel a part of that, and these artistes, these gospel singers, have served as a medium. There is hope in Harlem. *There is still hope in Harlem.*

Well, there are two senses in which it can be said that 'There is still hope in Harlem.' The first concerns the objective measuring of the likelihood that things will get better, and thereafter will continue to get better still. On that definition, 'There is hope in Harlem' will be denied or believed according to pessimists or optimists. But the other meaning of the phrase is far more important, and the assent in this case is unanimous. In that sense, 'There is still hope in Harlem' means that the kind of people whom I saw and heard at the Gospel Music Evening are full of hope. They hope in God and Jesus, and that hope is entirely self-contained, being affected by no exterior or material circumstances. Of course, with enthusiasm as powerful and dynamic as I had witnessed in the Baptist House of Prayer, the hope in Christ must inevitably expand to take in a more secular hope, the hope that things in Harlem which are now bad – poverty, unemployment, drugs – will get less bad. The obvious conclusion, at any rate to those who have experienced the fervour of the Gospel Seekers, the New York Specials, the Sunset Jubilaires, the Wearyland Singers, the Golden Sons of Brooklyn, the Sweet Tones of Israel and Elder Samuel L. Williams, is that the greater hope will surely help to bring about the fulfilment of the lesser.

But there are other kinds of entertainment in Harlem. I will have you know I am a member of the Colo's Sportsmen's Club, and I have a smart T-shirt and a hat to prove it. Moreover, I have been initiated into the mysteries of stickball. Way up in Harlem, at 109th Street, the Colo's take on all comers in this sport every Sunday, and a visiting Englishman – this one, anyway – may be press-ganged into the team.

Stickball may be described, more literally than the phrase usually intends, as a poor man's baseball. The game – which is indeed a simplified form of baseball – is played in the street rather than on a field, for the good reason that in these parts streets are much easier to come by than fields. The bases are chalked on the roadway, the pitcher's line likewise, one end of the street is barricaded with parked cars and the other end, which abuts on Fifth Avenue, now almost in sight of its end in the Harlem river, is shut, surprisingly, by a police barrier. Did the police really co-operate to that extent, I wondered, or had some of the more enterprising members of the team simply lifted one from its moorings? I asked, and was told that the police used to hassle them, but now all is peace, and the cops do indeed supervise the closing of the street.

Having been inducted, my first task is to learn the rules. The pitcher throws the ball – a soft rubber one rather than the hard sewn version that baseball uses – and it must be hit by the batter after one bounce. The batter, however, has the first advantage: he need not swing, bounce or no bounce, if he doesn't like the ball's length or pitch. If he does swing, however, he must connect – to miss is to be out. The same goes for a boss-shot that does not clear a V-shaped line chalked from the centre of the roadway to the walls on either side. If he connects properly, he throws down the bat and runs to first base; if he has sent the ball a long way, he will run on to second, even third, and occasionally – while the fielders are rescuing the ball and returning it – all the way to fourth base, which is home; whence a 'home run'.

I was astonished at the distance these players can hit the ball; the fielder on the boundary (as cricket would say) is on the far side of Fifth Avenue, with the traffic between him and returning the ball; defying death from the wheels, he is apt to weave in and out until he can throw the ball back with some hope of its being caught; if a fielder is on the base with the ball in his hand before the runner arrives, the runner is out. (So he is if the ball is caught by a fielder before hitting the ground.)

The rules – there are a few more, but they are easily grasped – having been mastered, the mysteries of the bat were explained to me. For budding stickball-players, I pass on what I learned. First, don't keep your elbows tucked in; swing the bat with arms fully stretched. Second, swing it horizontally, even though you are trying to sky the ball. Third, remember you don't have to swing unless the ball is coming up the way you want it (though skilled pitchers put wicked spin on it, to fool an innocent batter). Fourth, if you hit the ball, run like hell to first base, and obey the member of your team who will be stationed there to judge whether you can get to the next base or whether you should stop at the first. If you ought to stop, he puts out his hands, palms towards you, like a man pushing a stiff door; if you ought to go on, he (and the rest of the team) will yell 'Gogogogogogogogogogogogogogo'.

That is really all there is to it, other than the fact that a game consists of seven innings for each side.

Most of the players, on both sides, were young – in their late teens or early twenties; a few were older. They were friendly, easy, ready to laugh, though if they lived in a street like the one in which the game was being played (possibly some of them lived in this very one), laughter would not be the first thing that sprang to mind. This is not the poorest part of Harlem (it is mainly Hispanic, not black), but it is poor enough, and it was difficult to remember that the shabby tenements which lined the street were only a few feet from Fifth Avenue, and that the Fifth Avenue they were only a few feet from was mostly as shabby. More to the point, perhaps, the players and spectators, the children playing, the wives sunning themselves on the fire-escapes that snaked down the buildings, all of them seemed in good temper, and certainly there was no sign at all of 'crack' or other drugs. One youth was distinctly woozy and clung to a lamp-post for support, but it was clear that it was one drink too many that had slurred his speech. Another sign: the clothes were rough, but they were clean, particularly the shirts and hats that proclaimed their stickball allegiance. If these youngsters were streetwise, they were also street-proud; I guessed that, so far from dabbling in drugs, as takers or sellers, they were much more likely to be part of the campaign to get young people off them. Yet the surroundings were enough to daunt the strongest heart, and I was very conscious of the twin facts that twenty or thirty blocks to the south there were some of the most expensive apartment blocks in New York, and that twenty or thirty blocks to the north the conditions were a great deal grimmer.

I forgot to say that I certainly managed to hit the ball once, and I *think* I did so twice. But I distinguished myself in one way, to the immense hilarity of everyone on both teams, by setting off at an imposing speed towards first base, only to be given out when I was unable to find it.

But it was time for me to pay my last – and, as it turned out, most impressive – call. I had not forgotten the Grand Marshal of the Martin Luther King parade, and here I was, knocking at the door of Hale House. There had been a note about her in the parade programme which intrigued me; Mother Hale herself intrigued me a great deal more, when she came into the hall to greet me. A slender, though not frail, eighty-three, she exuded an air of calm and joy; her face was lined, but not in the least haggard, her bearing was upright, not bowed; her eyes were clear, and penetrating. I was clearly in the presence of a more than ordinary woman.

She began to talk, her voice very low, musical, full of fire. Outside the window were the street sounds of Harlem, and of an area rough and poor even by Harlem's standards. Within a few minutes, I knew I was listening to a woman not just extraordinary, but astounding; I realised at once what it must be like to talk with Mother Teresa. ('Mother' Hale, which I first took to indicate that she was, or had been, a nun, is only a – well, I was going to say a nickname or a pet-name, but neither fits the bill; let us say a name of endearment and admiration.)

How did it get started? But first, what is 'it'? It is Hale House, through which, in the last nineteen years, have passed more than six hundred infant children who were drug addicts – addicts, that is, in the full sense, but via a hideous route; they were all addicted through addicted mothers. Mother Hale, who from the start would rather have been weaning babies in the ordinary sense, set herself to a very different kind of treatment. She is at it still, and soon after we met she was due to open another Hale House not far away, where babies born with AIDS through infected parents can be similarly treated, the difference being that none of the children in Hale House Two are going to survive.

And how did it get started, Mother Hale?

I have always taken care of children. And one day my daughter saw a woman – that was back in '69, I think – who was obviously an addict and she was holding a baby, and she was nodding off, and my daughter realised that the baby was going to fall, so she ran over and said, 'You need help with that baby.' So she gave the girl my address and said, 'Take the baby to my mother, she'll help you.' Next morning, the girl was at my door, and said she was an addict, and that my daughter had sent her, and I said, 'My daughter doesn't mix with drug addicts, you've got the wrong place.' But she showed me the piece of paper where my daughter had written my address. So I said 'Wait a minute,' and I went upstairs and phoned my daughter, who had forgotten to tell me about it, and she told me what had happened. So I went back downstairs and the woman had gone, and the baby was lying on the floor. The next week the woman came back, and brought two more babies, two more babies of her own. Inside of two months I had twenty-two.

Mother Hale's quiet voice, with only the slightest emphasis, went on, carefully describing a circle of hell that Dante knew nothing about. Drug-addicted babies, it seems, have to go through all the agony that adults trying to get off drugs suffer, there being no other way. How, then, can they stand it? The answer was that they don't know they are addicted; their drug cries are indistinguishable from those of hunger or teething.

> You give them something in place – I gave them food and milk. Gave them a bottle every half hour, or every ten minutes even, if they wanted, so they would stop crying. They don't know the difference.

Born in Philadelphia, Mother Hale had lived in Harlem for fifty years, and seen it die. Once, 'They had nice homes, people lived well. And on Sunday it was a pleasure to watch them go to Church and everything. All of that's gone.'

> They took the drugs to Harlem first, to the Negroes. We were on drugs first, they had no idea that their children would take it up. Now it's gone round the world and there's no place that they don't have drugs. We as black people have been put down all our lives – we built America for nothing. So we take drugs, to forget the slavery, forget everything. Makes them think he's a man and as good as any other man – he takes it and feels good. For a time. For a time. Now you find babies out dead in garbage cans. People don't even tell they had a baby, they'll put in a garbage bag and drop it out. That's why I have this place, and I can't say no to a mother or father that brings them. They're good to me in this neighbourhood.

That was not difficult to believe. Indeed, it had already become clear that if Mother Hale stepped outside the door and someone lifted a hand to her in violence or threat, he would be dead the next second (and she appalled). But how does she bear the pain of what she sees and hears?

> I don't have any pain. I feel very good because I know that God doesn't make a mistake, and he knew what he was doing. Maybe this is one of the reasons that they sent drugs, he wanted people to know that there is no difference between white and black because now they have the same thing. Put a black

dog and white dog together, they don't know the difference. I've had white children here that were as happy as the little black ones. I don't need anything to lift me up. I don't need a cigarette, a drink or anything to make me feel any better. I know that I'm one of God's children and I'm as good as anybody else in the world so I feel good. And little children – I'd like to help them up and make them feel the same way. People say 'I love children', but they don't want to know why they're crying. You don't hear a lot of crying in here; we feed our children, we keep them dry, we give them a bath. And let you know you love them.

Mother Hale learned about hardship early. Her father died when she was a baby. She was the youngest of four children (the other three are dead), and her mother had to bring them up by herself. Hale House doesn't get enough funds from the city, but it is now so well known that it has almost more sponsors and helpers than it can use. 'Sometimes someone will simply walk into a store and order a huge box of children's clothes and just have it sent round.'

To judge from the children, someone must be in the habit of doing that fairly regularly, and doing it in good stores, too; the children were clean, and so were their clothes, which were smart and pretty, as far from institutional uniformity as could be imagined. Not long before his murder, John Lennon gave her $10,000, and his widow now gives her $20,000 a year, at Thanksgiving; not unnaturally, photographs of both of them are prominently displayed. On and on she went, the voice rising and falling like the gentlest sea; she is without bitterness, rancour or envy, constantly reiterating that God does not make mistakes, constantly casting out anger, constantly calling in love.

She had some duties to attend to, and left the room for a few minutes. I wandered up the stairs; from the next floor to the roof, the stairwell was completely covered in plaques, citations, certificates, awards of every imaginable kind for the work she has been doing for so long. On a whim, I counted them; there were 127. I heard her coming up the stairs behind me. 'Come,' she said, beckoning me into her bedroom. There was a child's cot beside her bed. She told me that every child taken into Hale House sleeps in Mother Hale's room for the first few weeks. On another whim, I asked her what was the worst she had ever come across. 'I've seen the lot,' she said, and fell silent. I sensed that there was more to come, and said nothing. She sighed. 'There's one girl', she said, 'who had three children boarded at Hale House all at the same time. She had the first when she was twelve, the second when she was thirteen, and the third when she was fourteen. Now she's fifteen. The middle one died.'

Are you *sure*, I wondered, that God doesn't make mistakes? But I didn't say it; there was no point in doing so, knowing what the answer would be.

I left Hale House, and wandered away in the early afternoon sunshine; I had had nothing to eat, and one of the helpers said there was a restaurant, Sylvia's, not far away. I thought about this woman, radiating holiness amid perdition. I thought of the children I had seen and played with; not cowed, not crushed, not timid. Some were going to die quite soon, well, *all* the AIDS victims in the new premises were going to do that. ('God doesn't send you a note, you know', she had said, 'when your time's up. But he knows when it is, and how you're going to go.') She had, only for a moment, glowed with pride, and it wasn't on the testimonial-laden staircase; it wasn't anything to do with Hale House at all. It was a memory from her early days looking after children – her mother, to make ends meet, ran a kind of crèche, and the daughter took to the life of child-minding. 'And not one of my children', she said, 'became a criminal or drug addict.'

Wrapped in a fold of her faith, I walked on, slowly; my very heartbeat had slowed with the certainty I had encountered, and I was hardly conscious of my surroundings. At an intersection, a huge truck thundered by, its slipstream shaking me as it passed. I came out of my reverie abruptly, to realise that I was in the heart of Harlem, and by no means the best part of Harlem either. Where was Sylvia's? More to the point, were all those warnings I had been given true? I looked around for a taxi; there wasn't one. Nobody approached me, and I walked on, trying not to look scared, patronising, furtive, brash, rich or lost. I comforted myself with the reassurances I had had from Jim Dwyer, the subway expert, who argued that the dangers of the subway were much exaggerated; let us hope that the dangers of Harlem were no less inflated.

But here was Sylvia's. Inside, I thought at first that mine was the only white face, but then I saw a table with a white family of five. The place looked very relaxed, and no crack-crazed Rastafarian was brandishing a knife at me. Sylvia approached with the menu. I murmured Mother Hale's 'God doesn't make mistakes' like a mantra, and ordered a salad.

★   ★   ★

Yet the last memory of Fifth Avenue was neither of Washington Square, where it began, nor of Harlem, where it finished. It was, perhaps appropriately, half-way along. There are balloon-sellers in New York, as there are in most cities where innocent pleasure is not forbidden. Like all balloon-sellers, the New York vendors keep their elusive wares in the same sort of tether; there is usually a thick leash, to which all the balloons are attached by a thin cord, and when a buyer comes along, the balloon-man plucks one of his fruit from the main stem, and hands it over. From time to time, since accidents do happen, the balloon slips from the grasp either of the seller as he detaches it or of the buyer as he takes charge of it. No great harm is done, for even the most upmarket balloons cost very little, and it is unlikely that even in a city as litigious as New York either seller or buyer will go to law for judgment as to which must pay for the one that got away.

But as I stood on the Park side of the Avenue, a little above 60th, I saw a sight that was pure magic. Against a brilliant sky untouched by cloud, a giant cluster of balloons, in a vast variety of colours, suddenly appeared; it was at once apparent that a balloon-seller had let go not of the fruit, but of the tree – indeed, it was obvious that he had, for the thick master cord could be clearly seen dangling from the bunch of balloons.

Now once, in the untechnological past, this sight was very rare, because it needed a powerful wind, blowing in the right direction, to lift a bunch of balloons into the heavens, and the moment the wind dropped, they began their descent to earth. That, however, was before the technique of filling balloons not with air but with helium had been discovered. Helium, it is well known, is one of the few substances which is lighter than air; it therefore follows that provided the balloon is made of some very fine, light material, the helium in it will ensure that it will soar upwards, and continue to soar, until the air it meets is so rarefied that it is lighter than the helium balloon.

That was precisely what was happening before my eyes, for it was clear that the balloons – there must have been thirty or forty – were helium-filled, and determined to reach the sun, the moon and the stars. I stood transfixed; it was not clear where the wonderful accident had occurred, but I first saw the cluster as it appeared beside the Pierre Hotel. It went almost straight up – the air was still – until it was level with the pinnacle of the Pierre. Then – a puff of wind had sprung to life – it veered downtown, still rising. It cleared the Sherry Netherland, the Pierre's neighbour on the south; it passed in front of the General Motors building, almost at its topmost storey; then it dared the undareable – it swept on towards *and above* the Trump Tower; I swear I could hear the angels cheering as the balloons committed their magnificent lèse-Trump. Still it was not finished; higher and higher went the bunch, its colours becoming brighter and brighter in the sunshine, and on it went downtown, as my heart sang at the sight, as splendid and comforting as a rainbow. Then, as a cross-breeze sprang up, it turned, still rising, and left Fifth Avenue; and so did I.

Index

Note: Shops, restaurants, institutions in New York are entered directly; elsewhere they are to be found under location.

n = note.

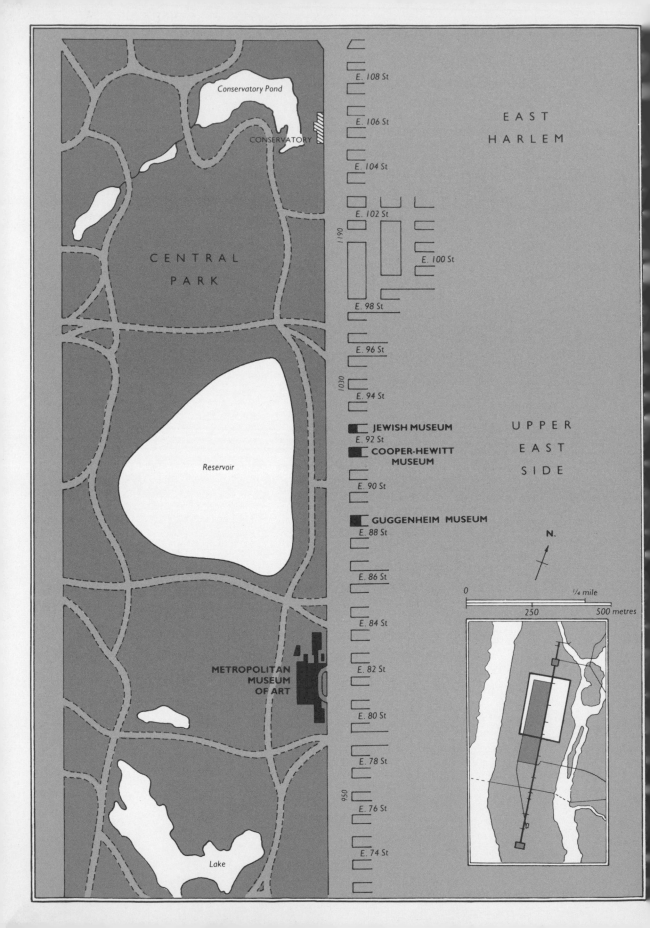

Conservatory Pond

CONSERVATORY

EAST
HARLEM

E. 108 St

E. 106 St

E. 104 St

CENTRAL
PARK

E. 102 St

E. 100 St

E. 98 St

E. 96 St

E. 94 St

Reservoir

■ JEWISH MUSEUM

E. 92 St

■ COOPER-HEWITT
MUSEUM

UPPER

EAST

SIDE

E. 90 St

■ GUGGENHEIM MUSEUM

E. 88 St

N.

E. 86 St

0   ¼ mile

250   500 metres

E. 84 St

METROPOLITAN
MUSEUM
OF ART

E. 82 St

E. 80 St

E. 78 St

E. 76 St

E. 74 St

Lake